Elizabeth Harriot Hudson

A History of the Jews in Rome

B.C. 160-A.D. 604

Elizabeth Harriot Hudson

A History of the Jews in Rome
B.C. 160-A.D. 604

ISBN/EAN: 9783744765237

Printed in Europe, USA, Canada, Australia, Japan

Cover: Foto ©ninafisch / pixelio.de

More available books at **www.hansebooks.com**

A HISTORY OF THE JEWS IN ROME.

"*Many shall be purified, and made white, and **tried; but the** wicked shall do wickedly: and none of the wicked shall understand; but the wise shall understand.*

DANIEL xii. **10.**

A HISTORY

OF

THE JEWS IN ROME.

B.C. 160—A.D. 604.

BY

E. H. HUDSON,

AUTHOR OF
"THE LIFE AND TIMES OF LOUISA, QUEEN OF PRUSSIA," "QUEEN BERTHA AND
HER TIMES," "THE ROYAL MAUSOLEUM, FROGMORE," ETC.

London:
HODDER AND STOUGHTON,
27, PATERNOSTER ROW.
MDCCCLXXXII.

PREFACE.

I THINK this book will not be found dull and lifeless, for while seeking, viewing in different lights, and blending the materials of which it is composed, I have felt myself carried back to my own youthful days. History was then my favourite study, which I ardently pursued, guided by a dear mother—the Reader to our happy home circle. Then I learned to love books suitable for reading in the family; consequently that is the character I wish to give to every one of my own literary productions.

With regard to this compilation, being unacquainted with the dead languages, I could not draw from original Greek and Latin sources, I could but make use of what has been given to the world by laborious students who have accomplished successful literary work, I could but select from among the vast multitude of events and facts, and the conflicting ideas which have resulted from them through many generations of men, such as most forcibly struck out sparks of thought from my own mind, and suited my purpose.

The history of the Jews and the history of Rome were not new to me; but while putting them together I have been led to see much that I had never before perceived, to see things worth reflecting on, which leads me to hope the book is worth offering to the public.

I studied my subject in Rome. The standard works from which I have collected information will be found foot-noted; I have most freely made use of "*The History of the Romans under the Empire,*" with the kind and full permission of Dean Merivale, of Ely.

From the lively, graphic descriptions by Dr. J. G. Sheppard in his *Fall of Rome*, and by Lord Mahon (afterwards Earl Stanhope) in his *Belisarius*, I have given ideas of the state of society, and incidents that occurred during the conflicts with barbarians; and when wishing to put before young readers a general view of the catacombs, I repeated Dr. Maitland's simple and clear statements of what he saw and what he learned in those sepulchral passages and chambers, yet not without reference to more recent works on the subject than "*The Church in the Catacombs.*"

This historical sketch begins with the first treaty made between the Romans and the Jews, and is carried up to the Barbaric or Chaotic period, out of which, a little later on, the modern nations emerged under the influence, and impelled by the increasing power, of the Church of Rome. Earnestly and undauntedly had she laboured for the conversion of the wild pagans, and had attached them to herself, and her alliance with Charlemagne was a master-stroke of policy by which she revived the Empire, and secured its allegiance to herself.

E. H. H.

CONTENTS.

CHAPTER I.
THE MACCABEES AND THE HERODS 1

CHAPTER II.
IN THE DAYS OF AUGUSTUS CÆSAR 35

CHAPTER III.
UNDER THE CLAUDII 67

CHAPTER IV.
ST. PAUL AND ST. LUKE 97

CHAPTER V.
THE FIERY TRIAL 123

CHAPTER VI.
THE ROMANS IN JUDEA 153

CHAPTER VII.

THE TRIUMPH 185

CHAPTER VIII.

UNDER THE YOKE 209

CHAPTER IX.

FINAL DISPERSION UNDER PATRIARCHAL RULE . 235

CHAPTER X.

IN THE AGE OF CONSTANTINE 271

CHAPTER XI.

DURING THE BARBARIAN INVASIONS . . . 295

CHAPTER XII.

WHEN IMPERIAL POWER FELL, AND PAPAL POWER ROSE 321

CHAPTER XIII.

WHAT THEIR BURIAL PLACES SHOW . . . 355

APPENDIX 379

THE MACCABEES AND THE HERODS.

I

"And I will make of thee a great nation, and I will bless thee, and make thy name great, and thou shalt be a blessing. And I will bless them that bless thee, and curse him that curseth thee; and in thee shall all families of the earth be blessed."—GEN. xii. 2, 3.

> " But then there came a voice, and still
> Its words through all my being thrill;
> Yet whether to the soul they came,
> Flashed inwards like the levin-flame,
> Or whether on the ear they fell,
> In spoken words, I cannot tell.
> 'Abram,' it said, 'I bid thee come
> Forth from thy kindred and thy home
> To a far land which I will show,
> Where I will make thy name to grow:
> The favour of thy God possessing,
> Thou shalt be blessed, and be a blessing.'"
>   *From " The Call of Abraham." By Hankinson.*

I.

THE MACCABEES AND THE HERODS.

JEHOVAH'S ancient people! The most wonderful people on the face of the earth, in the grandest of earth's many cities; for though modern cities may now vie with Rome, or may surpass her in world-wide power, in commercial activity, in internal magnificance, yet which of them has such a history—can show at once such evidences of a most glorious past, tokens of present life and growth—actual prosperity, bearing hopeful signs of future advancement?

When we read in the eighth chapter of the First Book of Maccabees of the beginning of intercourse between the Jews and the Romans, we see that they could previously have known very little of one another, scarcely as much as the Chinese knew of us when Queen Victoria ascended the throne; though more than five hundred and eighty years had elapsed since the foundation of Rome.

"Now Judas had heard of the fame of the Romans, that they were mighty and valiant men, and such as would lovingly accept all that joined themselves unto them, and make a league of amity with all that came unto them. * * *

"Also, that whom they would help to a kingdom, those reign; and whom again they would, they displace: finally, that they were greatly exalted. Yet, for all this, none of them wore a crown, or was clothed in purple, to be magnified thereby. Moreover, how they had made for themselves a senate house, wherein three hundred and twenty men sat in council daily, consulting always for the people, to the end they might be well ordered; and that they committed their government to one man every year, who ruled over all their country, and that all were obedient to that one, and that there was neither envy nor emulation among them. In consideration of these things, Judas chose Eupolemus the son of John, the son of Accos, and Jason the son of Eleazar, and sent them to Rome to make a league of amity and confederacy with them; and to entreat them that they would take the yoke from them; for they saw that the kingdom of the Grecians did oppress Israel with servitude. They went therefore to Rome, which was a very great journey, and came into the senate, where they spake and said—

"'Judas Maccabeus, with his brethren and the people of the Jews, have sent us unto you, to make a confederacy and peace with you, and that we might be registered your confederates and friends.'

"So that matter pleased the Romans well."

Four centuries had rolled away since the Prophet Daniel had interpreted Nebuchadnezzar's dream. All devout Jews, being acquainted with their Scriptures, must have been familiar with the words of that unfulfilled prophecy. Conjectures must have been formed as to the meaning of the signs, yet little could Judas and his councillors foresee that the nation who entrusted their government every year to one man, who wore neither crown nor purple robe, would prove to be the kingdom strong as iron which would break in pieces and bruise all other kingdoms. In happy ignorance of this hidden truth, the ambassadors must have been agreeably influenced by the favourable reception they met with, and deeply impressed with what they saw in the great city. Such impressions could not fail to produce lasting results on their own minds, which would naturally be communicated to their fellow-countrymen on their return to Judea: but of these two men, Eupolemus and Jason, we know only their names, and the names of their fathers. Of the general character of the Jews of that generation we have some means of judging, and a thoughtful historian who has considered the subject has distinctly put it before us.

"After the return from captivity in Babylon, a singular alteration in the character of the Jews displayed itself. Before they had been in Babylon they had been too prone on every occasion to adopt the practices and habits of adjacent nations; they now secluded themselves from the rest of the world in proud assurance of their own religious superiority. The law which before was perpetually violated, or almost forgotten, was now by general consent enforced to its extreme points, and even beyond. Their city, their native land, their religious ceremonies, became the objects of a too passionate attachment. Intermarriages with foreigners, neither forbidden by the statute, nor by the former practice, were strictly inhibited. The observance of the Sabbath, and even of the sabbatical year, was enforced with unprecedented rigour, such as we do not hear of in their earlier annals, even to the neglect of defence in time of war. In short, from this period commences that unsocial spirit, that hatred towards mankind, and want of humanity to all but their own kindred, with which the Jews are branded by all the Roman writers."*

Thus had the national character of God's own peculiar people deteriorated under trials which had tended to swell their hearts with unholy pride, and to lead them dangerously near to the hidden snares of selfishness and hypocrisy, developing the evil dispositions, of which we read in the New Testament, as being severely rebuked by our Lord Jesus Christ. Yet every generation, even the most crooked and perverse, had its righteous men— true sons of Noah, the preacher of righteousness, and of Abraham, who under God's blessing and direction went

* From Milman's "History of the Jews."

forth from his country, his kindred, and his father's house, that his faith and obedience might be a blessing to the world at large. Always the Hebrew Church, instituted by God's covenant with Abraham, has had members worthy of the calling, men who might well be likened to good seed widely sown by a careful prescient Husband-man. Numbers of Israelitish colonies had grown up out of families, or bands of exiles, which were prospering in distant lands. King Nebuchadnezzar had driven those men, or their fathers, out of the Holy Land and the surrounding countries; but under the most trying circumstances God will provide for His faithful people, so the exiles had increased wonderfully, and in course of time many of them had obtained freedom, and had planted themselves, or been planted by their rulers, all over Babylonia, in Media and Persia, and had even pushed their way to China. According to Hannenburg, the Israelites of China belonged to the Ten Tribes.*

The Jews who were carried away from Judea as prisoners by the Ptolemies, who afterwards made use of them as soldiers, settled very numerously in all parts of Egypt, especially in Alexandria, and in course of time scattered themselves in small colonies along the north coast of Africa.

Under the government of the Selucidæ the Jews prospered; their aptitude and taste for commerce, their intelligence and activity, and the faithful spirit in which they served their conquerors, was justly appreciated; and their being well placed in that part of the world, opened to their brethren in Judea the roads to Syria and Asia Minor, to Cyprus, Greece, Crete, and Italy. In most of the towns in those countries a Jewish quarter was formed, and a synagogue rose, perhaps near a

* "Rome et la Judée," page 108 of vol. i.

heathen temple. Colonies of other races likewise had their quarters, and their places of worship in every one of the towns of chief importance in the ancient world.

The Jews readily acquired the languages of the people among whom they sojourned, or whom they visited for the purposes of traffic or usury. At an early period they began to thrive on money lending.*

Then, as now, the Hebrew language was used in synagogues, and rabbis and well-educated Jews were acquainted with it, but did not speak it, consequently it rapidly became almost a dead language, as even the Jews in the Holy Land, after their return from the captivity, generally spoke Chaldean mixed with Syrian.

More than two hundred years before the Christian era the ideas and opinions of the Hebrews were strong enough in Egypt and Syria to attract the attention of the rulers of those countries, who began to see that these new elements introduced into society were important. Their action was not always checked; for when Antioch, the capital of Syria, was founded, equal rights of citizenship were given to the Jews as to the heathen. Subsequently there grew up in Syria and Asia Minor, and in some of the islands in that part of the world, a body of Greek teachers who positively taught monotheism. Three of these philosophers at different times emigrated to Athens.

The first who did so, Zeno, taught in a *stoa* or porch, whence those who followed his system were called Stoics. They grew into a highly esteemed and very numerous body of teachers, whose disciples passed on from Greece to Rome. May not faith in the God of Abraham, the one Almighty God, and morality, which

* "Rome et la Judée." Par Mons. le Comte de Champagny, de l'Academie Française. Paris, 1870.

inculcates a sense of duty towards God and man, be still justly looked upon as the porch at the door of the Church?

The Jews believed that the heathen gods were doomed to be destroyed and forgotten, so also thought the Stoics, who likewise derided idols and their temples. The Jews, excepting the Sadducees, believed in a resurrection, and they looked forward to the purifying of the earth by a universal fire, which would inaugurate a new era. They believed that God required men to obtain firm command over their passions and appetites; therefore, in that licentious age the Stoics set a good example, and notwithstanding the austerity of their sentiments and manners, many of them gained the admiration and regard of intelligent men, and the sect continued to increase in number, to spread, and obtain influence.

The books of the Maccabees relate to an interesting period of ancient church history. The heart of Judas Maccabeus is not laid open to us by the word of God, we can only know him historically as a brave patriot, who ended a noble, energetic life by an heroic death. As far as Judas was personally concerned, the alliance he had made with the Romans was quite unavailing; the treaty was concluded B C. 160, and before the close of that year the gallant chieftain had been defeated and slain in the battle of Azotus.

When we read of the struggle so earnestly, so strenuously made by the Jews under the command of the Asmonean princes, the question naturally arises, Why were they not blessed with success?

Was their strong desire and endeavour to free their country, and to establish its independence, the primary motive with many of them, rather than the promotion of God's honour and glory? Certainly it was not so with those who refused to save their lives by denying the faith. Or, was it contrary to the decree of the Almighty Ruler, that at this period of her history the kingdom of Judah should rise eminently, after a long career of wilfulness and disobedience, during which she, who ought to have been an example to all other nations, had shown herself unworthy of her high privileges, for she had not, as a nation, walked consistently in the light from heaven by which she was encompassed ?*

The time appointed for her visitation was drawing near, her King was coming quickly, and He was to find the land of His father David, not one of the great powers of the world, but a land about to be forsaken of both her kings, though the sceptre had not entirely departed when Shiloh came.†

The calamities of the Jews at this time appear like divine chastisements falling on a guilty, rebellious nation; but as we read the books of Maccabees, we are astonished by the numerous instances of individuals and of whole families who exhibited religious heroism in all its noblest and grandest aspects. We cannot help thinking that such men suffered more on account of the sins of their country and their kindred than on their own. Is not this Christ-like? The early Christians thought so, and included them among the Christian martyrs, whose deathdays they observed as festivals, in commemoration of patience, courage, resignation, self-sacrifice, and the trustful faith that gives everything up calmly into the hands of God, as the mother gave her seven sons, and they were ready to die, to give their lives for the covenant of their fathers.

The Maccabees and their loyal adherents, as Bishop

* 1 Macc. i. 11—13; Jer. vii. 2—5, viii. 3, 5—8, 12, 13.
† Gen. xlix. 10.

Wordsworth says, "were delivered by God, not *from* death, but *by* death. They were freed from this death-like life of ours into that glorious life which never dies, and which we hope will be ours on the other side of the grave. They looked upon their death-day as their birthday, their birthday to life eternal, and they rejoiced in it as such. The speeches of the Maccabean martyrs and confessors clearly show that they had a lively faith in the immortality of the soul, and in the resurrection of the body, and that they looked upon the grave, not as a dreary place, but as a bright passage to that blessed region in which they would dwell for ever in glory." Bishop Wordsworth points out most remarkable points of resemblance between their times and our own. There was no open vision,* no miracles were worked to guide or to save them; they had no prophets among them, but they were themselves the subjects of prophecy. They could read in the book of Daniel of martyrs who would not be delivered as he had been from the lion's den, but who would die for the truth; but their sufferings would not be for destruction, but to try them, and purify them, and make them white, and that the people who knew their God would be strong, and do exploits ; that the persecutor would be cut off; that at length the end would come, according to the words of the Prophet, "And at that time thy people shall be delivered, every one that shall be found written in the book. And many of them that sleep in the dust of the earth shall awake, some to everlasting life, and some to shame and everlasting contempt. And they that be wise shall shine as the brightness of the firmament, and they that turn many to righteousness as the stars for ever and ever."

"It was faith in these glorious revelations which

* As in the days of Samuel's childhood (1 Sam. iii. 1).

enabled the Maccabees to act and to suffer as they did."*

When Judas Maccabeus had fallen, Jonathan, who had generously submitted to a brother younger than himself, was called to the front. He was prudent as he was brave; for he affected a reconciliation with the Syrians, and placed himself on friendly terms with the new king.

Jonathan sent another embassy to Rome, which, like the former, was favourably received; but misfortunes again followed on this measure. Jonathan, lured to his own destruction, was captured and massacred with a thousand of his soldiers by the tyrant Trypho, who, while guardian of the young king of Syria, aimed at obtaining the crown of that distracted country, and as a preliminary step he deprived young Antiochus of an ally likely to have proved faithful to him.

Simon also perished, a victim of the basest treachery; thus the three great Maccabean princes prematurely fell. Nevertheless, the struggle fitfully continued long after their death.

The pontifical and regal powers were united in the Asmonean princes, though it is doubtful which of them was the first to assume the title of king.

Aristobulus and his younger brother, Alexander, who succeeded him, bore both the titles of high priest and king. Alexander, who was passionately fond of war, died while prosecuting a siege. He had bequeathed the kingdom to his wife, Alexandra. Their elder son, Hyrcanus, was, on the death of his father, made high priest, as he had no talent for the arrangement of state affairs, and no taste for war: their younger son, Aristo-

* See "The Maccabees and the Church," by Chr. Wordsworth, D.D., commenting on Daniel xii. 1—3.

bulus, was to succeed his mother on the throne. "The Pharisees, who were becoming a very powerful sect, gained undue influence over the queen, became directors of the state, assuming at their pleasure to banish and recall, to loose and to bind."*

Under this state of things the people became dissatisfied and refractory, and were easily excited and divided into factions by ambitious leaders. These times were terribly turbulent; while the Jews were quarrelling among themselves, and at last they dragged the Romans into the conflict. Aristobulus the Second entreated the assistance of the Romans, whose armies were then in Syria and Asia Minor, under the command of Pompey. The consequences of this step were fatal to the Jews. The Romans had never really done them any good, had rendered them little or no assistance, although they had accepted valuable presents from the Maccabean princes; and now Pompey and even his emissaries treated with both the contending parties, accepting all their gifts, and making fair promises to each in return. Aristobulus, on discovering this, with natural indignation, quitted the camp of Pompey without rendering him the customary tokens of respect. The haughty Romans immediately entered Judea and besieged Jerusalem. Twelve thousand Jews perished by the sword, besides numbers who destroyed themselves rather than fall into the hands of the enemy.

Judea was to be governed by a procurator from Rome; the whole country was completely reduced to a Roman province by the proud conqueror, who had received the homage of twelve crowned heads at once. Deeply was he to drink of the bitter cup he had often mixed for others—he was to be defeated, basely betrayed, deca-

---

* "The Jewish War." By Josephus. Book i., chap. v.

pitated, and his head despatched to his rival, Julius Cæsar. But Pompey the Great was in the zenith of his glory when he sent King Aristobulus and his family, consisting of two sons and two daughters, as prisoners to Rome. The elder son contrived to escape, all the other members of the Jewish royal family lived as captives in Rome. At the same time vast numbers of Jews were sent into the city, most of whom were publicly sold in the market-place as slaves.

Slavery was not altogether an unknown condition among the Jews; bond-service was permitted under the Mosaic dispensation, but the institution differed essentially from that which prevailed in heathen nations. Slavery among the Jews could arise legally either from captivity in war, insolvency, or from inability to make restitution in case of theft. But as it existed among the Jews, to those of Hebrew descent, it was little more than servitude or apprenticeship is now among ourselves, and the Jewish law gave many injunctions to secure the humane treatment of slaves.* But by the laws of Rome they were considered "chattels," were bought, sold, exchanged, could be punished to any extent, and even put to death by their master. They could not appeal to any court of law, unless some benevolent citizen allowed the appeal to be made in his name; for the slave had no legal rights; even the wives and children of slaves belonged, not to husbands and fathers, but to the master. Tyranny was in the ascendency, culminating to the highest point it has ever attained; and when we read of cruel despotism on the throne, we may be sure it as

* Lev. xxv. 39—55; Exod. xxi. 20, 21, 26, 27, xx. 10; Deut. v. 14, xii. 17, 18, xxv. 4. They might redeem themselves, or be redeemed by another, by purchase equal to the value of the remaining years of service (Lev. xxv. 47, 53, 40, 41).

a rule existed in families and in households of every description. Gibbon thus describes family life: "Woman was defined by the laws of Rome, not as a person, but as a thing, who could be claimed like other moveables. She was treated as the slave of man, not as his helpmate, companion, and best friend: the husband held most absolute power over the wife and daughter, could even put them to death for the most trifling offences. In his father's house the son was confounded by the laws with the other property, the cattle and the slaves. The parent was responsible to no earthly tribunal. According to his discretion, a father might chastise his children by stripes, by imprisonment, by exile, by sending them to work with the meanest of his servants. The parent held the power of life and death; infants and sickly or otherwise unpromising children were often put out of the way by fathers or mothers who did not care to have the trouble of bringing them up; and it was considered a disgrace, as well as a misfortune, for parents to have a family consisting only of daughters."*

Since such was the lot of members of the family, that of the slave must have been sad indeed. Even well-born, well-educated men and women might be, by force or fraud, in peace or war, converted into slaves, whose lives, in every sense of the word, were held entirely at the mercy of a fellow-man. In Rome the aristocrats were generally more cruelly disposed towards slaves, than were citizens of the popular party. Rich men held slaves by thousands, and perhaps took pride in having them from diverse nationalities. Many slaves were purchased for their capacity as pugilists, wrestlers, or gladiators, and not a few because of personal beauty, or for capacity as clowns or jesters. The

---

* Gibbon's "Decline and Fall," chap. xliv.

aggregation into one mass of human beings, without moral or other discipline, with no common objects, and many of them trained to fighting, could not but cause unhappiness and crime and danger to society.* Many masters thought chiefly of curbing their slaves rigorously and heartlessly, to keep them in order. Nevertheless, when the head of a house was a noble-minded man, and there were many noble Romans, the unlimited power he held enabled him to do a great deal of good, and to soften down the hardships, and brighten the lives of all around him. This is illustrated in the life of Terence, the dramatic poet, a native of Carthage, brought to Rome as a captive slave, and bought by P. Terentius Lucanus, a senator, who, perceiving that the boy had excellent abilities, bestowed on him a superior education, and then emancipated him, and permitted him to take his own name, which was often done when a master liberated a slave to whom he had become attached. Scipio, who had taste for literature, took great interest in this lad, one of the many who had lost their freedom and been expatriated by his own conquests, and those of his distinguished relatives; and being pleased with the young poet's writings, he introduced him into the most refined and intellectual circles in Rome. From the works of Terence we can gather that in his master's family, while still a slave, he was kindly treated. He saw home life under so happy an aspect, that in after years it was refreshing to look back on, when, as an author, he had to battle with the world, appreciated by some, envied and calumniated by others. Referring to his own hard experiences, he remarks:

* "Judaism at Rome, B.C. 76 to A.D. 140." By Frederick Huidekoper. New York. p. 89.

"I have found nothing so advantageous as mildness and a forgiving disposition;" and, "remembering that, as I am a human being, I ought to consider none of the incidents which befall my fellow-creatures to be matters of unconcern to me."

The sentiments expressed by Terence show that his impressions of domestic life were such as had tended to give refined feelings and a good tone of mind; his heart had not withered, as one might have imagined would be the case with a captive taken from his country, and sold as a slave. He writes of home, as the place in which children may receive the best instruction. He says, "As fathers form their children, so they prove. .... I know it is better to bind your children to you by a feeling of respect and gentleness, than by fear."

Philo, the Jewish historian, tells us that the Jews captured by Pompey were emancipated almost without exception by their generous masters, who were unwilling to do violence to their religious scruples. If this be true, surely it must be attributed to a wholesome fear of the great God of the Jews, of whose wonderful works they heard, not only from the Jews, but also from the soldiers lately returned from the East. Dean Milman suggests that probably there were opulent commercial Jews already in Rome, who with their usual national spirit purchased, to the utmost of their means, their unhappy fellow-countrymen, and enabled them to settle in freedom, to begin a new life in the great metropolis of the world. It is certain that from this time forward great numbers of Jewish freed men inhabited Rome. Jews themselves now tell us that the Roman masters found Jewish slaves unfit for service, and continual causes of difficulty and inconvenience, on account of the peculiar manners and customs to which they were so religiously attached, that it proved impossible to train them for servitude.

All that we read concerning the state of bondage, as it existed in the age or day on which the Sun of righteousness arose to lighten our dark world, helps us to realize the full meaning and force of the blessed word *Redemption*, as it must have been felt and understood in that day, when taught by the common experience of daily life.

Immediately on his arrival, Aristobulus was joined by his elder son, but they were both quickly put out of Pompey's way; the king was poisoned, and the prince seized and beheaded. Some time afterwards Antony sent the body of Aristobulus home to Jerusalem, where it was buried in the royal sepulchre.

Antigonus, the younger son of the deceased king, retired to Chalchis, where he waited the opportunity for asserting his right to the crown of Judæa.

Meanwhile that country and also Galilee and the adjacent districts constituted a Roman province, governed by a procurator. Generally speaking, countries subjugated by the superior power submitted quietly to their fate. Their people felt at first crushed, well knowing that further efforts to assert independence must be worse than useless, and under Roman government they soon became reconciled to the change. The legions stationed in their midst at first overawed them, but these were mainly recruited from the inhabitants of the land, and became fixed to the districts which they defended. This system had a tranquilizing effect on the popular mind; not a few of the men grew proud of being considered Roman soldiers, proud of their connection with Rome, though they had never seen that great city, the far-famed mistress of the world. "As state after state was annexed, the conquering general was allowed, with the help of a commission of instructions from the senate, to define the political conditions of the country, and to lay down the provincial laws. The object of this was mainly to fix the amount of tithe and tribute, to map out the countries lately acquired into assize districts for the courts of justice, and to give or to withhold special privileges in the case of those who had been most marked as friends or foes. But the Roman statesmen were always tolerant of local customs, and did not attempt to obtain uniformity of system. They broke up political unions, or federations that had been strong and might still be dangerous, but they respected the religion of conquered nations, and all other old forms of national life, and let their subjects manage their own affairs, for the most part, as they pleased. Each country held its separate life with varying customs that had been slowly shaped in the course of ages, and every part of it enjoyed a large measure of self-government.* In Egypt the laws of Ptolemy were still respected, as were those of Hiero in Sicily, and of Solon in Athens.

To this general rule the Jews formed no positive exception, although, for obvious reasons, those peculiar people did not mix with their fellow-subjects of the empire as readily and thoroughly as others; yet in process of time a kind of amalgamation was effected, and the people, when not stirred up by ambitious leaders, grew disposed towards submission and peace.

Antipater, procurator of the province including Judæa and the neighbouring districts, was an Idumean. Idumea and Galilee had, under the rule of the Maccabees,

---

* "Epochs of Roman History: The Early Empire." By W. W. Copes, M.A. pp. 181, 182. London: Longman and Co. 1879.

become converted to the knowledge of the one true God, though they had not adopted everything pertaining to the religion of the Jews. The people generally acknowledged God and forsook idols, though they were still very ignorant and superstitious; and the educated classes accepted with reverence the Hebrew Scriptures, which had been translated into Greek.

Antipater appointed his eldest son tetrarch, or military governor of Jerusalem and the country immediately round that city, and he sent Herod, his son next in age, into Galilee, with equal authority and the same title, although he was then a mere youth. The young Idumean chief proved himself equal to the position, and he gained a quite romantic reputation by the adventures he met with in his expeditions against the brigands, who infested the border-land between Judæa and Syria. Herod caught and put to death a notorious robber, who for years had alarmed and disturbed the country, and had made travelling or conveying goods so dangerous, that, for mutual protection, people congregated in very large parties to perform a journey. His achievements gave him the renown always gratifying to a young hero; made him so great a favourite with the people, that songs were composed in his honour, and sung in the villages and towns in praise of him who had come among them to deliver them from the terrible freebooter, and to give them the blessings of peace. The fame of his exploits made Herod known, through Sextus Cæsar, governor of Syria, to Julius Cæsar, who interested himself in the young Idumean Jew and his prospects.

Before the Christian era the ancient pagan religions had begun to be widely and forcibly shaken to their very foundations by the unseen, unsuspected power of Jewish influence in favour of monotheism. Jewish views had gained rapid foothold at Rome; multitudes of Gentiles, without adopting Judaism, had adopted monotheism. Wherever belief in a moral Ruler of the universe was diffused, civilization received an impetus. Belief in such a Ruler gave encouragement to, and sense of responsibility for, a right use of life. A difficulty experienced by modern missionaries confronted the Jews in their first efforts. The Greek and Latin languages contained no term for the one Supreme Being. The word "God" was a common noun, as our word man. The heathen use of the word "God" was analogous. We say, "Man proposes, God disposes."

By man we mean *any* mortal. A Greek or Roman would equally have understand the word "god" as meaning *any* divine being. To meet this difficulty the Jews connected with the word God, or substituted for it, adjectives which would partly at least convey their meaning. Generally speaking, the plebeians much more readily adopted Jewish ideas and opinions, than did the patricians; indeed, in Rome the aristocracy was the chief enemy of Judaism. The senate and the upper classes thought new light dangerous, likely to increase the difficulty of keeping those beneath them in subjection. Cicero advocated that no one should be permitted the exercise of any religion, either publicly or privately, except what had been established by the senate.*

In spite of all that man could do to shut out the knowledge of God, the light from heaven struggled through. Looking intently on those dark times, we may find a glimmering ray, and trace it on from generation to

* "Judaism at Rome." By Fred. Huidekoper. Published at New York.

generation. Take, for instance, Antonia, a daughter of Marc Antony and Octavia, the sister of Augustus—a beautiful, virtuous, and influential lady. She was probably a monotheist, for not only was her intimate friend in early life a Jewess, but also her business agent and superintendent of her estates in Alexandria was the Jewish ethnarch of that city, brother of Philo, the Jewish historian. This amiable Antonia brought up from childhood the freedwoman Cænis, educated her well, and she became the much-loved wife of Vespasian, who was raised to the imperial throne.* When the popular party under Julius Cæsar came into power, monotheists were introduced into the senate, and in his time Roman dignitaries on the first day of the passover threw away idol images. Cæsar's conduct had won the respect and grateful regard of the Jews, and his untimely end called forth their tears and lamentations. Many Jews were present at the burning of his remains in the forum. The pyre was erected in an open space in front of the Temple of Vesta, a spot overlooked by his own house. The wailing of the large body of oriental mourners was a most remarkable feature of that scene, which could never be forgotten by one who had witnessed it. After the funeral, for several following nights the Jews assembled at the tomb. The visitation of tombs was an ancient custom among them. There are two kinds of mourning for the dead; the one at the house, by relations and friends; the other more general, at the burial place of distinguished men, prophets, and teachers. Then the wailing chant was again raised, and prayers were offered towards the Holy City, commending the dead man to God, to whom they believed he still lived, though their ideas concerning a future life were very dim.

* "Judaism at Rome." By Fred. Huidekoper.

The sect of the Sadducees altogether denied the resurrection, believed in no angels or spirits; but happily those sceptical materialists were comparatively few in number.

After the death of Julius Cæsar, when the aristocracy again obtained control in B.C. 30, by the victory over Antony, they were hampered by members of the popular party. Some of these senators were at once got rid of by threats or other means, and in B.C. 18 or 17, by a preconcerted plot, nearly all the advocates of monotheism and popular rights were violently ejected. This reactionary senate, during a fierce conflict against Tiberius and the popular party, undertook to put Cicero's suggestion in practice. They drove the Jews out of Rome, and prohibited Jewish teaching. From this time forward no Roman could legally profess Judaism.*

Under these disadvantageous circumstances the Jews fell into disrepute; and it became the fashion of the day to deride their peculiarities. All their national customs greatly excited the curiosity of the Romans; the multitude strangely misunderstood the meaning of many of them. In the works of classical authors we read the most absurd explanations accounting for Jewish customs. Romans, being puzzled by the fact that Jews would not eat pork, which they themselves relished as delicious food, thought the Hebrew worshipped the pig. Plutarch has given us an amusing argument carried on by a little party of philosophers, who had met to discuss interesting subjects in a friendly social way. The chief speakers are Polycrates, Callistratus and Lamprias. "I very much doubt," says the first, "whether it is on account of the honour and reverence in which swine are held by the

---

* From "Judaism at Rome." By Frederick Huidekoper. Chap. i., pp. 1—7. New York, 1877.

Jews, or whether, on the contrary, it is not out of abomination, that they refrain from eating them; for the things they say about it themselves are like fables." "I think," said Callistratus, "that the animal is held in a certain honour by the Jew; and although it is an ugly, ill-favoured thing, I do not see that it is any more repulsive than the beetle, the griffin, the crocodile, or the cat, which are worshipped, some in one place, and some in another, by Egyptian priests, as most holy. The mole is deified by the Egyptians, because it is blind, and darkness is more ancient than light, and because it brings forth mice in the fifth generation at the new moon; and the lion is dedicated to the sun, because it sleeps very lightly, its eyes glistening when it is asleep; and because the Nile pours a fresh flood upon the fields when the sun passes through the sign of Leo, they make water fountains in the form of lion's heads. The followers of Zoroaster worshipped the hedgehog, and hated water-mice, and said that he who should kill most of them would render the most acceptable service to the gods, and therefore be himself most happy. This makes me think that if the Jews had abominated swine, they would have killed them as the Magi killed mice."

Lamprias agrees with Polycrates, being inclined to think that the pig cannot be a suitable object of worship, that it is not to be compared to the lion, the bull, the horned animals, or to the ibis cat, moles, and others reverenced in Egypt, because it in no wise illustrates power or noble aspirations, nor does it in any way set a good example to man, for it takes pleasure in nothing but wallowing in the mire. "Observe," he says, "that the eyes of swine are so bent and fixed downwards, that they can see nothing above, and cannot so much as look up to the sky, unless they are thrown on their backs, with their feet upwards, so that the balls of their eyes are turned quite contrary to their natural direction, and although, as a general rule, this creature is always crying or grunting, yet if the feet are turned upward, as before said, it will be perfectly silent with amazement at seeing the face of heaven, which it is not accustomed to do, and so at once it ceases to make a noise." These heathen "friends in council" carried on the discussion, and considered the question, Are the Hebrew God and Bacchus both one? The little they knew about the feast of tabernacles, when the Jews sat under tents or arbours covered with vine branches and ivy, had given rise to that idea. We do not know at what conclusion the philosophers arrived, as the end of that book of Plutarch is lost.*

Seneca gives a curious account of one of his early experiences. He tells us that when he was a young man, his most intimate friend, a disciple of Pythagoras, persuaded him to give up eating animal food. At the end of a year he was not only quite reconciled to the change, but really preferred the diet of bread and vegetables, and thought his mind was more active in consequence. But prejudices against foreign customs gained ground, and decrees were made for the expulsion of what were called other race religious observances. One of the proofs of adhesion to foreign superstitions was abstaining from the flesh of certain animals. Seneca's father had no distaste for philosophy, but he greatly

---

* "Peter Cunæus (*De Republica Hebræorum*, ed. Lyons, p. 273) complains bitterly that Plutarch should have tried to fix on the Jews the stigma of Bacchus worship, which Marcus Cato condemned in the strongest terms as the worst evil that ever afflicted the Roman state."

"Notices of the Jews and their Country by the Classic Writers of Antiquity." By John Gill. pp. 75, 76.

dreaded calumny, and therefore wished his son to resume his former way of living, to which the young man consented, not sorry to return to better fare.*

Possibly he had gained something by this training on the Samian philosopher's system, which, in a luxurious age, braced the mind and body by self-denial, study, and gymnastic exercises.

Although the Jew and his principles were so little understood, yet the Greek and Roman world adopted his division of time into weeks of seven days. For a long while the Jewish customs with regard to the Sabbath-day perplexed their fellow-citizens, before their meaning was perceived clearly enough to be respected.

Horace, Juvenal, Tacitus, and many other writers, derided the Jews, yet they were obliged to acknowledge that all over Rome they were making proselytes. Their Sabbaths, their festivals, and even their fast-days were becoming generally in some degree observed. Jewish festivals were getting popular, on which lanterns in the windows and other signs of festivity were to be seen, not only in the Jewish quarter, but also in other parts of Rome. Many Roman women were converted; the men were not so easily convinced, but the high-minded, who respected truth and justice, and philosophers of various schools, were attracted by the righteousness of the Hebrew law, and thus led to esteem the Hebrew, though they might feel no desire to embrace his religion. The multitude of heathen were not superior to the age in which they lived, and to this common herd the exclusiveness of most of the Jews, and their refusal to enter heathen temples, could seem nothing but absurd stupidity, or insolent national pride, or a heartless want

* Seneca, Epistle 108, xx. 21, 22, as the story is related in "Judaism at Rome," by Frederick Huidekoper.

of sympathy; accordingly, Molon describes them as godless, and hostile to all other men, and his words have been repeated by many writers; thus the opinion they express has gone down from generation to generation.

Yet always there were Jews who, on the contrary, yielded too much to circumstances, and to Romanizing influences. The Herods set this example; for although ostentatiously observing, when at Rome, their national rites, yet they were far from being genuine Israelites in heart and faith: of this their conduct continually reminded the Jews, as it now reminds us who read of them.

The first Herod, that gallant young prince who had distinguished himself in the guerilla war in Galilee, went to Rome before the death of Julius Cæsar, and was warmly received. We have an amusing account of the manner in which his birthday was celebrated in that city. The loyal Jews covered their door posts and the fronts of their houses with evergreens and a profusion of flowers, among which fragrant violets were the most abundant; but the writer of this description, evidently a conceited genius, more cynical than amiable, is pleased to notice the less pleasant odour of inferior oil in the lamps suspended from windows and trees. Such ill-natured satire, intended to ridicule the parsimony of the Jews, who did not keep the feast on this occasion in the luxurious Roman style, was likely to be popular, as the favour shown by Julius Cæsar to Herod and his family gave them immense influence, of which no doubt many Romans were jealous.*

The assassination of Julius Cæsar caused great disturbance throughout the empire; but although Herod had by that event lost a good friend, yet it did not

* "Notices of the Jews and their Country in the Classic Writers of Antiquity." By John Gill. Longman and Green, London.

impede his advancement. Octavius was even more favourably disposed towards him, than had been the late dictator. Between these two young men a strong friendship sprang up, which lasted till death parted them. Both were gifted with superior talents and abilities, but the character of the Roman became by far the nobler, because he attained the power of self-control; and the trying circumstances in which he was so suddenly placed tended to make him thoughtful and cautious. Though surrounded by magnificence, he maintained simple habits which pleased the people, and he attracted poets and other writers to his court, whose encomiums were of real service to him.

When he assumed imperial dignity as Octavius Augustus Cæsar, he, with admirable strength of will, put a stop to severe measures and other evils which had prevailed during the civil war, effectually producing order and peace, because he checked not only other men in authority, but also himself. He spent money liberally on his people, amused them with games and festivals, and in times of distress he gave bountiful provision to the needy. The affectionate title, "*Father of the country*," had long been generally bestowed on Augustus, before he received it from the senate and the people with the warmest expressions of gratitude.

As regards Herod, it was natural that a young prince whose strong arm and military skill had made all things yield to his will, who courted difficulties and hazardous adventures for the pleasure of overcoming, should, when in the heyday of prosperity, flushed with flattery, set his affections passionately on a beautiful daughter of a rival house. Mariamne, the Maccabean princess, was the most lovely and altogether attractive woman of the day. She was granddaughter of Hyrcanus the Second, one of those Asmonean princes, in whom, as we have seen, the pontifical and regal powers were united. He was both high priest and king. The union of those high offices had not tended to exalt the characters of those who bore them. The old man was proud, and fond of Mariamne, and for her sake pleaded Herod's cause with Marc Antony, who may also have been somewhat influenced by his admiration of a clever-spirited beauty.

He entrusted the government of Judæa to Herod and his brothers, and Mariamne's name was joined with that of her husband. As this marriage could not found a purely Jewish dynasty, the arrangements displeased the Jews, and especially the large important sect of the Pharisees; indeed, the Idumean family was generally unpopular. Antigonus, aware of this, quietly prepared his schemes. He obtained the promise of aid from Chalchis, hired a powerful body of Parthian soldiers, and then set up his standard, round which multitudes of Jews readily flocked. After some sharp fighting and much ignoble treachery, Antigonus obtained a temporary possession of the throne of Judæa. His first act was to mutilate the high priest by cutting off his ears, and allowing him to be carried away by the Parthians. Those barbarous enemies, before they retired, plundered Jerusalem and the surrounding villages. Unhappily for himself, Hyrcanus survived these indignities, to be restored to his country, and at last put to death by Herod's command, given in a fit of rage. Dearly did the high priest pay for having recommended and promoted the advancement of a bad man.

While the Parthians were ravaging his dominions, Herod escaped, and arrived safely in Rome, where his cause was warmly espoused by Marc Antony and Octavius Cæsar. Herod had never yet been honoured by the title of King of Judæa, and does not seem to have desired it, but his powerful friends thought him more competent than Mariamne's brother, who had a better hereditary claim to hold and exercise regal power.

In Rome Herod was made king of Judæa, and by the aid of the Romans he was established on his throne. It was not an ill-judged appointment, for he had displayed the qualities then required in a monarch, courage, subtlety, and capacities for ruling; all of the utmost value, because they were the characteristics most highly esteemed in the world. He was cruel, but as yet not more so than were many of his distinguished contemporaries. It was a cruel age. Men were brought up to think that taking a fellow-creature's life in the exciting and dangerous conflict for dominion and supremacy was as excusable as taking it on an actual battle-field. Even those who fell, if they were high-minded, took that view of the subject. Parents who destroyed their weak or deformed infants were applauded; and as to the aged, many persons agreed with Seneca, who considered it shameful to pray that life might be spared after strength and comeliness had departed.

Herod began his reign by endeavouring to gain the confidence, and to conciliate the feelings, of his subjects. He tried to attain popularity by much the same means which appeared to work successfully in Rome. He improved the city of Jerusalem, and built a grand palace for his own residence. He was condescending in his manner to the people, and often very liberal to them, and introduced Roman games and shows for their amusement. He made really zealous efforts to exalt the name of the Most High God, to whom he gave praise and glory by keeping up all the services and ceremonies of the divinely ordained religion, though he did not perceive and understand how indissolubly the honour of God is connected with the conduct of man, as exhibited throughout the course of every human life.

In the fifteenth year of his reign Herod restored the temple in a style of unprecedented magnificence, at an incalculable expense, and surrounded it with a wall, so as to enclose an area twice as large as its former extent. The Jews and their king were very proud of the splendid edifice, which surpassed Greek and Roman temples, and astonished Agrippa, the builder of the Pantheon, and other visitors from distant lands.

Yet, even while he was doing so much for the house and the city chosen and blessed by the God of Israel, Herod was also occupied with planning a new town which he built in the district of Samaria, and enclosed with a very strong wall. Into this city, which he called Sebaste, he introduced six thousand colonists, to whom he assigned an extremely fertile tract, and gave the inhabitants an enviable charter. In the centre of the buildings was erected a large and richly decorated temple to Cæsar, surrounded with consecrated ground. Indeed, there was not a suitable spot in his dominions which Herod permitted to be without some honourable memorial to Cæsar. One of the most beautiful, built of white marble, stood near the sources of the Jordan.*

Josephus commends the generosity of Herod, but his narrative shows that the king could be generous only to those who did not thwart his imperious will. He was not naturally devoid of the noble spirit of benevolence, which incited him to be a beneficent governor; and many favoured cities and individuals enjoyed the advantages bestowed by his liberality, and yet he was guilty of despicable meanness and atrocious cruelty.

* Josephus.

When any man stood in his way, whom he could not otherwise get rid of, Herod assumed absolute power, and put him to death. Thus died the high priest Hyrcanus, his wife's grandfather, and also her only brother. Then Mariamne's heart turned against her husband. The bitterness of her resentment gave her enemies pretexts for accusations against her; they fanned Herod's anger by every scandal they could invent, till at last he believed her to have been unfaithful, and the beautiful head of the queen he had been so proud of was struck off by his command. The commission of this crime almost turned his own brain. At times he could not believe she was dead, at others he suffered agonies of remorse: he retired into Samaria, where he diverted his thoughts by hunting. Mariamne had been beloved by the people; for her sake they now hated the king; her memory was sacred, and the hopes of the nation were set upon her sons, who through her, belonging to the Maccabean family, had, many thought, a better right to the throne than their father. Their grandmother, Alexandra, asserted their rights. She was put to death by Herod, but he spared the boys, and felt, or pretended to feel, great paternal affection for them. Six years later (B.C. 23) he took the lads Aristobulus and Alexander to Rome. Augustus received them most honourably and kindly. Herod left his sons under the Emperor's guardianship, to complete their education, and they had every facility given to them for growing up in the midst of high Roman life. Here, bright and promising were their youthful days, but on their return to Judæa they became victims of jealousy. Having neither respect nor affection for their father, they were drawn by conspirators into plots against him. Herod, who lived in a state of perpetual dread of losing his crown or his life, discovered a conspiracy, and ordered his sons to be strangled.

No man has ever developed a character more completely illustrative of the unsubdued natural man, nurtured in pride, than did Herod the Great. He was, we may say, selfish-pride personified. Following his career from youth to age, we see for years much that was promising. He was not only uncommonly handsome and strong, he had moreover excellent intellectual abilities, quick feelings, and abundant energy. Herod was capable of a true and warm friendship, as we see by his fidelity to Augustus Cæsar. He was not fond of money, not avaricious of wealth, but he loved praise, and no miser ever clutched his gold more selfishly than Herod grasped his power by wilful deliberate acts of heartlessless, injustice, cruelty, and crime; sinning more and more as the better part of his disposition became over-mastered by pride and self-will. The fully developed character is not lovely, even to the eye of the world; but the faults that constitute it, while they are growing, are looked on leniently, are even encouraged and applauded by flatterers.* Habitually giving way to his passions, Herod lost all power of self-control, and blinded by self-conceit, he could not see his own

---

* "Proportioned to his mind were Herod's personal endowments. In the chase, from his skill in horsemanship, he was always foremost. In a single day, accordingly, he sometimes overcame forty wild animals. The country abounds in wild boars, but particularly in deer and wild asses. As a warrior he was irresistible, and in the gymnasium exercise many have been astonished, seeing him the most direct javelin thrower and the most unerring bowman. But besides this mental and physical superiority, he was the favourite of fortune; for he rarely met with any disaster in war, and when he did, it was attributable, not to himself, but either to treachery, or to the rashness of his troops."—*Josephus*, Book i., chap. xxi.

conduct in the real light. In such a state of mind man is incapable of repentance, unless he be miraculously humbled; he cannot turn by any power inherent in himself, he can but do his utmost to kill his conscience, lest at any time it should awaken him to suffer the pangs of unavailing remorse.

Most strikingly does the character of this king of the Jews contrast with that of Him who came in great humility—the Babe for whom there was no room in the inn of the little town of Bethlehem—the young child whom Herod sought, that he might destroy him.

IN THE DAYS OF AUGUSTUS CÆSAR.

"Rome! the city that so long
Reigned absolute, the mistress of the world,
The mighty vision that the prophets saw,
And trembled; that from nothing, from the least,
The lowliest village (what but here and there
A reed-roofed cabin by a river-side?)
Grew into everything; and year by year,
Patiently, fearlessly, working her way
O'er brook and field, o'er continent and sea,
Not like the merchant with his merchandize,
Or traveller with staff and scrip exploring;
But hand to hand and foot to foot, thro' hosts,
Thro' nations numberless in battle array,
Each behind each, each when the other fell,
Up and in arms, at length subdued them all."

Rogers.

II.

IN THE DAYS OF AUGUSTUS CÆSAR.

A COURSE of 132 years elapsed from the taking of Jerusalem by Pompey to the final destruction of the city by Titus. During this period the Jews, as a nation, continued to live on their own land, but were tributaries to the Roman Empire. In return for the tribute money they obtained security, internal order, and protection against external foes, and a measure of indulgence as regarded their religion, so unusual, and so remarkable as to show us clearly that their God was lovingly, mercifully, holding them in the hollow of His hand till a time of tyranny was overpast. Not giving them independence, though they still boasted of their freedom, but holding them in a position in which they were safe in times of tremendous commotion, of great tribulation, when wars were raging throughout the then known world, and every little world within a human heart was so shaken by the general disturbance, that natural affection was lost, or preserved only by those who cherished it carefully, believing it to be good in the sight of God.

As it was in the days of Noah, so was it before the first, so will it be before the second advent of our Lord Jesus Christ.

At the period of history we are now considering, the passions of men, agitated and goaded on by the excitements of very trying times, if not checked by strong, firm principles, forced the mind off its balance, and unrestrained wilfulness ran on to madness. The many and various crimes of which we read could not have been committed by reasonable men in a right state of mind. Herod's jealous rage had maddened him, or he could not have caused Mariamne to be put to death, and then raved about his affection for her. He would thankfully have given all he possessed to bring her back to life, but he could not get rid of the consequences of his sin, which made him feel that his will was not omnipotent.

The Jews, firmly held under the guardianship of the only political power competent to protect them as a nation, and enlightened enough to preserve their existence as a religious community, were permitted to adhere to their institutions and customs. They were not at all prevented from maintaining the public worship of the temple in Jerusalem, in its appointed order and splendour. The changes that had occurred in the state of the world, though they had lessened the national power of the Jews, had increased their means of acquiring religious and moral influence among the people of many nations, by whom they were rapidly becoming more known than could have been the case in former years, when there were less facilities for travelling, less thirst for all kinds of knowledge. By clearing the Mediterranean of pirates, the Romans were making it a great highway on which people from all directions met, and interchanged ideas, and more or less it was the same on every one of the roads which the Romans made through every province of the empire. Those strong roads of which we see the remains, inaugurated a new era in the history of civilization, as effectually as in our time the railroads have done. The people then living under the widespread dominion of Rome travelled so much farther, and acquired so much more knowledge of all kinds than their ancestor had ever had, that they may have thought they were fulfilling Daniel's prophecy (chap. xii. 4), and so they were, in their wonderfully marked generation, though they did not run to and fro as fast as we do. How blind they were to the importance of the times in which they lived, and to their own duties, to the part assigned by God to His own peculiar people in those days! Motives connected with nothing beyond their prospects in this life led them to emigrate. Their own land had become over-populated, they adopted commerce as their pursuit, and dwelt in the great cities of other nations, but retained their nationality, their religion, and customs, which isolated them in a social sense from the rest of mankind. Everywhere their peculiarities attracted attention, and they were silent witnesses to the two great truths, the existence of one only God and the prospect of a golden age coming for the tired workers and unsatisfied loiterers in this weary world. Their ideas on this latter subject were vague and conflicting, but the faintest gleams of light are better than perfect darkness. It was the first breaking of a new day, the day appointed for the sons of Abraham to accomplish the duties of their mission, to diffuse among the families of the earth all the divine truth with which they had been entrusted, of which they had so long been the sole depositories, and to show forth God's goodness and righteousness by conducting themselves towards others according to His will.

When the Great Teacher of that day said to a vast multitude of Jews gathered round Him, "Ye are the salt of the earth," they knew what He meant. The men and women who listened to the sermon could see that the application of that simile extended beyond the family and the fatherland. Some of them must have had relations or friends dwelling or sojourning for a while afar off, along the shores of the Mediterranean, or in some distant busy city in which they were bartering goods or beginning to trade to a considerable extent. In Rome they had multiplied exceedingly, so as to form a formidable body. The common people disliked them and judged them harshly; indeed, this singular race seem to have excited a superstitious kind of fear in the minds of the vulgar, who fancied that the strangers had formed a secret society, the members of which unscrupulously sought their own advancement, to the hindrance and injury of others. But the wellbred, noble-minded Roman looked on the Jew, feeling that there was something superior about him. It was an inquiring age, and the Jew might help to solve some of the questions that had arisen. Greek philosophy had shaken the faith of all thinking men in ancestral heathenism. Philosophy was the order of the day. Every young Roman was to some extent a student of philosophy; and in each of the various schools there were men of riper years and judgment, honestly seeking truth, whom we now call "seekers after God." And even the barbarian, from beyond the borders of the empire, who might now and then be seen in the streets of Rome, even he might have notions tending Godward. Tacitus, writing of the age before his own, acknowledges that a nobler conception of the nature of the Divine Being subsisted among the wild Germans than among the highly civilized nations of Greece and Italy. He says, "They deem it unworthy of the dignity of heavenly beings to enclose their gods within walls, or to fashion their forms under human similitude."

The great Gothic race included Germans, Scandinavians and Saxons, who always had some dim belief in a Being that could never die. One superior to Odin or Woden, and their other deified heroes. They made no idol to represent this God of gods, they dared not name Him, but spoke of Him mysteriously by His attributes; generally choosing His most endearing quality—"The Good." These restless tribes were on their way—moving from the east: their migrations were very gradually made. The one idea that drove them on was that of finding, and very often fighting for, new ground, that would give fresh food. When the land on which they had halted for awhile was exhausted by their rapidly increasing families and flocks and herds, they struck their tents, or abandoned their crazy huts, and moved on.* Very faint and imperfect must be our conceptions of those wild people and their ways, though we have reason to believe that our own ancestors were among them; but very clearly can we see that they were impelled and guided by the One whose Name they could not utter, that they might be ready to sit down in their companies to take their portion of the Bread of Life, when it would be distributed by the disciples of Jesus.

Neither Romans nor barbarians were so debased as to have among them no men who could sympathize with the Jew in his deepest and purest feelings, none who could respect him for refusing to bend the knee to the statues of the gods in the Roman temples, none capable of obtaining through a son of Abraham elevating ideas of the Supreme God and of the higher life of faith in Him. At that time the Jew had every opportunity of being a blessing to the people among

* See Sharon Turner's "History of the Anglo-Saxons."

whom he sojourned. There were in Rome wealthy and highly educated Jews, Jews whose society was eagerly sought by senators and patricians, and through them attention was naturally drawn to their country. Its past history, its magnificent temple to the invisible God, became topics of the day—subjects on which men's minds were opening, and on which the good and intelligent heartily desired further information. Among the rich and learned Jews were some who attained the highest honours which the empire had to give, and more than once a Jew exercised important influence on public affairs. Although, like almost all the rest of the then known world, Judea was a Roman province, and paid tribute to Cæsar, yet the Jews were not destitute of moral power. Seeing this, reminds us of our Saviour's words, "If thou hadst known in this thy day the things that belong to thy peace." *

In one of the Hibbert Lectures of 1880, Ernest Renan tells us that in the time of Cicero, that is, in the reign of Augustus Cæsar, the Jews were so powerful and influential in Rome, that the word of Zechariah was verified to the letter: "The world laid hold of the skirt of the Jew, and said to him, Lead us to Jerusalem." †

Alas! as a nation, the Jews, notwithstanding the wonderful privileges they had enjoyed, were not worthy to lead. They had not learnt what God's dealings with them and their forefathers should have taught them; therefore, as regarded spiritual things, they were ignorant and blind, and they gave no heed to the signs of the times. Wrapt up in his own exclusiveness, each one felt sure that he was safe, because he was one of the chosen people, and had taken part in all the ordinances of a divinely instituted religious system. But in

---

* Luke xix. 41, 42.   † Ernest Renan, quoting Zech. viii. 23.

the visible church there is always a circle within a circle, a sanctuary beyond the outer court. This is equally true with the Hebrew and the Christian Church. Those members who have been drawn into the inner circle cannot fail to grow in grace, and in the knowledge and love of God, cannot fail to see that it is theirs to make Him known, to speak of His goodness and His wondrous works to their fellow-men. The number of Jews who were actuated by this love and trust in Jehovah, and this sense of duty, was large enough to be influential, of which we have abundant evidence in the works of heathen authors of that age, although, as the Hebrews held but few, if any, political offices and occupations in Rome, they are not often mentioned in political history. Moreover the Jews and their monotheistic and moral ideas found more favour among the lower classes than with the Roman aristocracy; and the patricians held control over the Italian literature, absolutely condemning what they disapproved, disbelieved, or considered dangerous. Yet, despite these difficulties, reliable evidence has been left to us, which proves that monotheism and morality made its way in Roman society, and leavened Roman literature, which we can fairly attribute to no other cause than that of Jewish influence.

Horace, at the end of the Satire, in which he jestingly claims the privilege of writing anything he likes to amuse himself and his readers, threatens that if this indulgence be not granted to him, he will assemble a whole company of poets, like proselytizing Jews, to help him in converting his opponent. This allusion evidently points to the great activity of the Jews in making converts to their faith.

Seneca bears testimony to the moral power of this

"most outrageous nation," as he calls it; for he regards the universal adoption of some of their customs as a remarkable instance in which the conquered have given laws to their conquerors. Slight allusions are found, which show that a considerable number among the Romans, though not converted to Judaism, in course of time watched these strange Eastern people with a not altogether unsympathizing curiosity, and became sufficiently interested in their sacred days to show them some degree of respect, and that a great many Romans went into the synagogues, looked upon the worshippers, and heard the service there, and the reading of the Word of God. These services must have been imperfect, yet the heathen who entered when a thoughtful Jew was reading or expounding, might listen to views which the range of heathen literature nowhere presented, to the idea that God takes interest in the moral education of mankind, that He is to be served by justice and kindness towards our fellow-men, and by maintaining a right frame of mind; that this is the service which He most desires. If the heathen listened to a judiciously selected psalm or hymn, he heard what might strengthen moral purpose, and quicken right affections, or aid devout aspirations. Heathen literature contained nothing which resembled it. The religious duties of heathenism consisted in rites and ceremonies and augury. Much of what passed for practical religion was merely fortune-telling under another name, and religious performances were utterly disconnected from thoughts of right behaviour between man and man, religious duties were treated as having no connection with morality or with human improvement.*

* "Judaism at Rome." See chapter ii., on Causes of Jewish influence. Zenophon represents Socrates as saying, "If we are

The managers of the senatorial faction in Rome had long ago created, and since nourished, a superstitious reverence for mystical books which they kept secreted in their own charge, and made use of when they desired to excite or direct the popular mind. These scrolls, attributed to a real or imaginary woman called Sibylla, or the Sibyl of Cumae, perished when the capital was burnt, B.C. 83.*

The people greatly lamented this loss, and an idea suggested itself to superstitious minds, which gained currency. Surely Sibylla, being no common mortal, might be yet alive, or other sibyls might exist, and be found if diligently sought.

A clever Jew, or a monotheist, took advantage of this excitement, and when the Capitol had been rebuilt, he turned the tables on the patricians by persuading the senate to bring from Erythræ, a city of Iona in Asia Minor, leaves in Greek verse, said to have been written by a sibyl who was, some believed, the Sibylla who sold her books to Tarquin.

The senate must have exercised little or no scrutiny with regard to this book, written in a foreign language, which afterwards proved so vexatious to them. Sixty years later, stringent measures were taken to prevent its perusal; but by that time it had made impressions on the popuplar mind, which could not be obliterated.†

unable to foreknow, touching future events, what course of action will be advantageous, the gods assist us by telling to inquirers, through divination, how things will turn out, and by teaching how they will be most favourably brought to pass."—*Zenophon, Memorabilia* iv. 3, 12.

* The old story of Tarquin the Proud and the Sibyl is well known. At Cumae, not far from Naples, the Sibyl's cave, in the midst of a wood full of beautiful wild flowers, is still shown.

† See "Judaism at Rome."

An extraordinary struggle—a storm of conflicting opinions, religious and political, was raging when our Lord Jesus Christ was born. On one side was heathenism, upheld by the Emperor and the patricians; on the other was monotheism, vehemently taken up by the opposite party, which was contending for popular rights, for civil and religious liberty. Augustus himself, the members of the senate, from which he had excluded monotheists, and the wealthy and influential M. Vipsanius Agrippa, headed the former party. The latter had its dauntless leaders; among the foremost was Tiberius, who afterwards succeeded Augustus; he was at that time out of favour, not banished, but being discontented with the state of things, he had gone to Rhodes, whence he was recalled in the second year of the Christian era.

In those tempestuous days, when old ideas were being rooted up and prostrated as trees fall before a mighty wind, the superstitious minds of the people were greatly disturbed. The verses of the Erythræan Sibyl, called also the Babylonian and Chaldean, because she was said to have at one time dwelt in Babylon, were causing great excitement. This book differed materially from the more ancient books or scrolls that had been burnt, which had referred only to the affairs of this life, and did not touch on morality, nor on a future state. Some Jew of Erythræ, or who operated from that place, had fabricated Homeric verses, teaching Jewish views drawn from the Hebrew Scriptures, and mixed up with fictitious prophecies of events that had already become historical, such, for instance, as the siege of Troy.

Readers competent to criticise must have found much in these poems which betrayed their real origin, and the mistrust engendered in such minds must have injured the cause of truth, which cannot be promoted, or faithfully and effectually served by falsehood, or by what are commonly called pious frauds. Yet the sibylline verses were so clever a forgery, that sincere men, not wanting in natural capacity, may have believed in their authenticity, and their teaching was in most respects superior to what could be found in heathen literature, as they inculcated belief in the one great God, and by imitations of genuine prophecies they startled even the heathen, and awoke many to look out for tokens of some wonderful change that might be expected.*

Only persons who are actually leading the NEW LIFE, beginning to lead it, or persevering in its course, can be deriving real strength and safe satisfaction from looking for the new heavens and the new earth; no tonic can strengthen the lifeless. Yet the first movement, the first sign of life may be partly attributable to some alarm which has struck the human heart with awe, and under the divine blessing such fear may prove the beginning of wisdom.

The following extracts from sibylline verses show the character of the poems.†

" Come, let us bow to the earth, let us invoke
The immortal King, the great God, the Most High,
Let us send to his temple, for he is the only potentate,
Let us consider the law of God the Most High,
Which is the most just of all things on earth.
We had wandered from the path of the Immortal;
With senseless minds we worshipped hand-made works,
Of carved idols, and of dead men."
* * * * *
As for the wicked, below Tartarus
They shall pay threefold the evil they have perpetrated;
Rocked by the sea of fire, they shall gnash with their teeth;

* " Judaism at Rome."
† See " Judaism at Rome," pp. 423—430, 456.

Consumed by thirst, and by their flaming torments,
They shall call it a blessing to die, but shall not be able.
But those who have done justice and good works,
With true monotheism and just thoughts,
The angels shall bear through the flaming river,
And bring them to light, and a life without care.
Where is the immortal path of the great God,
And three fountains of wine, honey, and milk.
And the land belongs equally to all, with no walks or inclosures,
And without divisions; it bears abundant fruits without labour.
Life is in common, and wealth undivided;
For neither poor men nor rich men will be there;
Neither tyrant nor bondsmen, nor yet great men nor small,
Nor king nor rulers, but all will be alike.

*   *   *   *   *

There shall not be multiplied days of care,
Nor spring, nor summer, nor winter, nor closing autum,
Nor marriage, nor death, nor buying nor selling,
Nor sunset, nor sunrise, for God shall make one long day."

*   *   *   *   *

And then he will establish an eternal kingdom
Over men; a holy law which he once gave.

*   *   *   *   *

For perfect peace shall come on the land of the good,
And the prophets of the great God shall do away the sword,
And they shall be judges among mortals, and kings shall be just,
And the wealthy among men shall be just.

*   *   *   *   *

Wolves shall play with lambs on the mountains,
Lynxes shall eat grapes with the stags,
And bears with calves, among all mortals,
The carnivorous lion shall eat straw in the manger,
And dragons nestle with unweaned children."*

The anticipation of a coming kingdom, a kingdom from the east, as Romans would say, was Jewish. The advocates of sibylline authority, whether Jews or Romans, must have found it for their interest to maintain the

---

* Abridged from the translation in "Judaism at Rome." By Frederick Huidekoper. New York, 1877.

existence of but one Sibylla, since, if but one existed, her authority had already been recognized by the Roman Senate in the most public manner.* So trusting in the credulity of the people, depending on the popular ignorance, the sibyl was supposed to assert her claims to extraordinary longevity.

> "Born at Erythræ—some will pronounce
> Me Sibylla, a crazy impostor:
> But when all things shall take place,
> Then you will remember me, and no one will longer
> Pronounce as mad the great God's prophetess.
> Did he not show me what occurred to my forefathers?
> The earliest events God enumerated to me,
> And all things subsequent he put into my mind;
> So I proclaim the future and the past,
> And tell them to mortals. For when the world was overwhelmed
> With waters, and but one approvèd man was left
> Sailing in his hewn-wood house on the waters,
> With beasts and fowls, that the world might be filled again,
> I was his daughter-in-law and his relative;
> To whom the earliest events happened, and all the last were unfolded,
> So that by my mouth all these truths should be uttered."

This reminds us of "The Wandering Jew." In dark times, history and poetry, truth and fiction, credible traditions and the very wildest legends were confounded together; as they were not in the days of Eugene Sue, whose book was accepted as a clever romance, founded on a legend.

The Roman aristocracy and their adherents, who were, generally speaking, unfriendly to Judaism, must, as a class, have derided this Jewish sibylline literature. Cicero had suggested its withdrawal from the public, a kind of suppression which was afterwards zealously undertaken by Augustus and the patricians.†

---

* "Judaism at Rome."   † "Judaism at Rome," p. 447.

With that strong aristocratic party in Rome the king of Judea sympathized and sided.

Their fears were not wholly without foundation: the dangers they dreaded and endeavoured to avert were not altogether visionary. Throughout the wide range of Rome's dominion, multitudes, including men of all classes, but chiefly the lower, were eagerly anticipating some wonderful revolution; a suddenly altered state of society, a kingdom quite different to any that had ever preceded it, which was to be characterized by monotheism and strict morality, liberty, and equality. Ignorant or base-minded men propagated their own imperfect or erroneous views and opinions concerning the coming kingdom, and its King, who was to overthrow all existing governments, and when he had conquered the whole earth, was to reign as the only Potentate; and then would come a golden age, like that described by Greek and Latin poets.

One of the finest fragments of the sibylline poems, translated by Frederick Huidekoper, begins thus:—

> "And then God will afterwards show a great sign,
> For a brilliant star like a crown shall shine,
> Brightly gleaming from the sparkling heavens,
> During many days. For then He will show a victor's crown
> From heaven, to men who wrestle in the conflict.
> For then shall be a great contest for triumphal entry
> Into the heavenly city. It shall be world-embracing,
> Open to all men, having immortality as its reward."

These verses continue by eloquently expressing the nobility and the necessity of morality, enumerating its many and various duties; and thus close the subject:—

> "This is the contest, these the strifes, these the rewards,
> This the gate of life, and entrance to immortality,
> Which the heavenly God has established as the prize

> For the most righteous of men.   Such as gain the crown
> Shall gloriously enter this gate."   *Sibl. Orac.* ii. 34, 153.

King Herod died shortly after the visit of the Magi to the infant Saviour. He was seized by a disease which caused intense suffering. On his deathbed he meditated a horrible massacre, but his last orders were not carried into effect.

His funeral was conducted in a style of unprecedented magnificence; all the regalia were brought out to grace the procession. The bier was of solid gold studded with precious stones, the bed of variegated purple. On this lay the body, covered with purple. On his head was placed a diadem, and over him a crown of gold, and in his right hand was a sceptre.

We have observed the contrast between this king of the Jews, and Him whose title was written, and put upon the cross, who was lifted up from the earth, that He might draw all men unto Him.*

The vivid description given by Josephus, of what he calls the end of Herod's history, reminds us of the purple robe, the crown of thorns, and the reed that mocked the sceptre.

Archelaus, Herod's eldest son, well knowing that the whole country was ripe for rebellion, prudently avoided assuming the title of king, but told the people he hoped it would be confirmed to him by the government of Rome. Notwithstanding this caution on his part, a violent dispute arose even at the funeral banquet. An insurrection ensued, the soldiers were called out, and the king's guard killed about 3,000 of the rioters.

The public declaration of Archelaus, that he considered the sovereignty at present in abeyance, encouraged his brothers and many of his own family to

---

* John xii. 32.

intrigue against him. King Herod had had ten wives, consequently the royal family was large, and dangerously devoid of union and sympathy. Selfishness seems to have been the only motive that actuated its members. Driven to despair by the difficulties of his position, Archelaus went to Rome, and literally threw himself at the feet of Augustus Cæsar. The Emperor raised him with the utmost courtesy, intimating that he believed him worthy to succeed his father, but still pronouncing no decision. He took time for considering the subject of the succession, and also that of the late king's will, which one of the contending parties was endeavouring to overthrow on the plea that Herod was not in a sound state of mind when he made it. The will was clearly expressed, and was far more consistent with reason and justice, than had been most of that man's acts and deeds. He had died immensely rich, and after dividing the bulk of his property among his offspring, he bequeathed several other legacies. To his patron and friend Augustus he gave ten million pieces of silver, (probably shekels) with his valuable plate and wardrobe, and five million pieces of silver to the Empress Julia, daughter of Augustus, wife of young Tiberius Cæsar.

While the affairs of Judea were being deliberated on in Rome, the country continued in a state of anarchy, and this present distress, and the recollection of Herod's tyranny, added to the number of Jews who desired "no king but Cæsar," they longed for the measure of independence that would be insured to them if their country were incorporated into the Roman Empire.

This body, which included many of the upper classes and superior men, sent a respectful petition to Rome, stating their grievances, and entreating to be heard. Fifty of the noblest men among the Jews conveyed this petition to Rome; where they were graciously received, and supported by eight thousand of their countrymen then residing in Rome. Cæsar convened a council of the Romans then in office, and of his friends, in the temple of Apollo on the Palatine Hill—an edifice which he had erected at his own charge, and ornamented at a vast expense. The Jews stood in a body, with the ambassadors, and Archelaus opposite, with his friends. Besides these, was present also Philip, Archelaus' brother, previously sent over, through kindness, by Varus, who then commanded the Roman legions stationed at Jerusalem. He had sent Philip with a twofold object, that he might assist Archelaus, and also be allotted a portion, should Cæsar distribute Herod's property among his sons. The accusing party, being allowed to speak, commenced with a recapitulation of Herod's violent proceedings, stated that they had found the late king, not a sovereign, but the most cruel of tyrants. Such were the miseries endured by those who survived the thousands murdered by him, that they accounted them happy who had perished. Through Herod, Judea had lost her ancient happiness and hereditary laws, and had become full of poverty and the lowest degree of crime. In a word, the Jews had undergone more calamities under Herod's rule than their forefathers had suffered in the whole interval since their departure from Babylon. To such a state of humiliation and habitual misfortune had they been reduced, that they had continued to submit to this servitude; and on the death of Herod they had acknowledged Archelaus as their king, and had prayed for the prosperity of his reign. But, as if apprehensive that there should be any doubt as to the stock from which he sprang, this son of a tyrant had prefaced his reign by the slaughter of three thousand citizens.

Those, therefore, who had survived such complicated miseries, now at length faced their calamities, wishing to receive their wounds in front, as by the law of war, and to implore the Romans to have compassion on the relics of Judea, to unite the country to Syria, and administer the government by their own officers; for though calumniated as seditious and inclined for war, they would show that they knew how to obey authority wisely exercised.*

The other party replied by refuting the charges against the deceased king and his eldest son, on whom the government of the kingdom had devolved. Nicolaus pleaded eloquently on behalf of Archelaus, and severely lashed those of his relatives who had joined his accusers.

Cæsar, having heard both parties, dissolved the council. A few days afterwards he gave one half of the kingdom to Archelaus, with the title of ethnarch, promising hereafter to make him king, should he prove himself deserving. The other half he divided into two tetrarchies for Antipas and Philip, also sons of the late king. Augustus, after having distributed the patrimonial property according to Herod's will, divided a thousand talents and the personal property bequeathed to himself among the members of the late king of Judea's family, selecting for himself only a few things which he kept in memory of his departed friend.

The appointment of an ethnarch was simply the establishment of a dependent king under another title.

Antipas, or Herod Antipas, as he is often styled, was tetrarch of Galilee when the holy family returned from Egypt (Matt. ii. 22; Luke ii. 39); yet this Herod

---

* Slightly abridged from Josephus' "Wars of the Jews." Translated by the late Rev. Robert Traill, D.D.

though generally considered a man of milder disposition, beheaded John the Baptist.

The return of Archelaus to assume the government of Judea under his altered title did not restore peace to the distracted land. The people feared him, and the country was rent with factions, and continually disturbed by seditious movements, false Messiahs, and alarming outbreaks; and by the intrigues of the Herodian princes, who were not satisfied by the decision of Cæsar. The state of things grew worse and worse, till Archelaus, having lost the confidence and favour of Augustus, was deprived of his office, and banished to Vienne in Gaul; then the urgent request of the Jews was granted; Judea was incorporated with the Roman empire. By the desire of her people, the sceptre of Judah was broken.

Augustus seems to have felt that, as the sovereign ruler of Judea, it was incumbent on him, or at least consistent with propriety, that he should show respect to the ancient national religion of the Jews, which was so closely interwoven with their past history. Ambassadors from Rome never entered the courts of the Temple that were open to Gentiles, without adoring the God of the Hebrews; and when M. V. Agrippa, as the minister of Augustus, was staying at Jerusalem, he went daily to the Temple, and offered rich gifts. Both Augustus and Livia presented golden vases and cups to the Temple, and the emperor, although he ordered the members of his family to abstain from personal homage or acts of worship, yet desired that in his name, and at his expense, a bull and two lambs should be sacrificed every day. This sacrifice, ordered by Augustus, and continued by his successor, was celebrated by the Jews with pious zeal—was felt to be the gauge of Roman tolerance and Jewish submission; a seal of friendship between Rome and Jerusalem.*

Yet Augustus did not at all encourage his Roman or other subjects to embrace Judaism. Towards monotheism in general he can never have seriously inclined; and when the excitement caused by the sibylline literature led him to dread its effects on the popular mind, he acted against it with despotic severity. At the beginning of his reign he had declined the post of supreme pontiff, and it remained in the feeble hands of Lepidus till his death. Then the emperor assumed the office and title, and immediately exercised the priestly power. He caused two thousand copies of various sibylline books to be at once seized and burnt. About the same time he ordered that every senator, before proceeding to senatorial business, should offer frankincense to the god in whose temple they were for the time being assembled.† He may have done this to exclude monotheists from the senate, or he may simply have acted in accordance with his sense of propriety.

We hear of the Jews in Rome at the time when an impostor pretended to be Alexander, one of the two unfortunate sons of Herod and Mariamne, who had been enducated in Rome, and whose lives had been cut short by their own father. The false Alexander was a Jew of Sidon. His plausible stories deceived many, and large sums of money were given to him to enable him to support his claims. He was imprudent enough to go to Rome. The whole Jewish body in Rome turned out to welcome him, his likeness to the deceased prince whom he personated was extraordinary.

---

* "Rome et la Judée." Par le Comte de Champagny. Paris, 1870.

† "Judaism at Rome."

Almost all the Jews believed in him gave him, royal honours, carried him in a litter, and provided him with attendants at their own expense. Cæsar, however, who perfectly remembered the features of the real Alexander, could not be imposed on: Augustus laughed at the whole affair, and gave the pretender, who was strong and fit for such employment, a place among the rowers of his fleet. But steps were taken to discover the author of the plot, a clever Jew, who was arrested and executed.

The thousands of Jewish residents in Rome who pressed in and around the new temple of Apollo when Herod Archelaus appeared before Cæsar to answer to the charges against him, must have thankfully felt that their lot as colonists in Rome was far happier than that of their brethren living in their own land; to which nevertheless their hearts were bound by associations most sacred as well as endearing. Under favourable circumstances the Jewish colony in Rome increased with inconvenient rapidity. The influx of their lower orders meeting the corresponding classes of the plebeians caused a clashing of interests, always very trying to vulgar minds, and uncommonly so in this case, on account of the singular customs of the Jews, and their unfitness for domestic service under the Romans of higher grade. Jealousies and disturbances arose, which did not escape the vigilant eye and prescient rule of Augustus, who separated the conflicting elements by assigning to the Jews that portion of the city which lay beyond the Tiber. Wealthy Jews then built houses on both sides of the river; as most of them were engaged in commerce, it suited them to live on the quay where the merchandise brought from Ostia on lighters was unloaded. Their residences and storehouses must have formed a substantial front, not far from what is now called the Porta Portese.*

Frederick Huidekoper justly remarks that Jewish habits of industry must have been partly due to Jewish religious views, to a sense of responsibility for the right use of time; and "if," he says, "the Jews were, as Josephus claims, and as some other circumstances might indicate, the mechanics of the Roman Empire, this would bring them largely in contact with their heathen neighbours, and give to those of them who were fitted for it an opportunity of making a favourable impression by their skill, industry, and fidelity.†

All the characteristics that command respect could not fail to co-operate in diffusing their religious views; and that the Jews throughout the world made converts to the main points of their faith is obvious from the frequent mention of such converts in the New Testament. Nevertheless, the absence of modern conversion to Judaism has blinded prominent writers to its influence on the teachers of antiquity.‡

---

* Ernest Renan.

† "The countries where monotheism had spread were the workshops of the Roman Empire. Josephus appeals to heathen cognizance of the fact that mechanical occupations were largely in Jewish hands. Philo mentions their workshops at Alexandria. The industrial prosperity of the countries where they settled is attested by patrician desire of obtaining office there. Cicero testifies that Asia Minor was the portion of the republic where reason and diligence effect most. Tacitus bears witness to the peacefulness and wealth of Syria. The Jews are mentioned by Dion Cassius as fabricators of arms for the Romans."—*Judaism at Rome*, p. 381.

‡ "At the present day the Jews exercise no perceptible religious influence in the Christian communities amid which they dwell, because, as regards accordance with reason, adaptation to human wants, and the evidence on which it rests, their religion has no advantage over Christianity."—*Ibid.*

The poorer Jews landed in large numbers where the more fortunate were founding the Hebrew colony in Rome. They were not compelled to dwell on that spot, they had not yet, as a nation, lost their place among the nations, they were neither captives nor outcasts. Naturally, almost all of them were glad to settle on the ground chosen for them by Cæsar; they felt in that yet unknown land the force of the everlasting truth, "union is strength;" and they cheerfully located themselves behind the edifices which their richer brethren were building, and all, according to their means, contributed and laboured to raise the synagogues in which they met together to worship the God of their fathers. The whole of the Hebrew Church no doubt took part in that work, for the intercourse of the Roman synagogues with Jerusalem was constant. In Rome they got their livelihood as they could; large numbers must have found employment under men engaged in business. It is known that many Jews were litter carriers and porters. The dirty dregs of the multitude took to bartering and huckstering, and tanning hides, and to keeping slaughter-houses for their own people, that the animals might be prepared for food according to the Levitical law.

We can understand why the Romans avoided these narrow streets, and that being avoided, they got worse and worse, till the smell of garlic was the least objectionable of the many which combined to offend the noses of persons brought up in cleanliness and refinement. The poor Jews in the *Transtevere* shared in the general largess of corn distributed among the poor inhabitants of Rome, and by a special command of Augustus, if the distribution took place on their Sabbath, their portion was reserved.

The Romans were not only the most highly civilized

people in the world, they had imparted civilization, had spread it in all directions—had thrown the world itself open. Men moved about regarding all the then known lands as one common country. The same interminable straight road led them with ease and safety from one extremity to another; everywhere they found themselves under the protection of the same strong government and the same laws. In every considerable city they came to, the temples, basilicas, theatres, baths, houses, and streets had much the same appearance, and everywhere Romans, and those who imitated them, were to be seen in the same dress, following the same customs, and speaking what had become almost the one universal language. Greece and Rome had filled the valleys and levelled the hills, and made the crooked ways straight, and the rough places smooth, and prepared the way for the coming of the Lord, that all flesh might see the salvation of God; and Judaism (no longer confined to Judea), like a herald, had raised a general expectation of His coming.*

Yet more wonderful still was the unanimous longing after "The desire of all nations." Men were tired of their ancestral gods, really believed in little or nothing of what they had been taught to say concerning them, or only believed as we believe in touching, heart-stirring poetry—the latter kind of faith animated the hearts of women. Men thought it was well that women and the ignorant multitude should be religious; religion was very useful in a state, as it helped to maintain order. On no higher motive thousands upon thousands continued to countenance what they did not venerate.

---

* Isa. xliv. 3—5, Luke iii. 4, as quoted by Rev. L. Cutts, B.A., in "Turning Points of Church History." Published by the Society for Promoting Christian Knowledge.

Every thinking man felt that something was wanting to make the religion of the day more real. Augustus thought about it; he evidently felt that the old deified heroes, Jupiter, Bacchus, Hercules, had lived so long ago as to have lost their hold on the sympathies of men. Actuated by his great talent for organization, he tried to effect a radical reformation in idolatry, and to establish it as the religion of the Roman state. He saw that great dangers might arise from hastily upsetting existing modes of worship, so he permitted the local cults everywhere to continue, but everywhere he set up the altars of Rome. He permitted the lares in every house and at every cross-road throughout his wide dominions to remain; but on every altar, and to every company of household and wayside lares—those cherished and revered images of the departed favourites and heroes of families and communities—was to be added the genius of the Emperor. He wished his people to feel that in him they had a living protector and friend. Not till after his death was his statue positively an idol.

Throughout the ancient world the word synonymous with our Saxon word God conveyed ideas very different from those awakened when we hear, or speak, or read that hallowed word; and words of ancient languages synonymous with our words worship and worshipful may have had a signification rather more like that which our ancestors attached to them, than is the higher meaning in which they are now commonly used and understood by us.

Throughout the Empire there were Romans whose loyalty was based on something better than mere selfish considerations, and such could look on the statue of Augustus as a symbol of the over-ruling Providence, which heathens could not think of as do pious Christians, but they felt that the highest guardian power of which they could form any conception, which had secured to them the blessings of prosperity, was represented by the statue of the Emperor.

This was felt in the provinces more than in Rome. In the imperial city the emperors were known as men, but very little of their personal characters was known by their distant subjects. Occasionally, dark reports of what had occurred in Rome made their way down into the country, but they floated chiefly in the upper circles, not among the people; and as far as Augustus was concerned, only in his last years were unpleasing stories of him circulated, and these did not go far enough to materially affect his popularity.

He seems to have set up a figure of his genius, not in quite the same spirit as that in which King Nebuchadnezzar set up the golden image, but rather under the pressure of the desire, then prevailing in all nations—the sense of a great want—the instinctive effort to try in some measure to satisfy man's need of a God to bless him with sympathetic blessings; to guide and lead every child of man through the intricate paths of life, and to dwell in every home. "God with us."

In a province of the Empire our Saviour was living, but His advent had not been revealed to the Emperor, nor even to the Jews in Rome. The world was no longer in darkness, the humble seeker after truth had light enough to find it; but men's minds were still shackled by the learning of the pagan schools, and Augustus was blinded by pride, which his position and all the circumstances of his life had fostered. We see that the heathen needed to be chastened, that they might know themselves to be but men, yet surely we need not unmercifully judge the Roman for thinking that he might do more for his people, whose welfare he had earnestly at heart, than could the lares of their ignorant ancestors.*

It is sad to read of the disappointment and sorrow which clouded the old age of Augustus. The defeat of Varus by Arminius, and the series of deaths, the trouble in his own family, and, above all, the shame, revolting to his best instincts, touching him so closely, grievously disturbed his latter years. Misfortune and failing strength made him more impatient and arbitrary than he had hitherto been. This was felt most by his subjects in Rome—Romans, Jews, and others—and they openly murmured against him, to which he was keenly sensible. Looking upon emigration as the remedy for over-population, he banished a large number of malcontents, but this did not tend to revive his popularity.†
Nevertheless the Romans were proud of their Cæsar, and most of the people were attached to him personally.

When Augustus knew that his end was approaching, he compiled a concise memorial of his acts. The ruined wall at Ancyra, engraved with this precious document, in both Greek and Latin, is one of the most curious of existing antiquities. The inscription gives a detailed

---

* "Thanks to this confraternity, all local gods, all private divinities, became Augustal gods. It was an admirable promotion for them. But this great attempt to produce a religion of the Roman state was evidently incapable of satisfying the religious wants of the heart. Augustus was even more a religious organizer than a great politician. The altars of Rome and of Augustus became the centre of an hierarchical organization of colleges of priests, which, to a much greater extent than is commonly supposed, furnished the basis for the division of dioceses and ecclesiastical provinces."—*Hibbert Lectures*, 1880, by Ernest Renan.

† In Rome, within a circuit of little more than twelve miles, more than two millions of people were crowded.—*Conybeare and Howson*.

account of his life and the events of his reign. The record extends over a period of fifty-eight years, and the great deeds it enumerates are not to be equalled by the achievements of any other hero of ancient or modern history. Yet even these are not so striking as is the marvellous sobriety and dignity of its tone. Certainly no pagan hero ever made a more becoming preparation for death.* We have no assurance that he was cheered by any kind of religious hope, but he died calmly, breathed his last in the arms of Livia; a few kind words to her were the last that passed his lips; a rare instance of conjugal fidelity in those times! Augustus died at Nola. His body was taken with the utmost pomp to the Forum of Rome, where the funeral oration was pronounced by Tiberius, the late Emperor's adopted son. Thence the remains were borne to the grassy fields on the banks of the Tiber, where the Roman youths met for athletic sports and martial exercises, and there the corpse was laid on an enormous funeral pyre. The fire burnt so fiercely and so long, that five nights and days elapsed before it was cool enough for the ashes to be collected; and during all that time the beautiful Livia, with ungirt dress, dishevelled hair, and bare feet, watched the pyre, attended by the principal senators. It was the widow's duty as chief mourner.

Augustus had built a mausoleum, in which he had laid the ashes of several members of his family. First, Marcellus, the nephew whom he loved with warmest affection, and afterwards that young man's mother, his sister Octavia, the widow of Antony. The mausoleum stood in a meadow not far from the river. It was a circular building, a lofty tower of white marble with

* Merivale.

three retiring stages, each of which had its terrace covered with earth and planted with cypresses. These stages were pierced with numerous chambers, destined to receive, row within row, and story within story, the remains of every member of the imperial family, and many of their most attached slaves and freedmen. There was an entrance hall, round which statues of Augustus and his successors were to stand. The top of the tower was, we may suppose, ornamented with friezes, and the entablature terminated by a circle of statues.* In the centre of that massive mound the founder of the empire was to sleep his last sleep, and his statue, conspicuous on its summit, was to be so placed as to overlook the beloved city.

The Roman mind, cultivated by the aid of Greek literature and art, had grown philosophical, and still more eminently dramatical. A governing idea, first expressed, as far as we know, by Pythagoras, had given its bent to many a Roman, had helped to mould the national character.

Their own authors perceived this. For instance, Petronius wrote, "I don't go in for vehement controversy (literally, don't drag the rope of controversy). It seems that we are generally agreed that almost the whole world is merely acting a stage play."

In another passage he says, "Almost the whole world appears to be simply taking part in a comedy." †

---

* As was generally prescribed for the Roman mausolea. (Hemans and Merivale.)

† "Totus fere mundus mimum implere videtur."

"Non dueo contentionis funem dum constet inter nos quod fere totus mundus exercet histrioniam." The quotations are given side by side under the 10th Fragment of Petronius in the

Augustus Cæsar made his exit, satisfied that an important part in the grand drama had been assigned to him, and that he had performed it well.

best edition—it is not known from what book of Petronius they come.

UNDER THE CLAUDII.

"What though in faded splendour Judah held
His trembling sceptre, darkness wrapt the arth. . . .
Each region had its dynasty of gods—
Primeval Asshur hers, whose altars blazed
Upon the plains of Shinar ; Persia hers,
Beside her founts of liquid fire : and where
The mighty Indus rolls its tide of wealth,
Innumerable shrines, sparkling with gems,
Studded the odorous banks. But none like Greece
Could boast its names of graceful deities—
For every fountain and for every wind,
For every stream, and wood, and ocean shore,
For night and day, for sunshine and for storms,
For every changeful phase of Nature's moods,
For every passion of the human heart,
For wine, for war, for laughter and for tears,
For nuptial dances, and for funeral dirge,
For all things from the cradle to the grave,—
And past the grave, in Hades—over all
Were gods, or goddesses, or demi-gods,
Sylphs, nymphs, fawns, muses, graces, president.
In Greece the sevenfold power of Ashtaroth,
Encamping with his limitary hosts,
First fixed his seat, in after-years removed
Where Tiber rolls beneath the walls of Rome."

" Yesterday, To-day, and For Ever."
By Rev. E. H. Bickersteth, M.A.

III.

UNDER THE CLAUDII.

THE Claudian dynasty sprang from the descendants of the Empress Livia, by her first husband, Tiberius Claudius.

When Augustus, having no son of his own, appointed Tiberius as his successor, the so doing amounted to a confession that he had previously treated his stepson unjustly. Throughout his early life Tiberius had been treated with an inconsistency, often harsh, and always unsympathetic, which had affected the formation of his character and manners. Naturally, his mother had been true to him, but she had frequently been obliged to conceal her maternal feelings and her hopes and designs on his behalf, while his training, education, and future prospects were depending entirely on the absolute will of the Emperor—so equivocal was the young man's position!

His heart had been ruthlessly crushed; for, while yet a youth, he had married Agrippa's daughter, whom he loved, but was forced to leave her for the vain, unprincipled, twice widowed Julia. Such a training could hardly produce even worldly wisdom, could not tend to make him grow up quite what Livia herself might have desired him to be. The will of Augustus had made her co-heiress, had given her the official title of Augusta, and raised her to the level of her son. She consequently in some measure shared with him the imperial dignity, and during the early years of the reign held considerable power, which in many respects she exercised judiciously.

When Tiberius ascended the imperial throne, the Senate and most of the public officers were controlled by an adverse faction, disposed, as far as possible, to resist the guiding power which was vested in the Emperor as the supreme ruler. In more than one instance the Senate acted in opposition to the new Emperor, and the haste with which it deified Augustus hampered his successor, as it rendered the undoing of anything that he had done apparently sacrilegious. Not that the Roman mind revolted strongly against such sacrilege, it was generally inclined to be too sceptical; and when the formal proposal was made in the House to confer divine honours on Augustus, and in course of time on each of his successors, the vote was commonly passed unanimously, as a matter of course, or withheld only as a token of abhorrence and contempt.

Livia, warmly desiring to endear the ruling race to the Roman people, enlisted the fine arts in her service; found employment for all the best painters and sculptors by multiplying portraits, busts, and statues of favourite members of the imperial family. She at the same time strongly supported paganism, as it had been established by her late husband. Under her influence priesthoods were formed, and temples rose in all parts of the empire to extend the adoration of Augustus, and inscriptions still preserved upon them testify to her pride and self-assertion, as well as to the policy with which she strove to surround the family with solemn associations of religious awe.* Yet deification signified little or nothing more than was in later ages signified by canonization. Vividly is this taught us in Rome, where we continually see representations of heathen gods and goddesses side by side with those of saints, gathered out of all generations since the Christian era. In the grand old Sistine chapel of the Vatican, in which so many deeply interesting scenes—most powerful assemblies have taken place —where the election of every new Pope is first proclaimed with impressive ceremonial—on the ceiling of that magnificent old chapel we see depicted Isaiah, Daniel, and the other prophets mingled with the sibyls, who are quite as attractively painted.

It is well for us to be reminded of the truth we are so apt to forget, though it interpenetrates all we can learn of the years that are past, all that we meet with, and all that we contemplate in the present day. *Imperfection* is the word that expresses man's condition, and that of all his faculties and powers. Well is it to be sometimes reminded that this state of existence has its appointed end, which Holy Scripture connects with the Last Judgment; so we may be thankful for the preservation of Michael Angelo's picture, though our conceptions of what that retrospective, searching, truth-telling day, or period, will be, may differ greatly from those which guided the famous old master's hand, as, year after year, he worked out the innumerable number of figures, by which he designed to show the joy of the blessed and the agonies of the condemned. It is a wonderful, a grand work of art, because earnestly devoted to a subject greater than the world itself, of deeper importance than all the deeds that have ever been done throughout

* W. W. Capes, M.A., "Epochs of Ancient History. The Early Roman Empire." Longman, Green, and Co.

all generations, whether they have been written on the pages of history, or have been consigned to what we call oblivion, until the revelations appointed for that day are made by God to man. Then, as the perfect history of the past comes before us, we shall clearly see its connection with the future, with the life that will energise perfected faculties, with what will lie before us when the stream of time has fallen into the ocean of eternity.

In Rome you come into such close contact with superstition, that it does not surprise you to hear that Augustus Cæsar was superstitious; that he, like the Athenians, erected an altar to "*The unknown God.*"*
The following story is still told of him in Rome:—

On the Capitoline Hill, near the spot on which had stood the ancient citadel, the first capital, of which relics might be then existing, and close to the temple of Jupiter, built by Tarquinius Supurbus, and magnificently restored by Sulla, Augustus raised an altar to commemorate the Delphic Oracle respecting the coming of the Son of God; on which he inscribed the words, "*Ara Primogeniti Dei.*" The spot on which stood that altar on the Capitoline Hill is now covered by the spacious church of Sta. Maria in Ara Cœli, hoary with age and solemnly picturesque. A quaint chapel within the sacred building marks the site of that altar.†

---

* Acts xvii. 23.

† "As we lift the leathern curtain and push into the church, a faint perfume of incense meets us. As the curtain of the west door sways forward, the golden sunset bursts in and illuminates the mosaic floor, and flashes here and there on the golden ceiling and over the crowd, on some brilliant costume, or closely shaven head. All sorts of people are thronging there. . . . A dim, dingy look is over all. But it is the history of the church, its great antiquity, the varied fortunes it has known, which gives deep interest to its faded

In the sixth year of his reign, Tiberius was threatened with a dangerous and widely spread rebellion. Whether the legions had really resolved on elevating their favourite Germanicus to the throne must remain a subject of conjecture, as the death of the young hero soon after his removal from Germany to Syria prevented the possibility of that consummation, and there is no positive proof that he actually took part in any conspiracy against his uncle. On the other hand, there is no proof that he was murdered, still less that Tiberius was privy to the deed. His death, in the prime of manhood, by a sudden illness, naturally suggested the idea of poison. Germanicus himself, on his deathbed, had charged his friends to expose his murderer, and avenge his death. Piso was to have been brought to trial, but committed suicide, which, even in those times, had a guilty appearance. Germanicus had been universally respected and beloved, and more than common sympathy was shown when his widow and her children came home with the funeral urn containing his ashes. This sad event happened when the minds of all classes of people were filled with apprehension that they were on the eve of some terrible disturbance of the peace. Such fear breeds many kinds of excitement, and a prediction was at that time sung in the streets, as sibylline, about some awful judgment decreed to fall upon Rome,

"When thrice three hundred years have passed away."

Generally speaking, the Jews in times of popular com-

splendour. Here Romulus, in the grey dawning of Rome, built the temple of Jupiter. Here the triumphal processions of emperors and generals ended. On the steps of Ara Cœli the first great Cæsar climbed on his knees after his first triumph, and if the tradition of the church is to be trusted, here Augustus Cæsar erected the '*Ara Primogeniti Dei.*'"—*Abridged from Roba di Roma*, i. 73.

motion, sided with the popular rather than with the aristocratic party. Habitually, they were quiet citizens, engaged in commerce, and were the chief mechanics of that day; consequently the wants of the industrial portion of the community, as well as their politics, would tend to draw together the Jews and the plebeians, and thereby to considerably swell and strengthen the popular party, making it appear too formidable. This explains why the Senate enlisted four thousand of the strongest Jews, and sent them to Sardinia. This decree of the Senate was imputed to Tiberius. Suetonius says, "He distributed the young men of the Jews, under guise of a military conscription, into provinces where the climate was severe. The others of that race he removed from the city, under pain of perpetual servitude if they did not obey." In the Annals of Tacitus we read (Ann. ii. 85), "Action was also held touching expulsion of the Egyptian and Jewish religions, and a decree was enacted by the Senate, that four thousand freedmen of suitable age who were infected with the Jewish superstition should be sent to the island of Sardinia to restrain the robbers there, as if they perished by the severity of the climate the loss would be a cheap one; and that the others should quit Italy unless before a fixed day they renounced their profane rites."

Dion Cassius tells us that the freedmen sent to Sardinia were not all Jews by birth, but also other men devoted to their institutions. In the reign of Augustus, discontented refractory Jews had been sent to that island. In spite of the unhealthiness of the climate, the Hebrew colony was flourishing there when St. Paul was a boy.

These severe measures have stained the reputation of Tiberius. Thus far the Roman law as it then stood was excessively rigorous against political offences—even the least; even a few seditious words, or words merely disrespectful to the ruling government, were punishable; but as yet there was no established law that authorised condemnation solely on religious grounds. But to the Emperor belonged the power of interpreting the old time-honoured laws, so he could strain them and bring them to bear on his own projects, and he had full power to issue edicts and decrees which had not the substantial and permanent character of laws, but were intended to overrule difficulties, and to promptly and despotically quell occasional disturbances.

From the writings of Cicero we learn that Roman law, which enforced as much of morality as pagans could appreciate, and which came within the scope of judges, was mainly derived, in past times, from the Stoics. The influence of Judaism upon the Greek Stoics seems to have reacted upon Roman law.* As emperor, Tiberius presided over the Senate, but he was often unsupported by that body, which was disposed to rebel against his authority.

Modern critics have come forward to defend the character of this emperor, as they think he has been calumniated by the chroniclers of his reign, whose political opinions differed from his own, which inclined to the popular rather than to the aristocratic side. A fine, pleasing statue of him in the Vatican pleads in his favour. Tiberius, when in the prime of life, had an active mind, well cultivated. He wrote a history of his own times, at least *Memoirs*, but the work is destroyed, lost, or undiscovered. His advocates say that he had nothing to do with the death of his nephew, Germanicus, although he may have been pro-

* "Judaism at Rome," p. 173.

voked to jealousy by the adulation bestowed on that favourite prince. The suspicion against Tiberius was no mere after-thought of later days, when the Romans had learnt to know the darker features of his character. He became more than commonly suspicious, and suspicious men are those most liable to be themselves suspected. The hardships and disadvantages of his early life account for the prominence of this dark feature of his character. Naturally he had warm feelings, he grieved sincerely for the death of his brother Drusus, and he dearly loved his first young wife; but when cruelly parted from her, he lived peacefully with Julia for a while, patiently resigning his will to those of the elders of his family in age and position. But when power came at last, it found him sullen and uncourteous, soured by rancour and resentment, afraid of the Senate and Germanicus, yet ashamed to own his fears; curbed by his mother, and spurred on by Sejanus; and at length, when he, the only man whom Tiberius had ever fondly trusted, played him false, his old mistrust settled into a general contempt for other men, and for the restraints of their opinion.* These safeguards gone, he plunged into the depths of intemperance, that lie beyond the bounds of reason, far down into which men may be driven, when mastered by their own passions; mysterious depths, haunted by evil spirits, who are sometimes permitted to take possession of those who make no resistance. John Milton must have conceived this idea of Tiberius when he wrote the fourth book of *Paradise Regained*. He makes the tempter say—

"This Emperor hath no son, and now is old,
Old and lascivious, and from Rome retired

* W. W. Capes, M.A. See "Epochs of Ancient Roman History," p. 70. Longman and Co., 1879.

> To Capreæ, an island small but strong
> On the Campanian shore ; with purpose there
> His horrid lusts in private to enjoy,
> Committing to a wicked favourite
> All public cares, and yet of him suspicious.
> Hated of all, and haling. With what ease,
> Endued with regal virtues, as Thou art
> Appearing, and beginning noble deeds,
> Mightest Thou expel this monster from his throne.
> * * * * * * *
> To whom the Son of God unmoved replies,
> * * * * * * *
> How gloriously, I shall, thou sayest, expel
> A brutish monster ; what if I withal
> Expel a devil that hath made him such ?'

The poet drew his view of the life led by Tiberius at Capreæ from Tacitus and Suetonius, whose works, when the learning we call classical was revived, were among those of the heathen authors most widely read. It has been suggested that misrepresentations may have arisen out of a joke on the name of the island—that some one may have called the Emperor Caprineus, which might mean either a resident at Capreæ, or by a play on the word, a grossly dissolute man. His evil doings, when in retirement, may have been exaggerated, but undoubtedly they left the serpent's trail. Those were wicked times ; but when human nature was at its worst, the Saviour thought it worth dying for. A dark shadow seems to rest on the life of Tiberius, and to blur his name. Let us hope that when all shadows flee away, the amiable features of the affectionate boy may reappear. Beyond everything that casts a shadow, light must be shining, even beyond the cross which has set its mark on this reign.

Pontius Pilate thought it would be an honourable achievement to introduce into Jerusalem those images of Augustus Cæsar which were loyally received in the chief cities of other Roman provinces. No doubt he felt encouraged to venture on this step, by his trustfulness in the fellow-feeling between the upper classes of the nations. For some time the Jewish aristocracy had in many respects sympathized with, or at least co-operated with, the Roman. Both Herod the Great and Herod Agrippa, who were closely leagued with the patrician faction at Rome, found support in the aristocracy of Judea, rather than in the middle and lower classes, from which we may infer that co-operation, direct or indirect, existed between the influential classes at Rome and Jerusalem.

Nevertheless Pontius Pilate was quite aware that he was attempting to do a very hazardous thing; so, well knowing that at least a large number of the Jews would be offended, he sent the images into the city secretly, by night. On the following morning a terrible tumult occurred. The Jews of all classes were struck with consternation at seeing their laws treated with contempt. The indignant crowds in the town were soon swelled into vast numbers, as excited people poured in from the country. A formidable body immediately went to Cæsarea, where Pilate then was, and besought him to remove the images from their city, and to preserve their ancestral laws. Pilate rejected their suit; whereupon, they fell prostrate, and during five days and nights remained immovable. On the ensuing day, Pilate having seated himself on the tribunal in the great circus, summoned these people, as if with a view to reconsidering their petition; but when they pressed near the tribunal, he gave a preconcerted signal, and the whole assembly of Jews was instantly surrounded by Roman soldiers. Then the

Procurator declared that he would cut them down, should they still refuse to admit the images of Cæsar; and at the Governor's nod every soldier unsheathed and brandished his sword, ready to execute the final word of command. The Jews, by one consent, fell prostrate in a mass, and offering their necks, cried out that they would rather die than trangress their law. Pilate, astonished at this courageous fidelity to their religion, gave the sign for the soldiers to sheathe their swords; and ordered that the images should be taken away from Jerusalem.

He subsequently occasioned another tumult by touching the corban, a sacred fund formed of the gifts of the people devoted to God's service for religious purposes. Pilate took possession of this accumulated money, and spent it on what he considered a good work for the benefit of all. He constructed an aqueduct which brought pure water from a distance of 400 furlongs. Indignant at this profanation, the populace, on his return to Jerusalem, collected with loud clamours about his tribunal. Having foreseen the tumult, he interspersed among the crowd a troop of soldiers in plain clothes, but armed. These men were directed not to use their swords, but to chastise the rioters with staves, and this they did so cruelly that numbers died of the blows they received; and in the confusion others were trodden to death. The rest took flight, and the multitude, terrified by the fate of their friends, were silenced.

The conduct of Pontius Pilate as Governor of Judea did not meet with the approbation of the Roman Senate; he was recalled in the fifth year after that in which he had given up a man whom he believed to be a just person to his enemies, to be put to death, contrary to

Roman law, which the accused had never broken. Pilate acted under cowardly fears and selfish ideas as to what course of action would be most likely to promote his own worldly interests, and was regardless of Roman law, which he was bound to uphold.

The cross was a Roman punishment, therefore the fitting instrument of death for Him who was to die, not for one nation, but for the whole world, of which Rome was at that time the acknowledged head and representative.

Pilate had held the office of procurator for ten years when he was summoned to Rome. The next time he left that city he was under sentence of banishment, and he died in exile. It has been said that he put an end to his own life; but so many legends have clung to his name, that it is now impossible to disentangle truth from fiction.

When Tiberius heard of the wonders that had occurred in Judea, he proposed to admit Jesus among the twelve most highly honoured gods of Rome.* The emperor was willing to add a thirteenth, but the senate raised objections which prevailed.

During the reign of Tiberius, young Herod Agrippa resided in Rome, where he was educated highly, and became the favourite companion of the Emperor's son, the second Drusus. After the death of that prince, being very little noticed by Tiberius, he bitterly felt this neglect, and suffered under it, falling into distress and poverty, but he afterwards attached himself to young Caius (or Caligula), whom Tiberius had named as his successor. In a moment of thoughtlessness Agrippa

---

* See "Rome et la Judée," vol. i., page 54. Par le Comte de Champagny. Paris, 1870. This author quotes Tertullian, Eusebius, Saint Jerome, and other early Christian writers.

expressed the wish that Tiberius were dead, which was reported to that tyrant, who threw the young prince of Judea into prison, and he was not released until his wish had come to pass, till Tiberius was no more, and Caligula reigned in his stead. The new Cæsar immediately released his friend, and ere long gave him a crown, reviving the kingdom of Judea, after an interregnum of twenty-six years. Thus at last were the Maccabean and Idumean families united in a sovereign descended from Herod the Great and Mariamne. Caligula presented him with a chain of gold of equal weight with the iron chain with which he had been bound. This chain Herod hung up in the treasury of the Temple, to remind him of the instability of human affairs, and no doubt under a feeling that the placing it there was an act pleasing to the God of that temple, who saith, "When a man's ways please the Lord, He maketh even his enemies to be at peace with him." Herod's religion was half-hearted, a striving to serve two masters.

By death in the one case, and by confiscation in the other, the territories of Philip, the tetrarch of Ituræa, and Herod Antipas, tetrarch of Galilee, fell into the hands of the Roman Emperor, who added them to the dominions of King Herod Agrippa. Antipas was accused of treasonable correspondence with the Parthians, and banished to Lyons. He was the murderer of John the Baptist, and before his judgment-seat our Saviour appeared.

The new king of the Jews was careful to show reverence for the Jewish religion, and anxious to gain the regard of his subjects. He relieved them from burdens —taxes they had borne when under the more immediate government of Rome, he still further beautified the temple, and effected useful and magnificent improvements in the city of Jerusalem, making it such as Pliny describes it to be, "the most glorious of all the eastern cities." Herod also gave especial attention to the fortifications, but there his building was checked by the Romans.

While the Jews were relieved from distress and enjoying prosperity, great sufferings fell upon the Christians. The rest which the churches had enjoyed throughout all Judea and Galilee and Samaria was now at an end, for Herod Agrippa cruelly persecuted the Christians. "He killed James the brother of John with the sword,* and because he saw that it pleased the Jews, he proceeded further to take Peter also" (Acts xii. 1—3).

That man seems to have done everything that he might be seen of men. He had his reward; more than he could have calculated on; but he did not long enjoy it.

Caligula, on his accession to the imperial throne, had been most enthusiastically received by all his subjects; for the Roman people had lost all patience with the gloomy, cruel Tiberius, and were consequently the more disposed to admire the free manners and lively disposition of this young son of the loved and lamented Germanicus. Caligula had a kind of quick wit, always ready with a jest, and as his character was not well balanced, it was natural with him to speak carelessly and to excite a laugh unwisely. His thoughtless words,

---

* Thus briefly does Scripture speak of the martyrdom of the Apostle who first suffered death for Christ's sake. He is often called James the Elder to distinguish him from James the Less, who lived to preside over the church in Jerusalem; but was martyred A.D. 62. Shortly before his death he wrote his General Epistle.

spoken with no other object than temporary amusement, might be easily perverted, or an undue importance, which he had never thought of, might be attached to them. He was fond of giving nicknames to persons in any way remarkable; thus he used to call the stately Livia, whom he knew well in his boyhood, Ulysses in petticoats. His name was Caius; but that of Caligula, or *Little Boots*, had been given to him in jest, when, as a mere baby, he was dressed as a soldier, and was very proud of his boots. Little did those who gave him the pet name foresee how deeply it would be dishonoured by cruelty and the wildest folly; and execrated, perhaps even more than he deserved, by the number of enemies he made, among whom were contemporary historians. Never were subjects more bitterly disappointed in a sovereign than were the Romans in Caligula; though he reigned only four years, the flattery they lavished on him quite turned his weak head. The Jews, having more sense of morality, were likely to hold such a man in even greater contempt and abhorrence than did the heathen.

The system of religion which Augustus had, in his heathen ignorance, tried to improve, and which he had but too well succeeded in establishing as the religion of the empire, had rapidly degenerated, and become corruption itself, as must always be the case with every kind of idolatry. In the hands of such a man as Caligula it was no better than the grossest paganism that ever degraded human nature. The Jews of Alexandria sent a petition to Rome, begging that they might be defended against the oppression of the Greeks; the Greeks in their turn retaliated on the Jews by commenting on their being the only people who refused divine honours to the Emperor. This mortified Caligula, and in his passionate vexation he sent peremptory orders to

Petronius then prefect of Syria to set up his statues in Jerusalem, and on the altars there, as on those in other towns of the Empire. Then, as both Josephus and Philo relate, all Judea and Phœnicia, the grey-headed, the vigorous men, the women and children, all feeling that a great cloud covered their land, made the heathen sensible of this by their deep unanimous distress and lamentation. So great was their wailing and crying, that when it ceased, the echo seemed still to fill the air.

Then they assembled on a plain near Ptolemais to address Petronius, first on the subject of their laws, and afterwards supplicating for themselves. As a Roman general, Petronius acted with good sense and moderation. He left his army and all the obnoxious statues in Ptolemais, went himself immediately into Galilee, and convened at Tiberius the mass of the people with all those of distinction. Petronius spoke to them of the power of the Romans, of the threats of Cæsar, and of the unreasonableness of their request; for, when all the subject nations had in every city placed among their gods the effigies of Cæsar, their opposition was little less than rebellion, and that aggravated by insult. The multitude cried out, "We will die rather than that our law should be broken." Petronius, having allayed the clamour, said, "Will you then war with Cæsar?" Then one from among them stood up and said, "For Cæsar and the Roman people twice a day do we sacrifice; but if he will erect these images, he must first sacrifice the whole Jewish nation, and we now present ourselves, our wives and children, ready for the slaughter. Petronius was touched, he dismissed the assembly, which quietly dispersed.

"This," says Gerovius, "is a striking scene in the great world's tragedy, and will ever remain a reproach against Caligula, and an abiding witness for the Jewish nation, which reflects nobler honour on them, than do the greatest deeds of David or of Solomon."

Under the influence of this example, affecting a mind not incapable of receiving good impressions, Petronius wrote immediately to the Emperor. By thus daring to refrain from promptly executing the positive orders he had already received, this Roman general put his own life and the fate of his family in most imminent peril. Happily for them the widespread conspiracy against the tyrant was at that time secretly forming, and ere long proved fatally successful. Among the numerous conspirators against the life of Caligula was one of the most wealthy Jews of Rome, Romanized as a patrician. This man some time afterwards stated that Caligula had given directions for the construction of a statue of himself to be erected in the Temple of Jerusalem. Frederick Huidekoper considers that this charge, made by a murderer against his victim, comes from a suspicious source, and he does not believe in its truth, although Josephus mentions it, and Philo treats the subject dramatically; describing the scene of excitement when a Jew arrived at Jerusalem, and told the news, that Cæsar had ordered a colossal statue of himself to be erected in the Holy of Holies, having his own name inscribed on it, with the title of Jupiter; and while the people were listening to him in astonishment and terror, others arrived, bearing the same sad tale. The Jews with one accord determined on making a firm resistance, but the assassination of the tyrant prevented the sacrilege.

King Herod Agrippa happened to be in Rome when the catastrophe occurred; he had gone thither in the hope of appeasing the rage of the Emperor, with whom he had pleaded for his people, and at the same time had begged that he might still continue to reign over them. Caligula had given no immediate promise of pardon; we know not what he might have done had not his own life been cut short by a band of assassins. Pierced with thirty wounds, he expired, and his dishonoured corpse was left in the corridor where it had fallen. Agrippa found it there, covered it with purple, and carried it into a garden, where he had it hastily burnt and buried, for he feared lest further insults should be vented on it: he knew that Caligula's memory would be hated even by his successor. When time had brought tranquillity, the ashes were exhumed, and received funeral honours.

The timid Claudius, uncle to the murdered despot, frightened by the awful event and the terrible commotion, hid himself behind some drapery, but was found by a party of the Prætorian Guards who were searching through the palace for conspirators. The soldiers respected the blood of the Cæsars, and remembered the relationship to Germanicus, whose name they greatly honoured; so, at first more in jest than in earnest, they saluted Claudius as emperor, and carried him off to their camp. Their officers, while yet the Senate was deliberating on the important question, decided that this brother of Germanicus and grandson of Drusus should sit on the imperial throne. Thoughts of restoring the ancient republic were being entertained, and some who desired a continuation of the imperial form of government had another candidate in view; but when the Prætorian Guard, making an imposing demonstration, descended in full force from their camp to the city, the citizens, with whom Claudius was popular, joined them, and the Senate, which had again assembled in the temple of Jupiter, submitted, and offered the crown to Claudius. He was really afraid to accept it; but, encouraged by the arguments and entreaties of Agrippa the Jew, he allowed his name to be proclaimed, and the crown to be set upon his head, and no doubt he ever afterwards felt grateful to the friend who had upheld him in every way in this moment of imminent danger and perplexing trial. The Romans generally were pleased with the part Agrippa had taken, and he left Rome loaded with honours. Additional territory had been added to his kingdom, and he had been made a consul of Rome, a dignity which seems never before to have been bestowed upon a Jew. Yet, if he had any feeling at all, he must have started from Rome with a heavy heart.

Caligula and Agrippa had been life-long friends—companions in boyhood. The survivor must have been struck by what he heard, and by the scenes in which he had been called on to take part. The excitement seems to have sharpened his insight into his own worldly interests; but what a wonderfully different view of the shocking event he must have taken, from that in which we see it! King Agrippa was well acquainted with the Scriptures, yet no thrill of awe turned his immortal soul towards the God of Israel, whom outwardly he honoured by beautifying the temple, attending the services, and duly performing the prescribed devotional exercises. When the Jews faithfully and firmly resisted the impious decree of Caligula, their king thought only of the safety of his crown, and the preservation of his territory. Rejoicing in having so wisely acted as to have secured the one and enlarged the other, Agrippa left Rome to return triumphantly to Judea. Though warned by example, he soon afterwards was guilty of the same presumptuous sin committed by Caligula, and was as signally, and more promptly, called away from all that he had set his heart upon. His return to Jerusalem was celebrated as a national triumph. In that city he acted the zealous Jew, at Cæsarea he could play the part of a Greek and a heathen. Here the sagacity he had displayed at Rome was highly estimated; and, feeling themselves exalted in the exaltation of their admirable sovereign, his subjects were very proud of him. Here it was that the populace greeted the speech he made to them with the cry, "It is the voice of a god, and not of a man."

While seated above the people in his royal apparel, he was smitten by a stroke of sudden illness, and died, as St. Luke describes in Acts xii. 21. This memorable feast was held in celebration of Roman victories in Britain. The tributary kings and the rulers of the provinces proclaimed a feast for rejoicing, and thanking the gods, that throughout the empire all people might participate in the triumph at Rome.

On that occasion Claudius on his knees climbed the stone steps that led up to the temple of Jupiter Capitolinus. Those steps, or whatever of them is remaining after repeated restoration, are now mounted by persons going on foot from the modern city to the church of Sta. Maria di Ara-Cœli. To the young and healthy it is a toilsome ascent; so perhaps we may give a man past the prime of life—a paralyzed man, with a weak spine, a halting foot, and a trembling hand—credit for having performed a real act of humility, in the face of the world over which he had reluctantly consented to reign. The war thus happily terminated in favour of Rome had been begun by Caligula in person, but he gained no decided advantage, and after his death historians and satirists threw contempt on the boasted achievements of this hated Emperor. Modern historians, looking impartially on things that happened so long ago, see that the expedition to Britain was not entirely a whimsical design, foolishly executed. The erection of a light-house bears witness in Caligula's favour. Dean Merivale points out that even the picking up of shells on our coast may be a grotesque misrepresentation of receiving a tribute in oysters or Rutupian pearls.* Claudius, at the beginning of his reign, favoured the Jews, perhaps for Herod Agrippa's sake, as after his death a change in the Emperor's conduct towards them is obvious, though he never abandoned them finally.

At this time there was in the city of Rome a very large number of Greeks, called Alexandrians, as they had at different times come chiefly from Alexandria in Egypt. When Alexander the Great of Macedon founded that city, one-third of its first inhabitants were Jews. The city had prospered, and become over-peopled, and large numbers had emigrated to Rome, with a view to bettering their condition by traffic. These people were more like the poor Jews in their habits and ways of life than they were like the Roman plebeians; consequently, in the Roman mind they became rather confounded together; the more so, as they also gained precarious livelihoods by the lowest kind of trade, and by such

---

* Rutupiæ, on the coast of Kent, where stood a grand old Roman Castle, is now Richborough, near Sandwich. Not far from the castle was a large oyster-bed which produced uncommonly fine oysters, perhaps also mother-of-pearl. In early times rents and taxes were paid in kind by the produce most abundant. Long after the Romans had left Britain the town of Sandwich paid a yearly rent of forty thousand eels to the Benedictine Monastery at Canterbury, and we read of an estate that was valued as worth thirty-eight thousand herrings per annum. (Hasted's "History of Kent.")

disgusting occupations as made them unfit for the better parts of the city. Consequently they had got mixed up together in the narrow streets of the *Transtevere*, and, no doubt, they became somewhat neighbourly one with the other, although the difference of religion prevented their fraternizing and blending. It had become a mixed colony of Jews and Greeks, among which the former preponderated. Disputes occasionally arose, but were not important enough to disturb the public peace, until Christianity had spread among the Greeks. Numbers of the poorest and most ignorant of them were admitted into the infant Church in Rome, and this caused a clashing with their Jewish neighbours, which created serious disturbances, such as needed to be put down by the strong control of the government. The Romans at that time generally looked upon Christianity as a sect, or offshoot, of Judaism. They did not clearly understand the distinction, and senators, patricians, and every class of the Roman people were partakers in a growing prejudice against the Jews; so that they were not disposed to bear with patience the outbreaks of religious animosity which they imperfectly comprehended, and in which they were interested only as far as concerned the maintenance of order throughout the city.

A bitter contest between the Jews and their inveterate foes, the Alexandrians, occurred just at a time when the whole population of Rome was suffering in consequence of a great scarcity. There was not food enough for all, and Claudius gave general satisfaction to his own people, when, exasperated by the continual feuds between the Jews and the Greek Christians, he turned them all out of the *Transtevere*, and ordered that the synagogues, in which riots had occurred, should be closed. Suetonius says that Claudius drove the Jews from Rome because they were incessantly raising tumults at the instigation of a certain *Chrestus*. This passage has been much discussed. Some have thought that there was a Jew named *Chrestus;* others, that the historian of the Cæsars mistook that name for the name of Christ, which may have been used unadvisedly by the ignorant and seditious. Or Chrestus may have been one of the many false Messiahs. The expulsion of the Jews from Rome, decreed by Claudius, was either not strictly executed or else soon repealed, as Scripture clearly shows by the little it tells us concerning Aquila and his wife Priscilla.* No doubt the memory of Agrippa, really cherished by Claudius, in some measure protected the Jews. Josephus thought the sudden death of King Herod Agrippa very unfortunate, as he was building a wall of extraordinary strength all round Jerusalem, and, had he lived to finish it, the Romans might have found the city impregnable.

Immediately on Agrippa's decease the Roman government resumed the ruling power over Judea, and held it until his son was old enough to be placed on the throne as Herod Agrippa the Second. This was the king before whom St. Paul was brought.† At that time there were many Jews in Rome. The Apostle had lately written his Epistle to the Romans, in which Jews are named. Nevertheless the decree of banishment, though so leniently enforced or so quickly rescinded, must have caused much trouble; but we may suppose that in the

---

* Compare Acts xviii. 1—3 with the salutations at the beginning of the sixteenth chapter of the Epistle to the Romans to the sixteenth verse. From verse 3 it is evident that Aquila and his wife were at that time in Rome.

† Acts xxv. 23.

days of Claudius, as in the days of Pompey, their wealthy and influential brethren helped them; for we read that among the Jews were men and women of great accomplishments, who ingratiated themselves with the highest families, and familiarized them with the rites and doctrines of their own religion. Such as these could stem the tide of fortune that had turned against the nation: each one in his or her limited sphere could, by winning esteem and regard, subdue the force of prejudice, although, as a nation, the Jews were now beginning to fall into adversity and disrepute. Their day was done, their light was passing away, and a long time of darkness must intervene before the faintest streak of dawn could break on the glorious morrow,—a day on which the sun has not yet risen, a day of which the noontide joy and splendour will exceed all that has ever gone before.

The growing and strengthening of prejudices against the Jews, and the rapidity with which this ill-feeling spread and deeply rooted itself all over the world, may in a great measure be attributed to the increase of the pharisaical spirit among themselves. There were several schools of Pharisees, and all of them partook more or less of the general character of the sect on which our Saviour so severely commented, which He branded as hypocritical. From the frequency of His warnings to the multitude against this spirit, we may infer that all classes were being deceived and led astray by it, and no doubt the Pharisees were followed to an extent which actually affected the national character of the Jews, and the opinion entertained of them by other nations.

The habits of thought in which they had been trained had contracted and cramped their minds so much that they could not grasp a grand idea, or obtain a wide or a thorough view of any subject. The learning of their reading-men, steeped as it was in sectarian prejudice, was nothing better than moral pedantry. They did not look beyond the letter, did not enter into the spirit of meanings which feed the spiritual parts of our triune nature. Their ostentation, though not at all greater or more inflating to vanity, was different to that of other men, and very offensive to them. Affectation of sanctity is sure to excite an antagonistic encounter with the pride of righteous indignation, which is generally only another form of self-righteousness.

When he was sixteen years old, Josephus joined the Pharisees, on considerations as mature as that age is capable of. He appears not to have regretted this step, although his descriptions of their feelings, aspirations, and habits are anything but attractive.

Pharisaical character did not commend itself to the Roman mind, which was disgusted by its blemishes, and could not appreciate its best points, its stricter morality, its habitual regularity, and conspicuous propriety. Josephus himself, renegade as he was, though not little in his own eyes, must have been looked upon with contempt by a Roman patriot.

We must not judge of the Roman mind by the Claudian Emperors, nor by the military despots who succeeded them; it is fairer to judge by the literature of the period. Likewise we should remember that as every Roman was not a Claudian, so every Jew was not a Pharisee, neither was every Pharisee a hypocrite. Among them we find Gamaliel, wise, merciful, watching for indications of God's will. Moreover, in all the great cities in which they dwelt, there were individual Jews, whose conduct was such as to gain the respect of those among whom they sojourned. A few of these were men who grew rich, and were not so absorbed in money-making, that they could not spend it liberally with a view to the public good. Now and then we read of a Jew who gained popularity with his fellow-citizens, but it clung to himself alone, not to the nation to which he belonged. These individual instances, so rarely noticed, throw us back upon the simple truth, that under every condition human life has its partially enlightened, as well as its dark side, that always "the best portion of a good man's life" consists "in little nameless unremembered acts of kindness and of love." Is not this a convincing proof that under the most depressing misery that can be produced by evil powers, as well as in unclouded happiness, the listening ear may hear Jehovah's voice declaring still, "All souls are mine"? *

Ever since the intercourse between Jews and Romans began, there have been Romanized Jews. When Judea became a Roman province, there, as in every other province of the empire, educated and deserving natives were admitted to all the privileges of free-born Romans. With a sum of money they bought their freedom, and they could make it an hereditary right, for the benefit of their heirs. Being Romans in the eyes of the law, they were bound to serve and to fight for the empire, not for their native lands in particular. For obvious reasons, the Jews were less disposed to Romanize, than were the people of other nations. Very many of them were prevented by religious scruples. Those strict Jews, and those who could not afford to buy their freedom, were apt to look on their Romanized brothers as unfaithful and worldly-minded. We do

* Ezekiel xviii. 4.

not read of many in the early times of the empire. Tiberius-Alexander, and Josephus are well-known representatives of this class. They were both living in the days of Claudius, but had not yet obtained celebrity. That emperor chose Augustus as his model, tried to imitate him in all things great and small, to a curious extent, although in his childhood he had suffered much through the unkindness of all the elder members of the imperial family. Augustus himself had set the example of treating the poor boy with contempt, because paralysis had affected his personal appearance, and stunted his growth. Possibly it had also touched his mental faculties, making them weak on some points, and leaving them strong on others. He seems to have been only now and then competent to wield the sceptre of the Roman Empire, which he grasped most despotically in his weakest moments. Throughout his reign he generally supported the Patrician party, which was doing its utmost, under strong opposition, to uphold heathenism, and to crush down every kind of monotheism. Had the Jews not been protected by Herodian influence, they might have fared far worse than they did in this reign.

Dr. Farrar, in his "Seekers after God," compares Claudius to our James the First, and his unfortunate matrimonial experiments to those of our Henry the Eighth.

The Roman put only one of several wives (a really abandoned woman) to death. She was avenged, as he was poisoned by his last wife, Agrippina, a sister of the late Emperor Caligula.

Taken altogether, the Claudii so conducted themselves, as to have suggested to modern historians the idea that the blood of the family may have been tainted by hereditary insanity. Under calamities consequent on this, the Jews in Rome must have suffered, at least equally with the Romans and others of that mixed population.

One of the most important architectural achievements of this period is the Claudian Aqueduct. Two channels are supported on the same series of arcades, which now, extending like a procession of ruins along the Campagna, are of the continuous length of six miles and a half. These are the most imposing, the loftiest, and in their present state the most graceful among all such constructions. In ancient times they brought, first three, and finally four springs of pure water into Rome. *

From the high ground on which stands the church of St. John Lateran very picturesque fragments of the Claudian Aqueduct are seen; indeed, it contributes to the pleasing effect of many an extensive landscape, and of many a charming little bit of Roman scenery. Perhaps the finest view of it is that obtained from the Appian Way, whence the line of arches is seen running along towards the foot of the Alban Hills. On that green range the towns of Albano and Frascati, and little villages and white villas catch the sunshine, and attract the traveller's eye, to cheer him while his feet are treading the barren moor-like waste below, or the hard hot road, or clambering over rugged ruins of bygone days—vestiges of homes that must have seemed built to last for ever, or of tombs and monuments reduced to nameless heaps of stones, among which wild flowers luxuriate. The sight of the bee orchis, or the scent of the mignonette, may send thoughts very far away.

* "Historic and Monumental Rome." By C. I. Hemans.

ST. PAUL AND ST. LUKE.

> "And as of old by two and two
> His herald saints the Saviour sent
> To soften hearts like morning dew,
> Where He to shine in mercy meant :
> So evermore He deems His Name
> Best honour'd, and His way prepared,
> When, watching by His altar-flame,
> He sees His servants duly paired."
>
> KEBLE.

> "And time passed on in spite of prayer or pleading,
> Through storm and peril, that that life might gain
> A peace through strife, all other peace exceeding,
> Fresh joy from sorrow, and new hope from pain."
>
> ADELAIDE A. PROCTOR.

IV.

ST PAUL AND ST. LUKE.

AS soon as it had been revealed to St. Paul that he was especially called to be sent far away to the Gentiles, his most ardent desire was to go to the great city which ruled all the kingdoms of the earth; but in a vision of the night God directed him to go to Macedonia. In the book of the Acts of the Apostles, written by St. Luke, we have connected details of St. Paul's travels in Greece, which make the abrupt conclusion the more remarkable, and we read the last chapter, wondering why we are not permitted to know more about his sojourn in Rome and his death.

His Epistle to the Romans, written from Corinth, shows us how earnestly he desired to go to them. His opening sentence after the salutation must have greatly encouraged them. He assures them that they are remembered in his prayers, and that he is praying for a prosperous journey to Rome. Oh how different was the answer from what he or they could have anticipated! and yet they met, and their intercourse was begun and continued under God's blessing.

How full of sympathy are the eleventh and twelfth verses! and then he goes on to say, " I would not have you ignorant, brethren, that I have often purposed to come to you, though hitherto I have been hindered, that

I might have some fruit among you also, as among other Gentiles."*

When St. Paul wrote this, he was hoping soon to be in Rome, was intending to return to Jerusalem for a short time, that he might be present in the Temple at the feast of Pentecost, and then go on to Rome, and thence to Spain.

St. James, called by the Christians James the Less, to distinguish him from James the Elder, was the chief pastor in Jerusalem; so much respected was he in the world, that it had given him the honourable title of James the Just. St. Paul was wishing to meet this brother apostle, and to speak with him and his counsellors.† (See Acts xxi. 18.)

St. Paul went to Jerusalem; there again he was hindered; that visit proved very distressingly eventful, fraught with circumstances which caused delay, and threw him again and again into imminent danger. At last he started from Jerusalem for Rome, not as a free man, but as a prisoner.

The letter he had lately written to the Romans shows how he had intended to proceed. Can there be anything more trying to an energetic man than the sudden frustration of carefully devised plans? It is

---

* Romans i. 11, 12, as translated by Conybeare and Howson.

† Origen says: "Such was James' reputation among the Jews for virtue, that Josephus, who wrote of the Jewish Antiquities in twenty books, wishing to assign a reason for the calamities of his people, affirms that they were inflicted by God as a punishment for their guilty behaviour towards James the brother of Jesus, who is called the Christ." "Strange is it," remarks Origen, "that this writer, who would not admit our Jesus to be the Christ, should nevertheless render such testimony to the virtue of James." (See Note on Traill's Translation of Josephus, by Isaac Taylor.) St. James was put to death A.D. 62, soon after he had written his General Epistle.

none the less trying if he be one who habitually makes his plans in a prayerful spirit, unselfishly, and wisely, as far as he can see; consequently he has felt almost assured that those plans were blessed, and must produce good results. When the frustration has been caused, not by death or sickness, or anything that comes directly from the hand of God, but by the injustice and ill-feeling of men, whose very conduct lowers them in the estimation of the higher minded; or through foolish misunderstandings, of which an innocent man feels himself to be the victim, so that those who naturally should be his protectors and friends, his own people, turn against him, this is trying to the inmost heart and soul of man. When this occurs to any one, it is to him as a day of battle. St. Paul fought the good fight; through the whole course of the battle he " kept the faith."

Follow him step by step, see how bravely he fought it out! Always self-possessed, true to the duty of the moment; whether he stood before the excited multitude thirsting for his blood, or before priests and their council, or before governor or king, or on the deck of a seemingly doomed vessel in a fearful storm. Then we hear of no cowardly rebellious wish that his disappointed life might be cut short by overwhelming waves, more merciful than the raging of his enemies. St. Paul prayed and worked, and exhorted and comforted his companions in distress. He was glad when the sun burst through the clouds; most thankful that through God's blessing on his prayers and exertions many lives had been saved.

We have been led to follow the adventures of Herod, Augustus, and Paul. The superiority of the Christian hero claims our highest admiration. We are inclined to suppose that St. Paul was upheld by superhuman power, so as to be above the weaknesses of human nature. A few simple words in the sacred narrative show us that when the excitement was over, and he had landed on the coast of Italy under circumstances so different to those he had comtemplated when thinking of his visit to Rome, he felt depressed even to dejection; yet, because he "kept the faith," his heart was not hardened, but rather softened by anxiety and sadness.

"And so we went towards Rome. And from thence, when the brethren heard of us, they came to meet us as far as Apii forum and the three taverns: whom when Paul saw, he thanked God and took courage."

St. Paul had not come unattended from Jerusalem; Luke and Aristarchus had come with him, not as prisoners, but as passengers. St. Luke, as a physician, might easily have procured a free passage. Dr. Farrar suggests that possibly one or both of them might have been sent with St. Paul by his friends in Jerusalem, many of whom were wealthy, and being much attached to the Apostle, they would naturally feel, under his melancholy circumstances and infirm health, it was better that he should not go alone. Julius, the centurion, who had several prisoners under his charge, was a humane man, and one capable of understanding that Paul was no common prisoner, but a man far superior to most of those with whom he had to do. From the first he was disposed to treat him kindly, but Roman soldiers were responsible with their own lives for the security of their prisoners, and therefore, to prevent the possibility of an escape, a custom had arisen of keeping every prisoner safe by chaining him with a long light chain by the right wrist to the left wrist of a soldier. Prisoners were not allowed to go anywhere without this galling protection; but we may hope that they were not always subject to it in the narrow fetid cribs and hatchways of the huge, unwieldy merchant vessels in which their compulsory voyages had to be performed.* It is also well to recollect that the chain was not looked upon, nor felt to be, a sign of moral or social degradation, which inflicted lifelong disgrace. When liberated, the man was free as ever, and was none the worse for having worn the chain, if he had not been convicted of crime.

After those never to be forgotten adventures on the sea and the island of Malta, which must have drawn them together, Julius and his cohort of soldiers, his prisoner, and the other passengers of the Castor and Pollux had landed at Puteoli. Very extensive trading was done at that busy seaport, especially with Egypt. We can still trace the ruins of seventeen piers of the ancient mole on which the light-house stood, and within which the merchant vessels were moored. Puteoli, the trading town, and Baiæ, an adjacent gay watering place, surrounded and crowned a rocky promontory on that indented coast. Many Jews resided there, and St. Paul had the happiness of finding a little community of Christians, who warmly welcomed him, and begged him to spend a week with them, to which Julius consented. The halt may have been convenient to him; so here they rested in one of the loveliest of earthly scenes.† Strikingly beautiful are its natural features, and the town on the projecting rock, and beneath it the fine temple of the Egyptian god Serapis, and Beulos, a marine palace of the Cæsars on a neighbouring height, were then in full splendour. The varied prospect over land and sea obtained from the high points above the

* Conybeare and Howson.
† See Lewin and Conybeare and Howson.

coast included the calm blue Lake Avernus and a thick wood, then as now enlivened by all sorts of wild flowers. In the depth of that forest lay concealed the cave of the Cumæan Sibyl, entered on one side from the wood, and on the other from the wave-lashed shore. Vesuvius was still a slumbering volcano, and Herculaneum and Pompeii were basking in the sunshine.

On the eighth day St. Paul and his companions started for Rome, which was a hundred and forty miles off. They journeyed on first to Capua; that town had recovered from its misfortunes and disgrace in the days of Hannibal, and was one of the most fashionable in Italy. Thence they passed through rich vineyards; then the scene changed, and they had to cross the Pontine Marches to get to Appii Forum, forty-three miles from Rome.

Horace describes this town as very noisy and busy. A canal brought up merchandise, and consequently bargemen and tavern-keepers abounded. It was a meeting place where travellers from all parts of the Empire crossed one another's paths. On that day, in the motley and vulgar crowd, some of the few Christians then in the world recognized each other, and emotions of holy joy and thanksgiving sanctified the place of coarse vice and vulgar traffic.*

The party who had come out to welcome Paul and his companions, Luke and Aristarchus, included no doubt most of those whom the Apostle had saluted in his Epistle to the Romans, and very likely the good Aquila and his wife Priscilla, with whom he had lodged at Corinth. Then again St. Paul's heart was lightened by the presence of sympathizing friends, and ten miles farther on he found another group at the Three Taverns.

* Conybeare and Howson.

Although this affectionate welcome from some who loved him in Rome could but be both gratifying and comforting to Paul, yet he knew that the number of his friends was comparatively few. He was well aware of the power of the Hebrew multitude, and the turbulence of the vast assemblage of the Jews in the synagogues of the great city. That people having been permitted to return to Rome, their synagogues had been re-opened, and Paul knew that on their favour or opposition his future destiny must much depend.

Cheered by conversation with his companions, the Apostle passed through scenes of ever-deepening interest, along a road more and more crowded with stately monuments as they approached the city. As they passed on, the warm-hearted brethren would point out to him the tombs of the Scipios and Cæcilia Metella, and the thousands of other tombs with their architectural beauty, and striking bas-reliefs, and touching inscriptions.* All along on either side of this Appian Way, for more than eleven miles beyond the walls of Rome, the illustrious dead repose. To be buried there was almost as great an honour to a Roman as the being interred in Westminster Abbey is to a distinguished Briton. Accommodation for travellers on foot was conveniently provided, seats being placed along the road at a distance of only forty feet apart; and there were roadside inns at which refreshment could be procured.

The Dei Viales were certainly not passed by unnoticed. The sight of such a group would help the Christian to lift up his heart in a prayer to the God of gods for a fuller diffusion of gospel light.

And so through ever-lengthening rows of suburban villas, and ever-thickening throngs of people of every

---

* Farrar's "Life of St. Paul."

class and of various nations, and carriages for travellers of every rank, and palanquins borne on the shoulders of slaves passing to and from the city, Paul and his companions pressed on. How many a look of contemptuous curiosity would be darted at the escort of soldiers with the chained prisoner and his Jewish friends! But Paul could bear this now he felt that he would not be utterly lonely amid the vast and densely crowded wilderness of human habitations, which he had caught sight of in the distance from the Alban hills, before he had descended to the plain. They must have passed near the fountain of Egeria and its colony of begging Jews, and by the pyramid of Caius Cestus, and under the Arch of Drusus; through the dripping Capenian Gate, leaving the Circus Maximus on the left, and going on amid temples and statues and arches till they reached the barracks of that section of the Prætorian Guards whose turn it was to keep guard over the person of the Emperor. It was thus that the dream of Paul's life was accomplished, and he entered Rome in March A.D. 61, the seventh year of Nero's reign.*

The household troops were quartered in a Pretorium attached to the palace of Cæsar on the Palatine. Here Julius gave up his prisoner into the hands of Burrus, the Pretorium prefect, whose official duty it was to keep in custody all accused persons who were to be tried before the Emperor. St. Paul may have been lodged in these barracks, or he may have been first quartered in the Pretorium camp outside the city. We do not know, and it is unimportant; but we do know that both among the soldiers and in Cæsar's household the seed of the Word of God was sown and bore fruit. We like

* Abridged from "Life and Works of St. Paul." By Dr. Farrar. Vol. ii., pp. 385—390.

to think of the good-natured Julius as one who may have sought Paul's company, and cheered him in his captivity, thereby gaining more and more knowledge and love of true religion, and recommending it by his example to the men under his command. We like to think of the long light chain by which St. Paul's hand was connected with that of a rough soldier, as a thing of earth which may be worth remembering in heaven. The Apostle, and at least some of those who in turn kept guard over him, and thus saw a good Christian man passing through a trial, the heaviness of which they could well understand, may now remember that chain as the first link in a chain of causes and consequences, the commencement of an intercourse which began

"'Mid toil and tribulation,"

and coupled this life

"in union
With God, the Three in One,
And mystic sweet communion
With those whose rest is won."

These are pleasant and refreshing thoughts, in which we may indulge; but it is not worth while to perplex ourselves over the much-debated questions as to where St. Paul was lodged on his arrival in Rome, and where stood the house he afterwards hired for himself.* Let us refer to the simple statement of St. Luke, that "Paul

---

* Three places are pointed out as the site on which stood the house which St. Paul hired in Rome.

1. The Church of Sta. Maria, in Via Lata, in the Corso, adjoining the Doria Palace. The subterranean part of this church is shown as the actual house in which the Apostle lived, and a fountain in the crypt is said to have miraculously sprung up in answer to St. Paul's prayers that he might have water for baptizing his converts.

2. Another Church, St. Paolo della Regola, not far from Ponte

was suffered to dwell by himself, with a soldier that kept him."

This was evidently an indulgence, probably due to the influence of Julian. Although a prisoner, St. Paul retained a considerable degree of freedom. Three days after his arrival he called together the principal Jews then in Rome; for although he had a special commission to teach the Gentiles, yet he was not regardless of the general rule, to preach first to the Jew and then to the Gentile. These chief men, though very cautious, were not uncourteous; they expressed a desire to hear what he had to say, although they candidly told him that they had heard nothing about him, and that the sect to which he belonged was everywhere spoken against. A day was appointed for a general meeting. Then many Jews came to him into his lodging, and he spake with them concerning Jesus, both out of the law of Moses, and out of the Prophets, from morning till evening; and some believed the things that were spoken, and some believed not." As fearlessly and truthfully as he had spoken to the Jews in Jerusalem, so did he now speak to those in Rome. His forcible arguments, and his reference to the words of their venerated prophets, were not ineffectual. He had awakened them to reflect upon these things, and they had great reasoning among themselves.

We have now reached the two verses which conclude the book of the Acts of the Apostles. They contain all that Scripture tells us concerning St. Paul's residence

---

Sisto and the ruins of the theatre of Balbus. To the right of the altar is the inscription, *Divi Pauli Apostoli Hospitium et Schola.*

3. The Rev. Dr. Philip prefers the tradition in favour of a house in Via degli Strengari, about 100 yards from the Ghetto. He thinks probably Paul resided near his Jewish brethren.

in Rome, except what we may glean from the epistles he wrote during those two years. The verses are very simple, do not express one dark idea, and clearly describe the life of a zealous missionary. We know that St. Paul was never so happy as when he was speaking of his dear Lord, or working or writing in His service; and he was cheered by the society of congenial friends, his two fellow-travellers, Luke, who was so devoted to him, and Aristarchus, a Macedonian of Thessalonica, whose life had been endangered by the mob at Ephesus and Epaphras, a Colossian.* There is reason for supposing that the two last named lived with him in his own hired house, and being in close attendance on the Apostle, might be said, though not quite in a literal sense, to share his imprisonment. We are glad to know that the repentant Mark, once dismissed on account of timidity and indolence, now assisted St. Paul, who grew so much attached to him, that years afterwards Paul sent for Mark to help him through the heavier troubles of his last captivity. Demas also came to Rome for a time, which was cheering, as he had not yet proved unfaithful through love of this present world.

These primitive Christians had no more foresight into what would happen to them on the morrow than we have. They were roughly rocked on the troublesome waves of doubt and fear and delusive hope with respect to their worldly position and concerns; but their minds were not tossed about on life's restless ocean, as they would have been without faith, that anchor of the soul, which fastens it to the everlasting Rock. Most likely, at the commencement of the captivity they had no idea that it would last two years, although that was not an unusually long time for prisoners to be detained. Tiberius

* See Col. iv. 10 and following verses, and Philemon.

had been in the habit of retaining accused persons in prison unheard, merely out of procrastination. St. Paul's prosecutors could not immediately arrive. The charges against him were divided into three separate heads. First, he was accused of having caused factious disturbances throughout the Empire; secondly, with being a ringleader of the sect of the Nazarenes, which involved heresy against the law of Moses; and thirdly, with an attempt to profane the Temple at Jerusalem, an offence, not only against the Jewish, but also against the Roman law, which protected the Jews in the exercise of their worship. In this case the accusers had to summon their witnesses from Judea, Syria, Cilicia, Macedonia, Corinth, and elsewhere—from all cities between Damascus and Corinth.* It is easy to see how repeated delays occurred; and, of course, when all the witnesses were in Rome, the proceedings would be adjourned from time to time to suit the Emperor's convenience.

Meanwhile the prisoner was treated as leniently as the strictness of Roman law would permit. All the members of the church in Rome could visit him freely. Besides the companions already named, were young Timothy, and Onesimus, a refractory slave, who had run away from his master, Philemon, but had been found and led into the fold of Christ. In these the faithful pastor took a loving and active interest, which must often have diverted his thoughts from anxieties with respect to his own future. Large congregations assembled in his house. Surely his eloquence was not the less effective when involuntarily he lifted the fettered hand, or when a sound of the shackling chain reminded his hearers of what he had said on the day when first he spoke publicly in Rome: "For the hope of Israel I am

---

* Conybeare and Howson.

bound with this chain." Nevertheless, "the iron entered into his soul," as we know by the repeated allusions to his bonds in all the epistles of this captivity.* It could not be otherwise than galling to a man of high spirit, strong will, and powerful energy. How strong must have been the self-control required, and by God's help attained, and exhibited. Under such a trial, how admirable and loveable must every indication of unselfishness and patience and readiness to forgive have seemed to lookers on, even to the soldier at the other end of the chain, who had to bear his share in the undeserved bondage! Had it not been for the blessed reconciling spirit of Christianity, both would have been in a worse case; for it is better to be under the eye and under the rule of one whose heart is not devoid of respectful kindly feeling, while he watches and curbs, than to hold command over a slave who hates and is disposed to rebel against the restraining power.

We know not, but we may fairly suppose that the favoured prisoner was allowed to take the air and exercise necessary to health; that he went out on the Palatine, among the noble edifices there. The palace of Augustus, still an imperial residence, was, as we have seen, guarded by the Prætorian barracks. Caligula had greatly enlarged the palace towards the forum, and had connected it with the capital by a bridge. The beautiful temple of Apollo, erected by Augustus, in memory of the battle of Actium, was near his palace, as were also the celebrated library, the academy, and the lecture hall, a kind of theatre in which poets and other writers read their compositions. On that side of the hill a venerable building linked together successive

* The Epistles of this two years' captivity are Philemon, Colossians, Ephesians, and Philippians.

ages, the days of the first kings and the first emperors—the temple of Jupiter Stator, begun by Romulus, and finished by his successors. An anxious thought must now and then have crossed St. Paul's mind when he passed the imposing BASILICA JOVIS, to which he was expecting to be summoned as soon as his accusers and their witnesses had arrived, that he might answer them in the presence of Cæsar and his councillors. The substantial and extensive palaces of Tiberius and Caligula, and the smaller but more elegant and highly decorated house of Livia, with their baths and pleasure grounds, stood near enough to one another to be connected by corridors, in one of which Caligula had been murdered.

This grandest quarter of Rome was adorned by many stately edifices elevated above the busy forum, which was incessantly alive with official and commercial activity. The upper end of the forum, near the capital, was the more aristocratic part. There, figuratively speaking, were planted the pillars that upheld the state. Below were ranged the equally important supporters of the manifold civic institutions, and the centres whence circulated business of all kinds necessary to the prosperity of this great metropolis.

At the corner of the extensive Basilica Julia stood the arch of Tiberius. Thence proceeded, down through the forum, the long straight street, formerly a crowded thoroughfare. It was so strongly paved, that the few persons who may now be seen pursuing their researches, are treading on the old stones; and the mosaic pavement of the Basilica Julia seems now wonderfully perfect, when we remember the centuries that have rolled away.

The Forum Romanum occupied an oblong space. One of the two short lines that marked that figure ran close under the steep Capitoline Hill. At its corner nearest the Palatine stood the temple of Saturn, and at its other angle the temple of Concord, near to which, on the slope of the Capitoline, just off the Forum, stood the strong Mamertine Prison, built in the most massive style of Etruscan architecture. It was begun by Ancus Martius, and finished by Servius Tullius. In ancient times a prison was a terribly sad thing to look upon; and this could tell many a melancholy tale besides its whispers about secret deeds of darkness, never to be truthfully revealed. The neighbouring temple of Concord was, on the contrary, a pleasing object that gave happy thoughts. It was founded by Camillus in memory of the peace made between the Senate and the Commons, when the office of consul was opened to the plebeian order. The temple had been restored by the Emperor Tiberius, in the Corinthian style; its portico of six columns, terminated by a group of three figures embracing at the top, had a graceful effect.

The temple of Saturn (already glanced at) was one of the most ancient and revered in the city; it had been repeatedly restored and beautified. In this temple the state treasures were deposited, under the care of the god Saturnus, one of the most revered of Roman deities, a more just god than Jupiter.

Sweeping the eye up over the Forum to the other short line that marks its oblong shape, we see at the corner nearest to the Palatine the temple of Castor and Pollux. When in its glory, that was one of the most admirable and attractive of the sacred edifices, ornamented with decorative work of the best period of Græco-Roman architecture, most delicate and perfect. The approach was raised above the Forum level, and projected beyond the line of the next building, the Basilica Julia. Within that spacious hall the fathers of men contemporary with St. Paul had crowded to hear Cicero speak. The ground on which he stood still speaks of Cicero. The Roman Forum recalled the departed and revived the past as much as it now does. St. Paul could discern more clearly than we can the spot in front of the temple of Vesta, on which the body of Julius Cæsar had been burnt, nearly opposite his own house, and the Julian rostra near it. The limit of the Forum on its short side, farthest from the Capitoline, may have been rendered indistinct when looked on from above, as a great deal of new building was going on there, even before Nero began to build his great golden house. That emperor seems to have had a mania for building; his foolish excess in that kind of pride was one of the characteristics of his insane or utterly ill-regulated mind. Before his wretched death had relieved the world from a despicable tyrant, he had covered not only the Velia, or low ridge of hill and dale that runs from the Palatine towards the Esquiline, with his superb erections and their surroundings, but also ground beyond. His golden palace, enormous though it was, is now reduced to foundations and fragments that blend with the relics of later periods, so as hardly to be distinguishable.

The spectator on the Palatine, having taken his bird's-eye view over the restless scene in the Forum, might turn away to look on what he called Old Rome, on the broken but massive walls and ramparts of the Tarquins, who had carried building and draining to unprecedented perfection, and on other strong masonry of the period of the kings, down to some foundations laid by Romulus, and vestiges of his house.

A general view of Rome taken by St. Paul and his companions from any one of the famous Seven Hills must have been very striking to men who had but lately come to the metropolis of the dominant Empire. As Rome had borrowed philosophy, science, and even mythology from her predecessor, Greece, as the school of Athens had completed the education of Rome, the city exhibited a good deal of Greek architecture, mingled with the massive walls, fortifications, basilicas, and other structures in the characteristic brickwork of Rome. The Corinthian order had been first introduced when the columns of the Temple of Zeus were brought from Athens, and used in the edification of the great Capitoline Temple of Jupiter. Babylon, the first of the four great empires, was represented in Rome; the mausoleum of Augustus being covered with terraces and trees in imitation of the Temple of Belus. The dwelling houses of the patricians were graceful mansions in Grecian styles of architecture; their level lines of marble masonry flanked airy colonnades interspersed with courts and gardens; those of the plebeians were chiefly either old houses of a bygone generation, built in heavy Roman brickwork, or of the Italian rustic style, and these small low dwellings must have been densely crowded together in that over-populated city: many of them had flat roofs, used for domestic purposes. This combination of ancient and modern, of the grotesque and the elegant, gave to the whole a strikingly picturesque character. Temples were numerous, and variously constructed. Among them, the Pantheon was then what St. Peter's is now among the churches. Its portico is the oldest specimen of the Corinthian order in Rome. Above that sacred edifice, dedicated to all the gods of heathendom, arose no higher dome, no spire, or *campanile*—only the obelisk, the memorial of victory over Egypt, the monument engraven by a Pharaoh or a Ptolemy to immortalize his deeds, re-erected by a Cæsar far away, yet again planted upon earth, and pointing to something above it, beyond the limited range of a mortal eye. The natural features of the landscape given by the Alban Hills near, and the Sabine Mountains in the distance, and the yellow Tiber, and the *campagna* beyond the city, looking like a sea-green heaving ocean, are features which time has scarcely changed. On the banks of the river the elegant circular Temple of Vesta in its full beauty was a pleasing object, and near it stood a very different one in the Ionic style, the Temple of Fortuna Viralis.

Of the theatres of Balbus, Marcellus, and Pompey, that of Marcellus was the most extensive and magnificent. Augustus had lavished a great deal of money on it, because, having named it after his favourite nephew and adopted heir, he, after the death of Marcellus, looked upon the building as a memorial of him. It was substantially Roman, but all its adornments were Greek. The theatre of Pompey was also a grand building. In the portico of a hundred columns attached to this theatre, Brutus sat as prætor on the morning of the murder of Julius Cæsar, and close by was the Senate House, where Cæsar fell at the base of the pillar on which stood Pompey's statue.*

Such was Rome when St. Paul and St. Luke, with others of the little Christian brotherhood, were residing there. The Pincian Hill was then in the suburbs; the wide view it commands was full of interest to intelligent

---

* Behind the remains of the theatre, perhaps on the very site of the Senate House, stands the fine modern church of St. Andrea della Valle.—*Walks in Rome. By Augustus Hare.*

minds. It was not then, as now, the fashionable pleasure ground, but was charming in all the wildness of natural beauty, enriched no doubt with varieties of the euphorbia, the aloe, and the cistus, or rock-rose, which daily sheds its white petals like snowflakes on the ground, with the star-like anemone and all the other indigenous flowers that are now abundantly gathered in the woods and meadows of the adjoining Borghese and Medici estates.

Being a physician, St. Luke must have been acquainted with plants and their properties, and being a disciple of the Master, who spake in parables, whose daily habits and conversations were still cherished recollections in the memories of living men, Luke must have found types and symbols in the unsullied flowers, must have gathered refreshing thoughts as he plucked the lilies of the field. When walking alone, he may often have been thinking of the true narratives he compiled in his Gospel and in the Acts of the Apostles.

Both these works were dedicated to his friend Theophilus, whose name only has come down to us. The author of the Acts, in his preliminary dedication, calls the Gospel his former treatise, which proves that they were written by the same person.

The chief object of the book of the Acts is not to give a continuous history of the Church, or a complete life of St. Paul; the author's main objects were higher than these. This book records the descent of the Holy Ghost on the day of Pentecost, the consequent effusion of the truth, and the astonishing addition so instantaneously made to the number of believers in Jesus Christ; and thus it teaches the Church that without the Spirit of God all other qualifications are impotent. Moreover it bears witness to the admission of the Gentiles into the Christian community.

Many of the expressions in St. Paul's epistles suggest at once the idea of a physician, ready to see a parallel between health of body and health of soul. They occur in the pastoral epistles, which were certainly written when St. Paul and St. Luke were together. In the case of one of them at least, if St. Paul made use of an amanuensis at all, he could only have used Luke, for he says that no one else was with him.

St. Luke, as a mutual friend of St. Paul and young Timothy, had doubtless often discussed with them questions referred to in the letters. The strong friendship between St. Paul and St. Luke is from some points of view very remarkable; for the educated Jew and the educated Gentile might have been widely separated. The one, a Pharisee of the Pharisees, entered manhood under the power of all the prejudices and bigotry of the narrowest of religious societies. A native of Tarsus, it is true, and by law a Roman citizen, acquainted with some of the works of heathen writers, but still a Jew,—a Roman only by accident, but a Hebrew of the Hebrews in his inmost nature. What we call accident is generally, and in the case of this man was certainly a special guiding providence; for did not the Lord Himself say to Ananias, "He is a chosen vessel unto Me, to bear My Name before the Gentiles, and kings, and the children of Israel"? St. Luke had culture of a different kind, and his training probably was broad, as that of St. Paul was narrow. Assuming that he was a Gentile convert and a physician, we may fairly conclude that the great writers of the ancient world were his study; that he had read the history and had witnessed the struggles of different schools of thought; that the artistic refinement of Greece and the broad justice of Rome had both their influences upon him, and we know that, to crown all, he had, by his conversion to Christianity, learnt all that which is most real and true in Judaism itself. The two were as different in their training as men could possibly be, yet, as Christians, they had that in common which united them in the closest bonds of friendship.*

Inspired authors were but men, in all other respects equal with their fellow-men, not raised above the commonest necessities, nor independent of the influences that combine to actuate our own daily lives. These two were earnest, faithful teachers and writers of truths in which they believed—careful pastors, zealous missionaries; they needed the same kinds of refreshment required by all hard workers, *re-creation* in the most literal meaning of that word, when the mind ceases for awhile to search into deep things, and gladly returns to the simplest ideas suggested by the familiar sights and sounds that catch the eye and fall upon the ear.

When St. Paul was a prisoner in the Pretorian camp, or in the barracks on the Palatine Hill, he continually saw the whole armour of a soldier, the shield, the breastplate, the helmet, and the sword; he heard all kinds of martial sounds, and at appointed hours the trumpet call, which gave no uncertain sound, but one well understood by every Roman warrior and citizen. Then time was marked, and people regulated the duties and habits of life, by sun-dials and trumpets. St. Paul may have heard the trumpet from his own house, and St. Luke may, at the same moment, have heard it while he was pur-

* "St. Luke as the Amanuensis of St. Paul." By Rev. John Healy, LL.D. Published in the *Homiletic Quarterly*, No. 19. Kegan Paul and Co., 1 Paternoster Square.

suing the active duties of life—endeavouring to convert the ignorant and wayward, visiting the brethren, going about doing good, while speaking of the Lord, whose example he faithfully kept in view. Sometimes, perhaps, he was on the hills, or on the plain outside the city, seeking plants and herbs from which he could distil medicine and healing balms to cure or to soothe the sufferings of the body. Then the trumpet was to him a call to the happy evening meal—happy, because received with genuine thanksgiving. Then, as with purest sympathy they conversed over the adventures of the day, were not that little brotherhood, including Jew and Gentile, free man and slave, each and all, one in Christ? Was not each one doing his part towards expressing on earth the answer to a prayer that had ascended from earth to highest heaven—the prayer of our Lord Himself—" that they all may be one"? *

Although the Apostles, and the earliest Christians cotemporary with them, believed themselves to be branches of the True Vine, members of a body of which Christ is the Head, yet they did not separate themselves from the Jews. When the Apostles arrived in a town, they always went to the synagogue on the following Sabbath-day, and expounded the Scriptures, often explaining passages from the prophets, as all doctors had a right to do. They were in the habit of speaking on the same subject on two, three, or more successive Sabbaths, and some of them gave long series of discourses which lasted for months. They never abandoned this practice, unless they were turned out of a synagogue because the new doctrines they inculcated alarmed and offended the rabbis and elders, or

* John xvii. 20 and following verses. Also, "Thy will be done on earth, as it is in heaven."

startled the people, who were not used to having God's eternal truth put before them in all its purity and force. At the same time, these first Christian missionaries fearlessly stood up to speak in pagan assemblies, in the basilicas and the forums, and in all other public places, even in the heathen temples, where they faced the idols, and endeavoured to convince the ignorant worshippers of the folly of such adoration. In short, while they continually prayed to Him on whom they depended, they left no means untried that could possibly serve to propagate the Gospel, and to touch the hearts and consciences of their hearers. Bravely did they carry out the Lord's injunction, "What I tell you in darkness, that speak ye in light: and what ye hear in the ear, that preach ye upon the housetops." *

From the memorable day of Pentecost, when thousands of men were brought together purposely from the ends of the earth, though not one of them previously understood why he was thus impelled; from that day forward Christianity was openly preached to the whole world. In so far as it was propagated by man's agency, its rapid progress may be ascribed to the free spirit of its chief teachers and preachers, who, looking up to a Master in heaven, felt happily independent of earthly authority whenever it attempted to counteract what was, they felt sure, the will of Him by whom all powers that be are ordained. They still obeyed in all sincerity, not in a rebellious spirit; for their loyalty to kings, priests, and rulers was grounded on the best foundation.

---

* Matthew x. 27; Luke xii. 3. Early Christian writers give this view of the trials and labours of the Apostles. (See Euseb. H. E. 11, 13, 15, 21; Cypr. Ep. 55; Irenæus 111, and others, quoted by Mons. le Comte de Champagny, of the French Academy, in "Rome et la Judée," vol. i., pages 58—60.)

Like Jabez, they were blessed indeed, and their view of this life, and of all that lies beyond it, was enlarged, and their ideas of boundaries extended, which did not confuse them, as it might have done, had they not at the same time been made to feel the loving pressure of the Hand holding and guiding them. They were kept from evil, that it did not grieve them; so they could be patient under inconveniences and sufferings. The tone of the apostolic mind is pitched above this world.*

We Christians use the word Apostle reverently, and it is well so to do, provided we bear in mind that it simply means a person sent, that every man, woman, and child that has ever been called into the Hebrew or the Christian Church has been, or will be, sent out into the world to act, to suffer, and to influence others by both precept and example. It has been so ever since the God of Israel began to call His people, and to be called on by them; and at this moment, numbers that cannot be counted, of whom the world knows as little or less than it now knows of Jabez, are living usefully and happily through evil times, under the same blessing.

* 1 Chron. iv. 10.

THE FIERY TRIAL.

Paul before Nero.

"And now these two men were brought face to face—imperial power and abject weakness; youth cankered with guilt, and old age crowned with holiness; he whose whole life had consummated the degradation, and he whose life had achieved the enfranchisement, of mankind. They stood face to face, the representatives of two races—the Semite in its richest glory, the Aryan in its extremest degradation; the representatives of two trainings —the life of utter self-sacrifice, and the life of unfathomable self-indulgence; the representatives of two religions—Christianity in its dawning brightness, Paganism in its effete despair. . . . But Roman law was still Roman law, and except where passions of unusual intensity interfered, some respect was still paid to the forms of justice. For the time, at any rate, St. Paul was rescued out of the lion's mouth. There was some flaw in the indictment, some deficiency in the evidence;"* or, as Merivale suggests, "his liberation was a further testimony to the acknowledged inoffensiveness of his sect."-

* "The Life and Work of St. Paul." By Dr. Farrar.

V.

THE FIERY TRIAL.

IN the large basilica in, or rather adjoining, the imperial palace on the Palatime, Nero presided over the trials of causes such as that of St. Paul. Basilicas were not roofed over until a later period. This splendid hall was open to the sky, but the interior was richly decorated with precious marbles. We may imagine the Cæsar, surrounded by his twenty councillors, all men of the highest rank and greatest influence. St. Paul was brought before the tribunal under the custody of his military guard. The prosecutors and their witnesses were called forward; for although the subject-matter for discussion was contained in the written depositions forwarded by Festus from Judea, yet the Roman law required the personal presence of the accusers and the witnesses.

When the parties on both sides had been heard, and all the witnesses examined and cross-examined, which perhaps occupied several days, the judgment of the court was taken, and each of the councillors gave his opinion in writing to the Emperor. Nero never discussed the judgment with the assessors, as emperors who were better men had done. He wrote his sentence according to his own will and pleasure, and it was read in his presence by his questor.*

* Abridged from Conybeare and Howson's Life of St. Paul.

There is now in Rome an interesting picture, "St. Paul before Nero," by Dr. Philip. As no writer of sacred or profane history has described the trial, this painting must be a work of the imagination; but the artist, who loves the Jews, and searches heartily into everything connected with their past history and present condition, has thoroughly studied his subject. He has strikingly delineated a scene in a hall of justice. The Emperor, the questor, the accused and his accusers, and senators and the vestal virgins. These women, many of whom were well born, formed a very numerous and influential class. They are shown as sitting in a gallery corresponding with that occupied by the senators. The vestals also had the power of expressing their judgment, not by word of mouth, but by the action of the hand; each one turned her thumb either up or down to indicate a vote for acquittal or for condemnation.*

We have no scripture to depend upon, but we may fairly suppose that St. Paul, when first tried in Rome, was acquitted, and that immediately on his liberation he went to Colosse, a city of Phrygia, in Asia Minor, where Philemon resided, whom Paul had commissioned to prepare for him a lodging.† The Epistle to the Colossians shows that the personal supervision of the Apostle was needed there. Thence he seems to have travelled quickly, visiting several cities in Asia Minor. We cannot be sure that he accomplished his long-cherished desire to reach Spain, and to plant the Gospel there. Some think he was disappointed, as we have never heard of a port at which he landed, or of a church founded by him in that country. The tradition among

---

* Dr. Philip's painting represents the last trial of St. Paul: the thumbs are turned down to vote for his condemnation.
† See Philemon, verse 22.

the earliest Fathers in favour of his having gone is credible, as it agrees with his expressed intentions.* His own disciple, Clement, mentioned in Phil. iv. 3, afterwards Bishop of Rome, writing from Rome to Corinth, states that Paul had preached the Gospel in the east and in the west, that he had instructed the whole world, and had gone to the extremity of the west before his martyrdom. Now in a Roman author "the extremity of the west" could mean nothing short of Spain, and the expression is often used by Roman writers to denote Spain.† Eusebius says, "It is currently reported that after defending himself successfully, the Apostle again went forth to proclaim the Gospel, and afterwards came to Rome a second time, and was put to death by Nero." ‡ St. Chrysostom says decidedly that St. Paul, after his residence in Rome, departed to Spain; and St. Jerome says he preached Christ's Gospel in the west. Bishop Stillingfleet and others have collected many ancient authorities to support their conjecture that St. Paul went on from Spain to Britain, which was well known to the Romans, and considered by them to be at the farthest extremity of the west. It seems likely that St. Paul may have visited our island, but of this we have no proof whatever.

We can only gather from Church history that while St. Paul was prosecuting his labours in the west, he received sad news from Judea, of the martyrdom of James the just, Bishop of Jerusalem, and of the cruel persecution of the Christians throughout Judea by King Herod Agrippa. It seems more than likely that he wrote immediately to the afflicted brethren, but opinions differ as to this part of the Apostle's life, with

---

* See Romans xv. 24—28.   † Conybeare and Howson.
‡ Hieron. Catal Scrip.

regard to which we really are left in the dark. Lewin says: "At this time St. Paul wrote his Epistle to the Hebrews; not long after that letter had been despatched, Timothy arrived from Philippi, when Paul and his young companion and other missionaries sailed for Judea, visiting Crete by the way."* The Apostle seems to have stayed but a short time with the Hebrew Christians; to have next made the circuit of the churches in Asia Minor, and to have gone on to Corinth; but details and dates given of this part of his life cannot be firmly depended upon. Certainly he intended to spend a whole winter at Nicopolis; but whether at all, or how far, he was permitted to carry out that intention, cannot be ascertained; possibly he may have been arrested there.†

There seems reason for supposing that before the widespread persecution excited by the great fire in Rome had finally subsided St. Paul was arrested on the charge of his being a non-worshipper of Roman gods, a follower of Christ; which, according to a decree lately promulgated by Nero throughout his dominions, was dealt with as crime worthy of death. It has been suggested that the Apostle was arrested at Troas, and thence taken to Ephesus, where he was imprisoned; this is mere conjecture on 2 Tim iv. 13, 14. At Ephesus, on Mount Piron, the remains of a tower are still pointed out, in which St. Paul is said to have been incarcerated before he was sent to Rome for his second trial: it is a local tradition.‡ Certainly on his return to Rome he

---

* "Life and Epistles of St. Paul." By T. Lewin. Published by George Bell.

† Titus iii. 12.

‡ The fact that St. Paul left his cloak and books at Troas has led to the conjecture that he may have left that place hastily, in

must have found that proud city like a mourning queen stricken by a grievous calamity, sitting in the midst of ashes. Most truly was it still a furnace of adversity in which all the elements of Roman society were chaotically separated. Blinded by the glare of that strange catastrophe, yet naturally seeking the cause, heathen, Jew, and Christian drifted apart, losing hold of every principle of common humanity, without which men cannot dwell peaceably together. The Romans, as a nation, had not yet learned to understand the distinction between Jews and Christians; they looked upon the disciples of Christ as forming a sect among the Jews. The nobler Romans of the Palatine were more favourably disposed, less prejudiced against Christianity than were their less educated fellow-citizens, though converts had been made among the plebeians in the unaristocratic parts of the city, and among the poor Jews in the *Transtevere*.

St. Paul had addressed his Epistle to the whole church,

consequence of his having been arrested. We have no evidence to support this supposition. There seems stronger reason for supposing that the prime movers in the accusation against him were his old adversaries, his own kindred, the Jews, who hated the Apostle to the Gentiles, because they could not bear that the Gentiles should be placed on an equality with themselves. The charge brought against him was simply adherence to Christ. Since Nero's edict had been proclaimed, Christians were considered malefactors (2 Tim ii. 9, iv. 13, 14, to end of the Epistle). The second arrest was brought about by Alexander the coppersmith, who ten years before had stood forward as the popular speaker against Paul. Soramus the proconsul seems to have been well disposed towards the Apostle. Whatever were the circumstances, Paul was again ordered to Rome; and as Soramus's period of office expired at that time, they may both have sailed in the same vessel, to perish by the same fate in the following summer of A.D 66. Soramus may have died a Christian death. Tacitus says "he was put to death by Nero for his virtues" (Ann. xvi. 23).—*Lewin*.

"To all that be in Rome," but one cannot read it without seeing that it appeals chiefly to the educated classes. It was precious to those who could only hear it read, and partially understood what they heard; it must have been most fully comprehended, most thoroughly appreciated, by the readers on the Palatine. Most likely it was read, not by baptized Christians only, but also by some of those who had not renounced all the religious ideas in which they had been brought up. Conversion among the native Romans was as yet rare and imperfect; they were sensitive, strongly attached to the traditions of their ancestors. Proselytism was not a vent for Roman enthusiasm; and they were not easily proselytised, though many were not indifferent readers and hearers of the books of the Old or New Testament. The wife of Aulus Plautius, the conqueror of Britain, was denounced to the Emperor as guilty of a foreign superstition; this shows that a Roman was not the master of his or her own conscience, that the making any charge with regard to religious observances was dangerous. Nero, perhaps out of regard for her husband, refused to listen to the accusation, and referred it to the domestic tribunal of Aulus Plautius and the chief members of his family. Pomponia was leniently judged, and escaped unpunished, but her subsequent behaviour must have annoyed her relations—it was so strikingly contrary to the spirit of the age—and she lived on for many years in self-chosen retirement and reserve. This story throws a little light upon the domestic difficulties of that day; yet, in spite of them, tranquillity prevailed until the great fire suddenly ignited the wildest and the worst passions of the variously constituted population of Rome.

On the 19th of July, A.D. 64, fire burst out near the Porta Capena, in that part of the Circus Maximus contiguous to the Palatine and Cœlian Hills; a part of the city that contained many shops full of inflammable materials, which renewed the force of the incontrollable element. It ravaged the Forum, and reduced adjacent temples and old palaces to blackened ruins. It swept round the base of the Palatine, and soon volumes of flame mounted the hill, where, notwithstanding the gigantic efforts of united strength that were made to stop it, great damage was done. A little subdued, it descended into the valleys, and for more than a week continued to burn on, though blocks of houses were purposely destroyed in the hope of arresting its progress. At last there was a lull, but it burst out again, and raged for three days longer. Of the fourteen districts into which the city was divided, three were totally destroyed, and seven were uninhabitable. During those ten awful days, scenes were witnessed such as no man who beheld them had ever seen before. We can readily conceive how some of the Christians, at least those who were excitable enthusiasts, as the newly converted are apt to be, in their amazement thought that perhaps this was the beginning of the end. That Rome was destined to be finally destroyed by fire, was an idea common to both Jew and Christian, and the Christian believed that fire would be let loose to do a work as awful as that done by water in the days of Noah. Earnest, faithful hearts were looking for that expected sign of our Lord's immediate return, which they hoped they should live to see. Is it not very likely that when feeling thus, expressions may have escaped many of them, which when misrepresented and exaggerated made them objects of suspicion, and laid them open to false accusations?

When at last the conflagration had ceased, the Romans could not look calmly on the devastation.

They were proud of their native city, and grieved to the heart to see its historical memorials laid low, the monuments of victories, the masterpieces of Greek art, lost for ever.

Many temples, among them the splendid one of Jupiter Sator, and all its surroundings, were destroyed, and wherever the fire raged, statues of the gods were left in a state that wounded the religious feelings of the Roman people, and must have suggested thoughts to the Jews and Christians, which some of them may have imprudently and provokingly expressed, and have thus drawn suspicion on themselves. Who was the author of the calamity? was the one question of the day. The Emperor's name was whispered; it was well known that he was passionately fond of building, and that existing parts of the city hindered him from carrying out extensive plans; all Rome knew that his will brooked no contradiction, and his foolish behaviour excited anger and strengthened suspicions.

We may suppose that Nero was not altogether ignorant of the reports that stealthily gained circulation; he knew that the people hated him. But soon the great popular outcry was against the Jews, by whom both Jews and Christians were meant. Were they not the people who had no reverence for the gods, no veneration for the temples, who rejoiced at their downfall, who had long been looking forward to the destruction of Rome, who had said that it would take place by fire?* At that crisis the smouldering embers of discontent were flickering here and there, all over Judea and at Jerusalem; were at that moment beginning to burst out into what proved to be the great Jewish War. The

* Jewish anticipations of Rome's destruction are scattered through the Sibylline Oracles and the Second Book of Esdras.

state of the fatherland could not fail to affect the feelings and condition of the Jews in Rome. The whole Roman world was exasperated against the Hebrew, and it was quite natural to imagine that the compatriots of the men who were levying war against Rome in Judea had kindled the flames by which they had intended to destroy the capital city of their enemies. Nero must have been glad to have so good an opportunity of diverting suspicion from himself; the slightest shadow of a reason for doubting the loyalty of a Hebrew to the Roman Government was thought sufficient to justify an arrest. Tacitus tells us they were condemned on the charge of arson; hence the extreme cruelty of the sentence, and the invention of a new punishment—the setting them on fire, which was looked upon as consistent with the crime attributed to them. The persecution fell on both Jews and Christians. Some represent that it began with the Jews, but Tacitus evidently thinks it began with the Christians; probably it was at the commencement indiscriminate. We know that all who refused to worship the gods of the Romans were looked upon as abominably irreligious; and the Hebrews were accused of being haters of mankind, because their ideas and customs differed from those of other nations. All historians agree in relating that on the whole this bitter persecution fell mostly on the Christians. The cause of this is not clear: their way of declaring that the world was soon coming to an end by fire might have led to the supposition that they had endeavoured to assist in the fulfilment of the prophecies they quoted. Some think that the Jews were first attacked, and did all they could to throw the odium and danger on the Christians; others think it was just the reverse, that, as Tacitus says, the Christians were accused, and that afterwards "a vast multitude discovered by them were condemned." It seems more likely that these should have been Jews, than that the Christians should have betrayed one another to so "vast" an extent.

We but too well know, on the testimony of all history, how bitter was the feeling between the baser sort of mere professing Christians and the Jews; we know, too, that the ideas of Tacitus concerning the origin and religion of the Jews were very cloudy. He could have been hardly capable of distinguishing Christian from Jew. The persecution is an historical fact. Unfortunate persons were crowded together, and very rigorously treated, before they were brought forward to confess their faith, and a profession of Christianity was deemed equivalent to owning that they had had some share in the crime laid to their charge. If condemned, they were treated as if guilty of both high treason and sacrilege, and the punishments were frightful. One of the most hideous features of Roman manners was to make a festival of public executions. The amphitheatres were turned into places of execution, the tribunals served for the arena and the criminals of the whole world were brought to Rome to supply the circus for the amusement of the people. The victims were reserved for a festival, to which beyond doubt an expiatory character was given.*

As to the punishment of the Dirces, there can be no doubt whatever. The colossal group called the Farnese Bull, now in the Museum at Naples, gave the horrible idea. Amphion and Zethus are binding Dirce to the horns of a wild bull, which is about to drag her over the rocks and briars of Cithæron. This indifferent work of Rhodian sculpture, transported to Rome about the time of Augustus, was the object of universal admiration.

* Ernest Renan.

What finer subject for this hideous kind of art, which the cruelty of the times had brought into fashion, the representation of celebrated statues by *tableaux vivants?* An inscription and a fresco at Pompeii seem to prove that when the criminal was a woman, this terrible scene was often represented on the arena.

An enormous brazen bull also appeared, made hollow, like the wooden horse introduced by the Greeks into the city of Troy; it was used as a furnace in which condemned persons were put to death.*

The amphitheatres, which had been originally erected for the combats of wild beasts, were now used for a more horrible kind of conflict. Criminals covered with the skins of beasts were thrown into the arena to be torn to pieces by dogs. In the persecution under Nero some were crucified, others had their garments saturated with oil, or pitch, or resin, and were fastened to gibbets, and reserved to illuminate the festival at night. When the day declined, these living flambeaux were lighted. In the glare of these torches the Emperor was sometimes seen. The circus races happened to be going on, so he appeared in his jockey's dress, or drove in his chariot when he mingled with the people. For this horrible show of his own devising he had lent his magnicent gardens beyond the Tiber, now the piazza on which stands the basilica, the cathedral of St. Peter's.†

---

* This, as well as the living bull dragging a female victim by the hair, and many other equally shocking scenes, are represented in the long series of fresco paintings round the interior of the large circular church, *St. Stefano Rotondo,* on the Cœlian Hill. These horrible pictures of the multitude of martyrs attract a wonderful crowd of spectators on St. Stephen's Day. Little children are lifted up by their parents to look at them.

† Hibbert Lectures for 1880. By Ernest Renan. Pages 80—90. The reader may like to have this in the words of Tacitus. " The

Having remarked that under this terrible tribulation the enmity between the baser-minded Jews and professing Christians was brought out, and that either in individual instances may have been ungenerous and unchristian enough to throw odium and danger off themselves and on their companions in misfortune, we must not leave the subject without referring to the testimony of the catacombs. They were then used not only for the interment of the dead, but also for the concealment of the living. Both Jews and Christians "*wandered in dens and caves of the earth*" (Heb. xi. 3, 8).

The catacombs afford evidence of the Jews having been confounded with the Christians, and that they also held underground services for public worship, and buried their dead in those sepulchres.

infamy of that horrible deed" (setting fire to Rome) "still adhered to him. To suppress, if possible, this common rumour, Nero procured others to be accused and punished with exquisite tortures, a race of men detested for their evil practices, who were commonly known by the name of Christians. The author of this sect was Christus, who in the reign of Tiberius was punished with death, as a criminal, by the procurator, Pontius Pilate. At first those only were apprehended who confessed themselves of this sect, afterwards a vast multitude discovered by them, all of whom were condemned, not so much for the crime of burning the city, as for their enmity to mankind. Their executions were so contrived as to expose them to derision and contempt. Some were covered over with the skins of wild animals, that they might be torn to pieces by dogs, some were crucified, while others, having been daubed over with combustible materials, were set up as lights in the night-time, and thus burned to death. For these spectacles Nero gave his own gardens, and at the same time exhibited there the diversions of the circus, until at length these men, though really criminal, and deserving exemplary punishment, began to be commiserated as people who were destroyed, not out of regard to the public welfare, but only to gratify the cruelty of one man."—*Tacitus, Annal* xv., c. 44.

In one of the galleries of the catacombs in Via Portuense, containing no Christian inscription whatever, there was found a lamp, having on it a representation of the golden candlestick of the temple, and upon the wall over it the word *synagogue* in Greek letters, evidently indicating the place of meeting for Jewish worship. The sign of the branched candlestick also is inscribed on tombstones: in one remarkable instance, it and the Hebrew word *shalom*, which signifies peace, occur in connection with Christian symbols, which has led to the conclusion that the sleeping-place is that of a Jewess who had been converted to Christianity, and a female with a decidedly Jewish name set up a slab to the memory of her Roman husband. The centre of the slab exhibits the monogram of Christ, with the ends of the side branches turned up to form the figure of the candlestick, ingeniously combining in a small compass the idea of Jewish origin with Christian belief. "Peace is inscribed on thousands of graves, suffering on very few."* The early Christians buried their dead under the feeling expressed by St. Paul, "Our light affliction, which is but for a moment, worketh for us a far more exceeding and eternal weight of glory." The catacombs show how widely Christianity had spread before it was tested by persecution, and how pure, when tried, it came out. The inscriptions bear no signs of resentment—only such as betoken sentiments of composure, gentleness, trust in God, and love to all among whom He had cast their lot in life. They show how impossible it is for the sincere Christian to wilfully injure a fellow-creature. What is tribulation but threshing, which would not be needed if chaff did not

* "The Catacombs of Rome." By Benjamin Scott. Longman and Co.

exist? We must not be so blinded by the chaff that we cannot see and be thankful for the heaps of good ripe wheat made ready for the garner, yet still possessing power to make earth fresh and fruitful, and to sustain the children of men; for "the blood of the martyrs is the seed of the Church."

It is generally believed that both St. Peter and St. Paul were martyred in the latter part of Nero's reign, and that St. Paul suffered, not in the full heat of the persecution, but when it appeared to have passed off. We have no scriptural account of his last days. The Second Epistle to Timothy is the only portion of Holy Writ that throws the slightest gleam of light upon them.

In the utter absence of information that can be entirely depended upon as authentic, traditions have gained attention, and even some wild legends related in connection with them, have excited interest.

About two miles beyond the noble Basilica church outside the walls, built long ago, and dedicated to St. Paul, but recently restored by Pope Pius the Ninth, there is another smaller church, one of three churches enclosed in one garden, and taken care of by the monks of La Trappe. It is called *S. Paolo alle Tre Fontane.* This little church covers the spot on which St. Paul is supposed to have been beheaded: within are three springs of pure cold water. The custodian points to the remains of a broken pillar, and tells you that on it St. Paul's head received the death stroke; that the head bounded three times, and that where it struck the ground a spring of water issued. It used to be added that the three fountains were warm, tepid, and cold, but that most extravagant part of the legend has died out.

Undoubtedly this is a fable, one of those against

which St. Paul warned Timothy and Titus in his pastoral epistles to those shepherds of the flock of Christ.* But on the authority of standard ecclesiastical historians we may believe that St. Paul was a second time arrested, and after an imprisonment, more rigorous than the former one, was put to death. He must have been permitted to see or to communicate with friends in Rome, as he sent their greetings to Timothy.† Peter's name is not mentioned, although, according to Eusebius, he was in Rome, and he and St. Paul took their last missionary journey together before they were imprisoned. This does not harmonize with the story of Paul's arrest at Troas, and incarceration at Ephesus; but he may have been liberated, or partially so, for a short time. Not long before this, when the Neronian persecution was raging, St. Peter was at Babylon, safe there, as that city belonged to Parthia. At Babylon he wrote his first epistle, while St. Mark was with him.‡ He may have gone thence to Rome, and there have met St. Paul; but we cannot rely on Eusebius, as all the earliest ecclesiastical chroniclers accepted traditions that would be rejected by modern historians; but whatever we may say of such stories, it remains probable that St. Peter came to Rome, and there suffered martyrdom. Germs of truth are likely to exist in traditions beginning in the age to which they refer; and with regard to St. Peter, Papias, Irenæus, Clement of Alex-

---

* 1 Tim. i. 4, iv. 7; Titus i. 14.

† Possibly Linus, named in 2 Tim. iv. 21, may be the first Bishop of Rome mentioned by Irenæus and Eusebius. Archdeacon Williams suggests that Pudens, also greeted by St. Paul, may have been a Roman of that name, who was once stationed in Britain, who married a British lady, possibly the daughter of Caractacus; . but as Claudia was a common name, this is uncertain.

‡ 1 Peter v. 13, 7, iv. 12 to end of chapter; 2 Peter i. 13–15.

andria, Tertullian, Origen, and Eusebius agree in stating that the apostle suffered martyrdom at Rome. Papists assign more importance to this fact than really belongs to it; but that is no reason why Protestants should deny it. It has no connection whatever with the far more important question as to the supremacy of St. Peter, or of the Church of Rome.

If Eusebius be correct, as to the meeting of St. Peter and St. Paul, and their travelling together, then it would in that case appear possible, and even not improbable, that they should have been imprisoned together in the Mamertine prison on the declivity of the Capitoline Hill, near the arch of Septimus Severus, according to the story still told when the dark dungeon beneath the church of *S. Giuseppe dei Falegnami* is shown. It is impossible to imagine a more horrible dungeon, one more dark, damp, and low; indeed, the darkness is total, and there could never have been one ray of daylight given to cheer the captives. Its existing state answers perfectly to the description of Sallust, who relates the circumstances attendant on the fate of the Catiline conspirators who were confined there about sixty-three years before the Christian era. That historian says, "In the prison called the Tullian (because, though it was built by Ancus Martius, it was enlarged and completed by Servius Tullius) there is a dungeon ten feet deep; when you have descended a little to the left, you are surrounded by walls, closed above by a low, vaulted roof of stone. The appearance of it, from the filth, the darkness, and the smell, is terrific." The Mamertine prisons were used especially for state prisoners. We can imagine that St. Peter and St. Paul may have been confined there; but few among the many visitors are credulous enough to believe the guide who holds up his torch against a pillar, to which he tells them the apostles were chained, yet allowed to preach and to baptize with water miraculously provided for that purpose. The pure taste of the water in that awful place speaks to the heart more forcibly than words can do; it says, "Let him that is athirst come;" and the greatness of his misery, the wretchedness of his earthly condition, will only make the living water more reviving. But the delicious spring cannot literally verify the legend of that subterranean spot.*

Scripture fully manifests the genuine invincible faith of those holy Apostles, though it does not put before us any details of their last earthly trials and human sufferings, but we know that they were indeed "faithful unto death."

We cannot be certain as to the exact spot from which St. Paul departed to receive "the crown of life," but most likely he was beheaded in the valley about three miles from Rome, anciently known as Aquæ Salviæ, now called the *Tre Fontane*. We have no reason for contradicting the tradition which has clung unswervingly to that spot, although we reject the legends connected with it.

We may picture to ourselves the venerable Apostle going forth from Rome for the last time, to lay his grey head on the block, passing under the gate which now bears his name. It is a modern structure, but near it stands a conspicuous object, which St. Paul must often have seen, which he may have noticed as he was being

---

* "No positive proof has been discovered that the conical cell was ever anything more than a water tank, and the name of dungeon which has been attached to it is probably a medieval legend, invented to indicate a spot which might be venerated as the prison of St. Peter." (See "Old Rome." By Robert Burn, M.A.)

led out of Rome, the city he had so longed to enter. The Pyramid of Caius Cestius, which in olden times was thought to be the tomb of Remus, stands close to that gate. We may feel certain that disappointment was not at that moment the predominant feeling in the mind of him who was going out to die, but rather "for me to die is gain." Then he thought of "the city that hath foundations," but most of Him who saith, "I am the Resurrection and the Life."

Blessed words, which near that very spot awaken, not the dead, but the living—awaken the fainting spirits of broken-hearted mourners to the realities of everlasting life, at the gate of our English cemetery; and further on, the Word of God, written by St. Paul's own head and hand, gives unfailing comfort.

As to the last days and death of St. Peter, Scripture is absolutely silent, and traditions and legends are perplexingly abundant and inconsistent. It is generally believed that this Apostle was crucified with his head downwards, either on the height called *S. Pietro in Montorio*, on the Janiculum Hill, or in Nero's pleasure ground, which is now occupied by the grand cathedral of St. Peter's and the piazza in front of that edifice: indeed, Nero's gardens extended over all the ground now appertaining to St. Peter's and the Vatican. That ground received the baptism of blood which marked out Rome as the city of martyrs, to play a special part in the history of Christianity, and to become its second holy place. It was the taking possession of the Vatican Hill by a triumphant army, of a kind which the world had not yet known. The hateful madman who governed the world did not perceive that he was the founder of a new order of things, and had signed for all future time a charter, the results of which would be claimed for mankind after the lapse of 1800 years. . . . Next to the day on which Jesus died on Golgotha, the day of the festival in the gardens of Nero (we may fix it as the 1st of August, A.D. 64) was the most solemn in the history of Christianity. The solidity of a construction is in proportion to the sum of virtue, of sacrifice, of self-devotion, which has been built into its foundations.*

Thus were the foundations of the Church of Christ laid upon Him, the chief corner-stone; thus was His death followed by that of a multitude that no man can number, who now stand around His throne, on the right hand of God the Father Almighty." We may believe that among them are St. Peter and St. Paul, enjoying the sweet repose of Paradise, each realizing the promise, " Him that overcometh will I make a pillar in the temple of my God." Each retaining his own personal character, and yet not quite what he was during the struggles and collisions of daily life. Apostles were men of like passions as we are, not always subduing their passions, and only subduing them at all by that grace which is offered to us as freely as to them.† These brother Apostles were the leaders of two distinct schools of theology. St. Peter's was Judaism saturated with, nay, rather regenerated by, Christianity; for it was life through Christ animating the ancient religion and worship of the Israelites. St. Peter still loved the types and shadows, and looked through them up to the antitype. St. Paul, the Apostle of the Gentiles, though by birth a Jew, and educated as a Pharisee, rejoiced in the liberty of the Gospel, and held that circumcision was not required.

* Hibbert Lectures for 1880, by Ernest Renan, pages 89, 90.
† Dr. Goulburn.

This rite, ordained by God's command to Abraham, was the very badge of Jewish nationality, and among Jewish converts were many who were afraid or unwilling to give up this and other ceremonial observances of the ancient religion according to the Old Testament. It seems as if there were many converted Jews in the church at Rome, for St. Paul wrote on this subject very strongly in his Epistle to the Romans, reasoning with them thus: "He is not a Jew which is one outwardly, neither is that circumcision which is outward in the flesh; but he is a Jew which is one inwardly, and circumcision is that of the heart, in the spirit, and not in the letter, whose praise is not of men, but of God;"* and again, "The gospel of Christ is the power of God unto salvation, to the Jew first, and also to the Greek."† St. Paul declared that to maintain the old law was to dishonour Jesus, who was made a surety of a better Testament. He feared lest Christians should trust in the mortal priest and his ministrations, more than in Him who hath the unchangeable priesthood.‡

It has been suggested that soon after St. Paul left Rome, at the expiration of his first imprisonment, St. Peter may have gone to that city with a view to counteracting what he considered dangerous in St. Paul's teaching.§ This is mere conjecture; it seems far more likely that the extraordinary, unprecedented calamities which fell upon the Christians, when those in Rome were falsely accused of having set fire to the city, excited the deepest sympathy throughout the whole church, and thus strengthened the bonds of brotherly love; and that the common danger may have induced the two chief pastors to meet that they might consult

---

* Romans ii. 28, 29. ‡ Hebrews vii. 22—24.
† Romans i. 16. § Römische Petrussage. By M. Lipsius.

together and unite their efforts to protect and encourage the terrified flock, driven hither and thither, pursued by enemies more cruel and savage than wild beasts. It is pleasant to think that these brothers in Christ may have taken their last journey together, may have been companions in captivity, and that after death had released their happy spirits, their bodies may have been laid to rest in the same burial place. We cannot be sure of this, but certainly, about the middle of the third Christian century, the mortal remains of two men, said to be those of St. Peter and St. Paul, were brought up to light from the catacombs of St. Sebastian, near the Appian Way, and were reverently interred; the one in what had been Nero's garden, but the ground was changed, everything had been altered, for nothing was cherished in which Nero had delighted: there St. Peter was buried, and the grand basilica that bears his name arose to mark the spot. St. Paul was laid outside the gate that bears his name, through which he passed on his way to execution, on the Ostian road.

The first church on this site was built by Constantine, the first Christian emperor. Lucina, a Roman matron, gave the ground, which had been a vineyard. Succeeding emperors enlarged the building into a basilica, and under the popes it increased in magnificence and beauty. Before the Reformation the sovereigns of England were protectors of this church, and contributed towards its preservation. On the 15th of June, 1823, the night which preceded the death of Pope Pius the Seventh, the noble building was almost destroyed by fire. No one dared to tell the dying man, for he was very fond of that church, having lived in the convent when he was a quiet monk, when his life was spent in reading, teaching, and simple recreations. His successor, Leo the Twelfth, began the restoration without delay, and in a truly catholic spirit, as he readily accepted contributions of rare marbles, gold, silver, and precious stones, from all who desired thus to do honour to the memory of the great Apostle. Even Russia gave the malachite altar, and the sultan of Turkey presented four columns of oriental alabaster, brought to Rome by Mahomet Ali. The restoration was completed, and the church re-opened by Pius the Ninth. Though costly, the exterior of the building is heavy and unattractive, the more so, as it stands on a desolate, abandoned part of the Campagna, which has been deserted on account of the increase of malaria having rendered it very unhealthy during great part of the year.

The interior of St. Paul's Church is magnificently spacious, the roof being supported by eighty granite columns; and strikingly splendid is the decoration. It surpasses the basilica that was burnt, and everything that betokens its connection with historical associations has been carefully restored, even to the badge of the Order of the Garter, which tells of bygone times.

In the open space between the transept and the nave is a gorgeous baldachino, supported on four pillars of the finest marble, with gilded capitals and a Gothic canopy. This heavy structure surmounts the traditional tomb of the Apostle, and bears this inscription :—

"Tu es vas electionis Sancte Paule Apostole,
Prædicator veritas in Universo Mundo."

Beneath the high altar and St. Paul's shrine is a smaller shrine and a very plain altar, on which is inscribed the one name "Timothei." Here the ashes of Timothy are said to rest. "Strong is the temptation, for once, not too exactingly to demand or to scrutinise authority for the truth of a legend in itself so beautiful; that these two honoured servants of Christ, who had loved and laboured, and wept and prayed, sorrowed and rejoiced together, are now resting side by side—the father and his own son in the faith."*

Timothy was by birth both a Jew and a Greek: his mother, a true daughter of Israel, having married a Greek who lived at either Derbe or Lystra when this child was born.

The question whether Clement of Rome was of Jewish or Gentile origin has been frequently discussed and answered in opposite ways. Dr. Lightfoot, Bishop of Durham, who has sifted the question, is inclined to agree with those who believe that this venerable father of the early Church was in a worldly as well as in a spiritual sense of the expression a redeemed man, one liberated from the state of bondage—that either he or his parents had been set free, according to the custom of the times, and that consequently he was a loving and beloved subordinate member in the family of a Roman nobleman of high position, near the imperial throne. Having stated his reasons, Dr. Lightfoot adds, "I venture therefore to conjecture that Clement the Bishop was a man of Jewish parentage, a freedman, or the son of a freedman belonging to the household of Flavius Clemens, the Emperor Domitian's cousin. It is easy to imagine how, under these circumstances, the leaven of Christianity would work upwards from beneath, as it has done in so many other cases; and from their domestics and dependants the master and mistress

---

* "St. Paul in Rome." By the Rev. J. R. Macduff, D.D. See pages 89—91.

† "St. Clement of Rome." By J. B. Lightfoot, D.D. Page 263. Macmillan.

would learn their perilous lessons in the gospel. Even a much greater degree of culture than is exhibited in St. Clement's Epistle to the Corinthians would be quite consistent with such an origin; for amongst these freedmen were frequently found the most intelligent and cultivated men of their day. Nor is this social status inconsistent with the position of the chief ruler of the most important church in Christendom. . . . At a still later date, more than a century after Clement's time, the papal chair was occupied by Callistus, who had been a slave of an officer in the imperial palace. The Christianity which had thus taken root in the household of Domitian's cousin left a memorial behind in another distinguished person also. The famous Alexandrian father who flourished a century later than the Bishop of Rome bore all the three names of this martyr prince, Titus, Flavius, Clemens. He too was doubtless a descendant of some servant in the family, who, according to custom, would be named after his patron when he obtained his freedom. The imperial household was henceforward a chief centre of Christianity in the metropolis."* Jews were found in large numbers at this time among the slaves and freedmen of the great houses, even of the imperial palace. Dr. Lightfoot tells us that every time he reads the Epistle of St. Clement to the Corinthians, the conviction of a Judaic authorship is strengthened in his mind. The name of Clement was a very common one among Romans and Romanized people of the conquered nations. Tacitus mentions five persons of that name, and it is often found on sepulchral monuments.

St. Paul, in his Epistle to the Philippians (iv. 3), men-

* "St. Clement of Rome." By J. B. Lightfoot, D.D. Pages 265, 266.

tions a fellow-labourer named Clement. Origen thought this man was Clement of Rome, and later writers have followed him, but they cannot be identified with any certainty. We hear of them as living at different places, the one at Rome, the other at Philippi; dates also do not seem in favour of the identity, though they do not prove it to be impossible. The Clement commendably mentioned by St. Paul might have been a young man who lived forty or fifty years longer in the world.

The newly recovered portion of the first or genuine Epistle of Clement, which has been found in the library of the Most Holy Sepulchre at Constantinople, contains an earnest entreaty to the Corinthians to obey the injunctions contained in the letter, and to heal their unhappy schisms; a long prayer, ending with an intercession for rulers and governors, and a strong protest against the sin of disobedience. The Epistle is peculiarly valuable, as it enables us to more fully understand the secret of papal dominion. This letter does not emanate from the Bishop of Rome but from the church in Rome. There is every reason to believe the early tradition which points to St. Clement as its author, and yet he is not once named. The first person plural is maintained throughout. "We consider," "we have sent." It is a letter from a community, not from an individual. Irenæus thus describes it: "In the time of this Clement, no small dissension having arisen among the brethren in Corinth, the church in Rome sent a very sufficient letter to the Corinthians, urging them to peace." Now that we possess the work complete, we see that Clement's existence is not once hinted at from beginning to end. The name and personality of Clement are absorbed in the church of which he is the spokesman; and the words of the letter are those of earnest entreaty, of wise and affectionate exhortation. "It may seem strange," says Dr. Lightfoot, "to describe this noble remonstrance as the first step towards papal aggression; and yet undoubtedly this is the case. There is all the difference in the world between the attitude of Rome towards other churches at the close of the first century, when the Romans as a community remonstrate on terms of equality with the Corinthians on their irregularities; strong only in the righteousness of their cause, and feeling, as they had a right to feel, that these counsels of peace were the dictation of the Holy Spirit, and its attitude at the close of the second century." The original primacy of Rome was a primacy, not of the bishop, but of the whole church—a primacy, not of official authority, but of practical goodness, backed, however, by the prestige and the advantages which were enjoyed by the church of the metropolis.*

On this valuable work by Dr. Lightfoot, now Bishop of Durham, which puts before us the Epistles of this humble-minded though important person who appears to have been at the head of the church in Rome in the last years of the first century, Ernest Renan remarks, " I am happy to find myself in accord with one of your ablest and most enlightened critics with regard to Clement of Rome. In the half shadow in which he remains enveloped, and as it were lost in the luminous dust of a fine historic distance, Clement is one of the great figures of a nascent Christianity; but we may liken him to some head in fresco of Giotto's, old and faded, but still to be recognised by its golden glory and the pure and mild brilliancy of its indistinct features. Everything leads us to believe that Clement was of Jewish origin. He seems to have been born in Rome,

* Dr. Lightfoot.

of one of those families from Palestine which for one or more generations had inhabited the capital of the world. His knowledge of cosmography, and his acquaintance with secular history, testify to his having received a careful and superior education. Without having any decided proof of the fact, we may admit that he had had some intercourse with the apostles, especially with Peter. The high rank which Clement held in the purely spiritual hierarchy of the church of his times, and the unequalled reputation which he enjoyed, are beyond doubt. His approval was a law in itself. All parties claimed his leadership, and desired to shelter themselves beneath his authority. It is probable that he was one of the chief actors in the great work which was in process of accomplishment—the posthumous reconciliation of Peter and Paul by the fusion of the two parties.

Clement is the first type of pope which Church history presents to us. His lofty personality, which legend makes more lofty still, was, after that of St. Peter, the holiest figure of primitive Christian Rome. Succeeding ages looked upon his venerable face as that of a mild and grave legislator, a perfect homily of submission and respect. Already the idea of a certain primacy belonging to Rome was beginning to make its way to light. The right of warning other churches, and of composing their differences, was conceded to that church. Similar privileges, so at least it was believed, had been accorded to Peter by the other disciples.* Thus a bond which gradually grew closer was established between Peter and Rome."†

* Luke xxii. 32.
† Hibbert Lectures for 1880, by Ernest Renan. See pages 123 to 125.

In the hazy distance in which we see Clement as a chief pastor of the early Church, we cannot distinctly trace the details of his life work at Rome, or the circumstances of his death. Much more clearly are the fine features of his character perceptible in his writings. The Church which places him as the third bishop of Rome, reckons him among the martyrs; yet Eusebius, when he mentions the death of Clement, does not even allude to his martyrdom. He says, " In the third year of the above-mentioned reign (Trajan's), Clement, Bishop of Rome, committed the episcopal charge to Everastus, and departed this life, after superintending the preaching of the Divine Word for nine years."

He lived on the Cœlian Hill, where his house has been wonderfully preserved. Of course it is below the present level of the ground, but hitherto it has been accessible when the water, which at times rises, does not overwhelm it. Over this old home now stands one of the most interesting churches in Rome. Its extensive crypt between the upper church and the buried house is lighted up on St. Clement's day, and most picturesque is the primitive simplicity of the time-worn walls and arches of Roman brickwork, though nothing in the dark recesses can be clearly discerned. But light enough is given to show the frescoes which are among the most precious of Rome's art treasures. They may be referred to the periods between the ninth and twelfth centuries, scarcely in any instance to an earlier date. The mosaics, also, in the upper church are curious from their great antiquity. In spite of modernizations, that upper church retains more details belonging to primitive ecclesiastical architecture, than does any other building in Rome.

THE ROMANS IN JUDEA.

An angel said—" The light of heaven
Soon faded, and the transitory rent
Through which it streamed was blocked with denser cloud,
But it had lit imperishable hopes
In human hearts and ours. How could we faint,
Or how despond, when men of flesh and blood,
Weaker than we in power, but strong in prayer,
Wrestled, and wrought, and vanquished? Oft herein
They ministered to us, as we to them :
Without us haply human faith had failed,
Without them ours."
" Yesterday, To-day, and For Ever."
By the Rev. E. H. Bickersteth.

VI.

THE ROMANS IN JUDEA.

EVER since St. Paul's last sojourn in Jerusalem—ever since he left the city as a prisoner—a guiltless man, who, accused by the Jews, had appealed to Rome for justice, the condition of Judea had been growing more and more gloomy. The city that was ready to kill God's faithful messengers was justly sentenced to be left desolate.

The chosen people, blessed with the knowledge of the glorious truth that Jehovah, the righteous God that changeth not, is the King of all the earth, had sunk into the very depths of unrighteousness, through disregarding the eternal attributes of their God, and rebelling against His rule of truth and justice. While thus living and acting in a state of antagonism against the Divine will, heartlessly and superstitiously worshipping the God of their fathers, how could they recognize their Messiah, or form any higher conception than that their expected King would be a man of selfish will and imperious passions like their own, endowed with almighty power to crush every other nation of the earth? Such was the national feeling, but we may hope that then, as in Elijah's days, when the prophet said, "I, even I only, am left," the Lord saw many who were true to Him.

Perplexing, sometimes overwhelming, must this state of things have been to thoughtful, religious, simple-hearted Jews under their own narrow-minded, self-asserting priests and elders, men too blindly bigoted to perceive the fine features of superior character, as their treatment of St. Paul proves. That form of tyranny must have been far more galling to the nobler spirits than was the pressure of the foreign yoke.

Rulers unworthy of position and power seem to have been the instruments chosen by God for the execution of His sentence against the Jews, as a nation, condemned, because it had not accomplished its appointed mission, to set, by precept and example, before less favoured nations, the glory, goodness, and righteousness of God, that all might be drawn nearer to Him, the eternal, immovable Centre of Love, Truth, and Omnipotence to bless.

A succession of evil-disposed, incompetent governors were sent from Rome to Judea, men not restrained by the fear of any god, or of any righteous judgment, not actuated by any genuine love for their fellow-men. Great must have been the trials of the Jews under such proconsuls as Felix, Festus, Albinus, and Florus, governors who were both scourges in themselves, and snares whereby the people were provoked to desperate proceedings. Of Felix, a ransomed slave, Tacitus remarks, "With the true genius of a slave he exercised the tyranny of an eastern despot." Festus found the priests quarrelling so bitterly, that the Temple was often polluted with their blood; and he took advantage of this to serve his own worldly interests, little thinking that the first year of his proconsulship was to be the last of his life.

Albinus positively encouraged the brigands, by whom the country was overrun, by allowing those who were captured to purchase their freedom. Equally injudicious was his hasty decision to stop the public works, and at once to discharge eighteen thousand artificers and labourers. The idle, starving rabble thus let loose increased the difficulties of all persons who were endeavouring to maintain order in spite of civil dissension and the discontent naturally felt under a foreign yoke. Large numbers of the discharged labourers quitted the city to become freebooters and robbers of the baser kind; thus the bands of the brigands were recruited. Already they had been swelled by numbers of the ignorant, who had been deluded by false Messiahs, and when they had become convinced of their mistake, finding their worldly prospects ruined, and themselves unfit for settling down to the sober pursuits of life, they had joined the brigands.

Florus felt no sympathy for the people whom he governed. No grievance was redressed, no complaint listened to, and the most respectable citizens were in his time rudely treated. Josephus goes so far as to say that Florus purposely drove the Jews into open revolt with a view to their being at last really and thoroughly subdued: he thought their independent spirit could and must be broken. Herod Agrippa the Second still bore the title of king, though his mind and his aims were more Roman than Jewish, and he had lost all actual power over his people, who were growing more and more refractory. For the purposes of supervision and coercion the king had devised a peculiar scheme. He had built his palace close to the Temple, and he now elevated it sufficiently to overlook the courts of the Temple, which had become debased into places of business and intrigue. The faction of the zealots was very strong and truly dangerous; they were destroyers of pure faith, of peace, and human life. The people looked upon the king in his watch-tower as a spy, and raised the walls round the sanctuary to shut out his view. The zealots met in secret; their aim was to exterminate the supporters of the foreign government. The sentences pronounced by this horrible secret society were executed by their sicarii, or dagger-men, in the streets, or even on the steps of the Temple on occasions of public festival, and no precautions prevailed to protect the objects of their hatred.

Hitherto the Romans, from motives of policy, had refrained from occupying Jerusalem with a military force. Now they were requested by the chiefs of the priesthood, of the nobility and inhabitants to protect the city. This was the point to which the zealots themselves had wished to lead. Roman troops were sent in. On entering Jerusalem, they found the housetops thronged with an excited mutinous population, who assailed the soldiers first with stones, and then with deadly weapons. Agrippa in vain spoke to the people in favour of his patrons: finding himself utterly powerless, he hastily withdrew to Berytus (now Beyrout), where he had lately built a residence to which he might retreat, for he well knew that he did not reign over the hearts of the Jews, that the patriots had no regard for him, and looked back to the glorious era of the Maccabees. The lower city and the Temple were abandoned to the people, while the Romans held the citadel, with the palace and other heights and towers of the upper city on Mount Zion, where the Roman banners waved. For seven days the possession of these respective strongholds was contested, but the conflict resulted in the destruction of the palace and other buildings on Mount Zion by fire, the capture of the citadel, the murder of the high priest, and finally the capitulation of the Romans. But the zealots were resolved to render accommodation impossible, by involving the nation in unpardonable guilt. The capitulation was ruthlessly violated, and every armed invader was slain by the sword.*

Florus was at Cæsarea when he heard that the rebellion which he had long been fanning had burst at last into the flames of war. The inhabitants of Cæsarea immediately rose against the Jews in that city, and slew in one day twenty thousand. Florus was suspected of having instigated this horrible massacre; certainly he caused all who endeavoured to escape to be seized and sent to work as prisoners in the dockyards. This happened on the very day on which the Roman soldiers were being perfidiously butchered in Jerusalem.

Cestus Gallus, the Governor of Syria, at the head of a large army, hastened to the relief of the Romans; but moved by the earnest entreaties of King Agrippa, before he advanced upon the city he offered terms of accommodation. The Jews, led on by the bold Simon, son of Giora, not only refused the terms, but received the bearers with a shower of arrows. Thereupon Gallus led his troops to the gates, and Cestus assaulted the city for five days. Again the Romans were repulsed, Gallus retired, and all Judea rose in rebellion. This occurred early in October, A.D. 66, and the report reached Nero in Greece. Understanding the importance of the crisis, the Emperor immediately sent his most trustworthy captain, Vespasian, to the scene of action. Vespasian was to proceed by land, collecting troops and war engines on his way; and his son Titus was to go by sea to Alexandria, and summon from

* "History of the Romans under the Empire." By Dean Merivale, D.D. Vol. vi., page 534, etc.

thence the fifteenth legion to serve in the impending campaign.*

Both Cestus Gallus and Florus were summoned to Rome to answer for their conduct: the former died before his sentence was pronounced, the end of Florus is not recorded.

The Jews made strenuous efforts to prepare for defending their country and city. The Sanhedrin, which was converted into a council of war, divided Palestine into seven military districts, besides the capital city. It placed Josephus, then thirty years of age, in command of Galilee. He was a descendant of the illustrious and beloved Asmonean family, and distinguished by his extraordinary abilities, which had been cultivated by a superior education. His mind had been expanded by travelling in foreign lands, and he had spent some time in Rome. In his autobiography, Josephus gives the following account of his journey to Rome, and his sojourn there:—

"I had not long completed my twenty-sixth year when a circumstance happened, which induced me to make a voyage to Italy. At the time when Felix was procurator of Judea there were some priests with whom I was well acquainted, honourable and good men, whom, on a mere frivolous casual pretext, he had sent in irons to Rome to render account of their conduct to Cæsar. I was anxious to find some means of deliverance for these priests, and the more so as I heard that even under this depressing affliction they were not neglectful of religious observances, and abstained from all food except figs and nuts. I reached Rome after a very perilous voyage, for our ship foundered in the

---

* "History of the Romans under the Empire." By Dean Merivale, D.D. Vol. vi., pages 533—538.

Adriatic, and about six hundred of us were throughout a whole night swimming on the sea, till at break of day a vessel from Cyrene providentially came to our rescue, and saved eighty of us. I landed at Puteoli, and there I met with Aliturus a comedian, a Jew by birth, a particular favourite of Nero. With this fellow-countryman I formed a friendship; he introduced me to Poppæa, Cæsar's consort, and I availed myself of the first opportunity to solicit her influence in favour of the priests. Their liberation was granted, and in addition to this kindness I received costly presents from Poppæa. On my return to Judea I was grieved on perceiving how the seeds of revolution were developing. I found many persons greatly elated at the revolt from the Romans. Convinced of our own inferiority to the Romans in military skill, I warned them not thus rashly, with utter recklessness, to expose our country, our families, and ourselves to the most extreme perils. My arguments were unavailing, so completely were they infatuated to desperation!"

His opinion of Roman invincibility made Josephus an object of suspicion, and probably also of misrepresentation, to those of his countrymen who were prejudiced against the Romans. But at that moment the Herodians prevailed in the Jewish councils; Josephus obtained the appointment, with full power to conduct the defence of Galilee, as he might consider most conducive to the general interest. His post proved a most important one; for Vespasian's plan was to isolate Galilee from Samaria and Judea, and completely to reduce it, before he turned his arms against the hostile metropolis.*

At the opening of spring, a season made by the genial sunshine and the flowers particularly beautiful in

* Merivale.

Palestine, Vespasian marched into Galilee, immediately took the fortress of Gadara, and proceeded to besiege Jotapata, which Josephus defended vigorously for forty-seven days; but at last the town was taken by surprise, and all its inhabitants were either put to the sword or taken prisoners. Josephus himself was among the captives. He and forty of his bravest soldiers escaped the general slaughter by cutting their way through the enemy's ranks, and taking refuge at last in one of the many caverns of that country. Vespasian found out his retreat, and offered him his life on honourable terms, if he would surrender. Josephus was willing to accept the conditions, but his comrades would not for a moment listen to them. Then Josephus, according to his own account, advised that as they were resolved to die rather than to surrender, their lives should .be taken, not by cruel enemies, but by their own countrymen and brethren in arms, who in love and mercy would give the death stroke. He proposed that lots should be drawn to mark two men, the one who was to die, and the one who was to kill him with the sword; and this drawing was to be repeated until only one man would be left, who must take his own life. This was carried out until there remained only two survivors, Josephus and a soldier, whom he persuaded to agree with him in thinking that the wisest thing they could do would be to immediately give themselves up to Nicanor, the Roman officer in command. This they did, and were courteously received. A military escort, headed by Nicanor, conducted Josephus to Vespasian. The Romans crowded to obtain a sight of him; the multitude of lookers-on of all classes pressed together, pushing forward to get a nearer view, and his quiet fortitude touched many a brave and generous heart. Titus, who was looking on, felt deeply for the captive, of whom he had heard enough to be aware that he was no common man.

With cold formality he was received by Vespasian, who informed the prisoner that it was his intention to send him to Cæsar.

In reply Josephus requested that he might be permitted to speak in private to Vespasian. That a prisoner should ask such a favour, must have been surprising, but Vespasian immediately ordered his attendants, and all who were present except Titus and two friends to withdraw. When they had retired, Josephus broke silence by thus addressing the Roman General :—

"You think, Vespasian, that you have possessed yourself merely of a captive in Josephus, but I come to you as a messenger of greater things. Had I not received a commission from God, I knew the law of the Jews, and how it becomes a general to die. Do you send me to Nero? Wherefore? Are there any remaining to succeed Nero, any nearer than yourself? You, Vespasian, are Cæsar and Emperor, you and this your son. Bind me then the more securely, and keep me for yourself. For you, Cæsar, are master, not only of me, but of sea and land, and of the human race. And I should deserve greater punishment and stricter ward if I could speak to you lightly, especially on a matter pertaining to God."

Vespasian either was, or affected to be, but little impressed by this address; he at first thought it only an ingenious artifice to save the speaker's life. Gradually, however, he was led to believe it, as he grew more powerful, and perceived other signs foreshowing the sceptre.*

The young, unsuspicious mind of Titus responded directly to the words of Josephus, whom previously he

* See translation of Josephus by the late Rev. R. Traill, D.D.

had admired and pitied. He could not fully express his feelings, but he had no greater pleasure than that of doing everything he could do to alleviate the trials and discomforts of the captive. Like St. Paul, and those priests whose liberation Josephus had obtained by taking a journey to Rome, he now had to bear the galling chain himself. Painfully irksome it must have been, but not a mark of moral degradation, as it now is. In our free land a chain is never seen upon a human being, except on Portland Island, or near some other convict station. In ancient times the chain was associated with misfortune, but not necessarily with the deep disgrace of punishment for the basest crimes. Josephus tells us that he was kept in close custody, though presented with raiment and other articles, and treated with kindness and attention; Titus contributing much to these respectful courtesies.[*]

It appears that Vespasian retained Josephus under his own control, and did not at this time send him on to Nero. The distinguished captive was carried about for some years by his conqueror, in a custody which he had no inclination perhaps to evade.[†] Certainly it was safer than freedom could have been to him, and literary occupation may have continually refreshed him under the tedium and weariness of captivity. He wrote a great deal that has come down to us, and probably some works that have not lived through eighteen centuries. Vespasian and Agrippa consulted together at Cæsarea Philippi to arrange the best mode of co-operation. Very sumptuous entertainments were given. Bernice, Agrippa's sister, continued to reside with him. Perhaps it was at this time that she first met Titus, who,

[*] See translation of Josephus by the late Rev. R. Traill, D.D.
[†] Merivale.

though twelve years her junior, was captivated by her beauty and her fascinating manners, and ten years later she was still as great a favourite with him.

The Emperor Nero may have suffered from an uneasy conscience, which he could not kill, for he became very restless. We hear no more of his putting on the garb of a driver, and driving his chariot round his pleasure grounds, as he had been in the habit of doing, and at last did on that fatal night when with festive hilarity the most atrocious crime of his life and reign was perpetrated. We hear no more of those gardens. Perhaps he felt fearful lest he should meet one of the ghosts with which they were said to be haunted. Popular feeling had turned quite against him, and even persons who most disliked and despised the Jews and the Christians compassionated the sufferings of those who had been so cruelly put to death. "This horrid sacrifice," says Merivale, "so deeply impressive to sixty generations of Christians, ruffled then, for a moment, the feelings of Roman society. But a few days passed, and when the people looked again around them they beheld the reconstruction of their city commencing with extraordinary vigour. The city of the plebs, a collection of narrow winding lanes, which crept along the hollows at the foot of the seven hills, thronged with high unsightly masses of brickwork or woodwork, among which its shifting crowds could with difficulty wind their way, had long been an eyesore to the denizens of the patrician mansions above. The upper growth of aristocratic luxury culminating above the smoky hives of vulgar industry had made Rome a double city, half Greek and half Italian."

The restoration after the fire was done by government, while Nero occupied himself by extending in various directions the limits of his own residence. His *domus transitoria*, or house of passage, by which he had connected his palace on the Palatine with a villa on the Esquiline, spanning perhaps the hollow between those hills by arches, had fallen a prey to the flames. He set about building a still larger palace, which was still the old mansion of Augustus and the villa on the Esquiline, connected a second time by a longer series of arches, under which the public below could pass. The long colonnades, the baths and terraces, and other buildings connected with this Golden House were so extensive, that Pliny described the city as encompassed by the palace of Nero. Its name was due to the splendour of its decorations; it was adorned with gilded roofs and sculptured friezes and panels of many-coloured marble, and the choicest works of art were collected in its halls. The grand entrance from the Forum was adorned by a bronze statue of Nero, 120 feet high. It is worthy of remark that these vast constructions were planned by Roman architects, Severus and Celer; these men must have ably combined engineering with architecture. The rapid rebuilding of Rome tasked all the energies of the Italian workmen, and the expenses of these extraordinary renovations and improvements rendered it necessary to tax the people. This was done recklessly, and even the sacred treasures of the temples were seized. Nero was neither respected nor loved by his subjects, and at last they would not submit to his exactions, and conspiracies were formed against him. One was discovered, and many victims put to death, among them Lucan the poet, and Seneca, Nero's old tutor, who, being allowed the privilege of choosing his death, caused his veins to be opened in the presence of his friends, with whom he conversed calmly, as long as possible, while he lay in a warm bath, to lessen pain by accelerating the flow of blood. He happened to have friends dining with him when he received Cæsar's command to destroy his own life. The soldiers who brought the mandate were to wait till all was over.

We are glad to know that Seneca wrote, "*This day, which thou fearest as thy last, is the birthday of eternity.*" (Ep. 102.)

A heart such as Nero's could not but hate the preceptor who had earnestly striven to make him a totally different man and monarch to what he was. No doubt he was glad when false witnesses helped him to get rid of his mentor with some deceitful show of justice.

Surely pagans, who have lived up to their light, and have died faithful to the dictates of persecuted morality, have their appointed place in the ranks of the noble army of martyrs!

"*The gods stretch out their hands to those that ascend. Dost thou wonder that man goes to the gods? God comes to men, nay, what is nearer, comes into men. There is not any soul that is good without God.*"—Seneca, Ep. 73.

Seneca expressed so many ideas in accordance with Christianity, that some of his many readers of many generations have supposed that he was converted, probably by St. Paul. But as we have no record of this, the degree of enlightenment to which a heathen philosopher attained during, or perhaps after, the Apostle's two years' residence in Rome, seems rather to indicate that the influence of the Apostle's teaching and example extended far beyond the hearers who habitually attended the meetings at his house. Persons who, being impelled by no higher motive than curiosity, seldom availed themselves of the opportunity, and some not personally acquainted with St. Paul, may have heard of his exhortations and discourses, and have derived some benefit by reflecting on them.

Seneca died A.D. 65. In the following year Nero carried out his long-intended visit to the East, which hitherto, by various untoward circumstances, had been prevented. He had thought of going to Egypt, but did not get as far, being fascinated with Greece, where he was flattered and homaged to his heart's content, and where he was able to throw off all the restraints of decorum more completely even than he could do in Rome, gratifying his passion for dancing and singing without the least reserve.

Some writers say that St. Paul's last trial and execution took place during Nero's absence from Rome, but this has never been proved. We have no certain date of that event; but we know that while the Emperor was in Greece the rebellion in Judea burst out, and Vespasian was sent to quell it.

At Delphi, Nero consulted the oracle, which bid him beware of *the seventy-third year.* This answer to a man of thirty seemed to promise length of days; another significance was afterwards discovered. But at the moment Nero, who had been feeling really alarmed by murmurs throughout the Empire, that were no longer stifled, and by other threatenings of an approaching crisis, was reassured by the prophetic words of the *Pythia.* He returned to Rome, completed and dedicated a temple to Poppæa, his last wife, whose death he had accidentally caused when she was in a delicate state of health and he was in a furious temper. Poppæa was a clever woman, with some qualities such as Josephus could admire, and she liked him. She was a Jewish proselyte, one of the Roman ladies of rank and fashion who frequented the synagogue and adopted some of the Jewish customs. We may hope that some of the ladies gained real good there, although Juvenal severely satirized them. It is supposed that the Jews who came to Rome to accuse St. Paul or to bear witness against him, sought access to Poppæa to request her aid for the destruction of a traitor to the Jewish faith. The intrigues of the imperial court were very complicated, and persons of high station were not above taking a bribe.*

Poppæa did her utmost to retain the affection of her husband: careful to preserve her fine complexion, she kept five hundred asses, and bathed every day in their milk. Sad was her fate, yet she deserved it, for she had wickedly supplanted the young Octavia, Nero's child-wife, whom from motives of policy he had married, and soon wished to divorce. Her unmerited degradation had excited the sympathy of the people, who crowned her statue with flowers. A pretext had been invented for putting her to death before she had attained her twentieth year, and most likely Burrhus had been poisoned, because he had dared to say to the despot, "If you dismiss the daughter of Claudius, restore at least the empire which was her dowry."

This prefect was in the habit of speaking his mind boldly. He commanded the Prætorian guard, therefore there is reason to suppose that he was the captain of the guard into whose custody St. Paul was given by Julius the centurion, who had brought him from Judea. Burrhus was just the man to be influenced by Paul's example, even if he were not converted to Christianity by the Apostle's teaching.

Having done honour to the memory of his lost Poppæa, Nero resumed his usual life of vicious and fri-

* See "The Life of St. Paul," by Conybeare and Howson, p. 745.

volous pleasure. Once more he celebrated the games of the circus, and drove his chariot there. The Circus Maximus was in the valley between the Palatine and the Aventine hills. The arena had been made for these chariot races and other spectacles in which the Roman public greatly delighted. All the emperors had patronized the chariot races and the Circensian games and other entertainments on the circus, but not one had taken part in them in the undignified way in which Nero did. This year he was intending to favour the public by playing to them on a new kind of water organ lately invented. The Circus Maximus could accommodate about 250,000, besides about 150,000 who could stand under the porticoes encircling the arena. Trophies of war gave a degree of grandeur to the circus, although it was thronged with idle loungers, itinerant venders, market-criers, and fortune-tellers. Sanguinary combats sometimes took place there, and the *Porta Libitinaria* was used only for carrying out the slain. The *Porta Pompæa* served for the entrance of the grand processions with which the entertainments commenced, and through the *Porta Triumphalis* the victors made their exulting exit.*

The enjoyment of these amusements was damped by bad news. Courier after courier came dashing into Rome with reports of the defection of generals and legions. It soon appeared that the army had revolted. Vindex had fallen, but Galba had raised the standard of rebellion. Great was the excitement among the senators, as well as among the people. The household troops, the Emperor's own Prætorian guards turned against him, and then Nero saw that his only chance of safety was in flight. He begged some of the centurions

---

* "Historic and Monumental Rome." By C. I. Hemans.

to protect him, to go with him as far as Ostia; but they refused, and one of them, blunter than the others, said, "Is it then so hard to die?"

The next morning at daybreak he secretly left the palace, attended by four servants, and they safely reached the villa of his freedman Phaon, about four miles from the city. On the following day a slave brought papers from Rome. Nero snatched them from his hand, and read that the Senate had deposed him, proclaimed him an enemy, and decreed his death. He said he should kill himself, and the few persons about him seem to have expected that he would do so. He lacked the courage, but was heard talking to himself aloud, trying to nerve himself to do the deed. "Fie, Nero, fie!" he muttered in Greek; "be a man; come, rouse thee!" Thus he hesitated till he heard the trampling of a large body of horsemen. At that moment he was alone with the slave Epaphroditus. "Sound of swift-footed steeds strikes on my ear," exclaimed Nero, quoting Homer, as he pointed his sword to his own heart, and commanded the slave to drive it in.* His ashes were quietly buried in a private sepulchre on the Pincian Hill. The people rejoiced over his death, thinking it would bring them a freedom they really would have been unfit to exercise, had it been granted to them, but this they did not understand. Such was the almost universal feeling; yet some unknown friend loved Nero well enough to strew his grave with flowers—a tribute not altogether unmerited by one who had cultivated a taste for poetry, which might have tended to refine the fountain-springs of thought, the nobler passions of the soul, had he not allowed his imagination to run wildly on into poetical frenzies. We can believe that the man who met death

* From Homer's Iliad, book x., 535.

with words from the Iliad on his lips, might, in a moment of terrible public calamity, have thought of nothing better that he could do, than to take up his lyre and mount to the top of a high tower, whence he could survey the flaming city, and at the same time sing about the destruction of Troy.

Nero had disappeared so strangely and suddenly, that the Roman people could hardly believe he was dead. An idea that he might be living in concealment lingered among them. More than twenty years after his death a false Nero was protected by the Parthians. This popular notion was the foundation, perhaps, of a common persuasion among the Christians that he would return as the predicted Antichrist—a thought not unlikely to occur to some of the martyr's relatives and friends, and to circulate among them.

Much more than a dynasty expired with the last of the Claudian Cæsars. That event caused a radical and complete change in the character of the imperial power, and a change of times and circumstances. Then began a new epoch which was to bring in quite a new state of things. Galba, who was first proclaimed Emperor, was to have but little to do with this. He was in his seventy-third year, and thus fulfilled the prophecy of the Delphic oracle to the satisfaction of the superstitious. Moreover the steps he took to mount the throne in that year proved fatal to himself. He assumed the purple in the June of A.D. 68, and was assassinated in the following January.

We have digressed from our subject to contemplate the last days and the death of one man who had caused the death of many, the author of the first great persecution, in the miseries of which Jews and Christians, and Christianized Jews of Rome, were all more or less involved.

Even the Parthians had protested against the barbarity of the Romans, and had requested that, for decency's sake, Nero's remains might not be savagely mutilated. Perhaps this foreign interference tended to prevent posthumous insult; but how little had that proud tyrant thought that he should ever owe anything to the rulers of Parthia!

The struggles of Galba, Otho, Vitellius, and Vespasian to obtain the supremacy, belong to the history of Rome, as likewise the details of the never-to-be-forgotten war in Judea, belong to the history of the Jews. Those residing in Rome were but remotely, though sympathetically, affected by the distress in their fatherland. They were now unmolested, for the madness of persecution had spent itself. The Romans were ashamed of what had been done, they wished the odium of it to rest entirely on Nero's memory, and so there was a strong reaction in favour, not of Jews or Judaism, or of Christianity, but of humanity; and public attention was now fully occupied by intrigues and wars at home and abroad. In Rome only the pen could be wielded against the Jews, and that was effectually done.

As soon as he had power to do so, Vespasian released Josephus from bonds, but he remained with Titus as an attendant. Vespasian, having been elected, hastened to Rome, leaving his son to prosecute the war in Judea, and to make preparations for besieging Jerusalem. Two parties existed in that city. The more moderate of its inhabitants saw the hopelessness of contending against Rome, and desired to submit, on the best terms that could be made, rather than to risk the loss of the capital, which would be inevitable destruction to the nation. The other party, consisting of the desperate and fanatical zealots and the lower classes of the people, clamoured for uncompromising resistance. A few educated men, animated by enthusiastic patriotism, joined them. Civil dissensions had run on to civil war and fighting in the streets. The zealots, being hardly pressed, took refuge in the precincts of the Temple, where they were closely besieged by their antagonists. Thus was Jerusalem anything but "a city that is at unity with itself." Its actual condition was as great a mockery of the meaning of its name—*A Vision of Peace*—as any mockery with which it had insulted Christ. Is not this an impressive lesson? for does not God deal with individuals as with nations, especially with every one whose baptismal name was given as a Christian sign with no hidden meaning?

When Titus first approached the city, he committed an imprudence which very nearly cost him his life. He, with a few men, got entangled in some gardens, and the Jews sallied forth and separated him from the main body of his escort. Titus cut his way through his assailants, and was saved by the fleetness of his horse. The whole army soon came up and encamped about Jerusalem.

Josephus was still a prisoner in the Roman camp, and Titus made use of him, hoping that by his persuasions the Jews might be induced to surrender. He was repeatedly put forward to deliver a message proposing terms, which, considering the customs and the temper of the times, were not severe; but the Jewish leaders treated all the offers of the Roman general with contempt. Again Titus sent Josephus to intercede. He addressed the leader John, but spoke in the Hebrew tongue, often appealing to the multitude, beseeching them to spare their country, their city and temple:

his words, broken by tears, and blended with expressions of sympathy, were received by the people in silence and dejection; but John, after venting many invectives against Josephus, finally said that no one need fear that Jerusalem would be captured, for it was Jehovah's city. It was more than commonly crowded; for when the Romans were marching on Jerusalem, prepared to lay siege, the Jews were preparing to celebrate the passover—it was the last!—and was kept thirty-six years after that at which the true Lamb of God was sacrificed. The festival was attended by an extraordinary multitude of Jews from all parts of the world; for the war-party, anxious to obtain reinforcements, had written to their brethren in all countries, inviting and urging them to come, and if need be to take part in the national struggle for independence, and especially in defending the holy city of David. Many Christians had left the city and retired to some hill country, secluded from the turmoil of these unquiet times. They had watched in faith, and had recognized signs predicted by their Lord: mindful of His warning, they had fled from danger; numbers of them had found safety in the little town of Pella, beyond the Jordan.

The Jews felt great confidence in the strength of their ramparts and triple city, within which were several forts. The principal of these, the citadel, was called the Castle of Antonia, having been so named by Herod after his patron, the Triumvir. The Towers of Hippicus, Phaselus, and Mariamne, with probably some others, were separate fortresses, constructed for mutual support. The Temple itself, surrounded by an outer and inner wall, was capable of resisting very formidable attacks. It comprised an outer court, equal sided, of six hundred feet each way, lined with double or triple porticoes. Within this was an area subdivided into compartments, which secluded and guarded the innermost, mysterious most holy place—a shrine without an idol.*

All the efforts Titus made to induce the Jews to capitulate were in vain, and at last, weary of the protracted siege, he determined upon a decisive attack.

The preparations for assault occupied the Romans twenty-one days, the Jews were too weak to hinder them. When all was completed, the battering-rams and other engines were brought to bear upon the walls, and at night a portion fell; the Romans rushed in, but, to their disappointment, found an inner wall, which was obstinately defended, and at last taken by stratagem. After every fort and post that could be defended had been bravely held, but quickly taken, at last nothing remained to the Jews but the Temple itself. All the Roman soldiers looked upon the Temple with awe. Titus desired to save it, not only from destruction, but from pollution. " I appeal," said he, "to my own army, and to the Jews beside me, aye, and to you yourselves, that it is not I who compel you to defile these things; and, would you but change the scene of conflict, no Roman should approach or profane the holy places; nay, I will preserve the sanctuary even against your will." Many Jews gave themselves up to the Romans; they were all, for the present, sent to Gophna, with a promise that when peace had been restored they should be reinstated in their respective possessions. One day Titus sent for these Jews, and ordered them, with Josephus at their head, to make the circuit of the city wall, in order to be seen by the people, and to implore them to leave the insurgents. A considerable number did escape and flee to the Romans. In his last speech,

* Merivale.

Titus said, no doubt in all sincerity, "It seems to me that the God of this place has deserted it." Convinced at last that Jerusalem must be taken by force, he reluctantly proceeded to further hostilities.

The awful calamities of that siege—malicious internal disagreement and strife—the tyranny of the strong over the weak—pestilence—famine that tempted a mother to butcher her child—are well known. With the energy of despair the Jews defended their temple. Titus greatly desired to take the wonderful edifice without destroying, or even materially injuring it; but it was so resolutely held, that his forbearance was attended with danger and slaughter to his own troops; seeing this, he reluctantly gave orders that the gates should be set on fire. The flames rose very quickly, mounted in continuous columns, and seized on the galleries. The Jews, struck with consternation, stood motionless spectators. All through that day and the following night the fire continued to rage. The next morning Titus directed a division of his troops to extinguish the flames, and to prepare a way to the gates for the more easy ascent of the legions. He then convened his six generals in council, and brought before them the subject of the sanctuary. Some were inclined to enforce the rights of war; for the Jews, they said, would not desist from rebellious projects while the Temple remained as a point of concourse to them from all quarters. Others thought the Jews could be prevented from occupying the Temple as a military position, and that it might be spared. But, said they, "If it be used for purposes of war, it is a fortress, and no longer a sanctuary." Titus maintained that they ought not to wreak their vengeance on things inanimate, instead of on men, nor to destroy so magnificent a work, which, if preserved, would ever after be an ornament to the Empire. These arguments prevailed, and orders were given with a view to extinguishing the fire as quickly as possible.

Only the courts of the Temple and the fine colonnades and other surroundings had suffered; as yet the sanctuary itself was in full beauty—the flames had not touched it; and though war had raged round its walls, that central edifice wanted nothing that could strike the eye or the mind. Overlaid throughout with massive plates of gold, it reflected at sunrise so fiery a lustre as could not be steadily gazed upon; the eye averted itself as from the solar rays. Seen from a distance, it looked like a mountain covered with snow; for in those parts not faced with gold the building was of the purest white. On its summit were fixed sharp golden spikes, to prevent the birds from polluting the roof. In front of the sanctuary stood the quadrangular altar, with corners projecting like horns. This superb edifice was ascended on the south side by a gently sloping acclivity. In its construction no iron was used, nor was it ever touched by iron. It was built of the largest stones that could be hewn; each one, before it was fixed in its place, had been cut by rule, shaped to a given form and size. A barrier of ornamental stonework, about a cubit high, enclosed both the sanctuary and the altar, and served to separate the people outside from the priests.*

Twelve steps led up to the first gate, which had no doors, for it represented the invisible and unobstructed heaven. The portal was faced with gold, as was all the wall around it, and above were golden vines, from which hung down clusters of grapes, a man's stature in length. The inside portal had golden doors, fifty-five cubits high and sixteen broad. Before these was spread a veil of

---

* Josephus, book v. 6.

equal length with the doors. It was of Babylonian tapestry, variegated with blue, scarlet, and purple, and fine linen wrought with admirable skill. Nor was the mixture of the material without design; it served as a symbol of the universe. The scarlet and the blue were emblematical of fire and air, being similar in colour. The fine linen was emblematical of the earth which produces it, and the purple of the sea, also on account of its origin. Embroidered on this tapestry was a representation of the entire heavens, the signs of the zodiac excepted.

"Within this compartment stood three pieces of workmanship most admirable and universally celebrated—a candlestick, a table, and an altar of incense. The seven lights represented the planets, for so many were the branches of the candlestick. Loaves on the table, twelve in number, symbolized the circle of the zodiac and the year. The altar of incense, by the thirteen fragrant spices with which it was replenished from the sea, and from lands inhabited and uninhabited, signified that all things are of God and for God.

"The innermost recess of the Temple measured twenty cubits, and was separated from the outer by the veil. In this nothing whatever was deposited. Unapproachable, inviolable, and to be seen by none, it was called the Holy of The Holy." *

Every Roman capable of appreciating this most magnificent work of art, this wonderful Temple, desired to save it; but it was doomed to destruction. Every pillar of that Temple was to fall, not one was ever to be reared in another land. A Roman soldier who had received no order to do so, flung a firebrand through one

---

* Josephus, book v. 4. 5. Abridged from the translation of Rev. R. Traill, D.D.

of the windows of the sanctuary. The dry cedar wood was instantly in a blaze. Shouts and shrieks rent the air. The flames rapidly rose, and a scene of the utmost confusion ensued. Titus himself, with his staff, ran to the spot, and ordered, and with his own hands did, everything that could be done to check the devouring element, but in vain. In the excitement of that terrible catastrophe the Roman soldiers became quite uncontrollable. No quarter was given or looked for on either side. The Romans, losing all discipline, rushed from every quarter to the scene of action, the Jews resisted them with equal fury, howling and wailing as they fought. John, by an astonishing feat, made good his retreat to the upper town, where he found Simon. In the indiscriminate slaughter a number of women were put to death. They had assembled under the guidance of a false prophet, who assured them that at the very crisis of the siege the Messiah would appear to deliver them. Tacitus thought their prophetical books had led them to believe that it would be so.

Josephus thus describes the indiscriminate slaughter: "One would have thought that the hill itself on which the Temple stood was seething hot, full of fire in every part, yet there was more blood than fire, and those that were slain were more in number than those that slew them. Nowhere was the ground visible, so covered was it with the dead; and over heaps of the slain the living ran after those that fled from them. But Simon and John were still living, and a few brave men were with them, who took up a position in the upper city, on the hill of Zion, and still held out. For the last time Titus demanded a parley, and, standing on a bridge that connected the Temple with Mount Zion, he again offered terms to the insurgents. They declined them, and eighteen days later Jerusalem fell. The Temple had stood more than 1,130 years, from its restoration, according to the words of the Prophet Haggai, in the second year of Cyrus, King of Persia. Josephus remarks, "It waited until the very month, and the very day on which the first temple had been burnt by the Babylonians." Both downfalls are still solemnly commemorated on the 9th day of the Hebrew month *Ab*.

With the destruction of the Temple, the temple service was abolished, the traditions of the Levitical system were no longer guarded by a recognized succession of interpreters, nor maintained as the title-deeds of an authorized ministry. They were long remembered, and in some degree observed in private families, but, as time went on, they became less and less truthful, more and more mixed up with legendary lore. The distinction of tribes and families was lost; and the threads of descent have never been recovered.

Such were the results of the astounding blow struck by the Flavian Emperors. The idea that the great kingdom which they ruled was being actually led on by them under the guidance of Divine providence, and was wonderfully accomplishing prophecy, does not seem to have impressed their minds, nor the minds of their contemporaries. They were all absorbed in the one idea of looking, not for a mighty power either territorial, or moral, or religious, but for the personal Deliverer whose coming had been predicted, and who would, the Hebrews believed, come forth from the house of David; and the Romans as strongly desired, wished, with enthusiasm that merges into faith, that he would appear in the person of one of their own emperors, and be acknowledged and received as the Lord of the whole earth. "We have seen," says Dean Merivale, "the wide diffusion of the Sibylline prophecies, pointing towards a new advent or development in the time of Augustus, and that emperor's efforts to compel the anticipations of mankind to centre and terminate in himself. We have remarked the ready acquiescence of the Roman world in the hope that each succeeding emperor would be in truth its expected preserver, and how willingly it ascribed divinity to the lords of the human race." The ignorant multitude worshipped Augustus with an honest kind of reverence, and would have felt and done as much for each one of his successors, but bitterly were they disappointed in the Claudian sovereigns.* Vespasian, coming from Egypt and Judea seemed likely to literally fulfil the promises of both the Jewish and Sibylline oracles. Against his own will, for he was a simple-minded man, miraculous powers were ascribed to him. In his military sphere, before he had begun to entertain ambitious views on his own account, those who loved and honoured him thought him capable of tranquilizing the disturbed Empire. When with him in the east, they heard the prophecies concerning Messiah, and saw that the suggestion of such an idea, as that Vespasian might prove to be the expected deliverer, would further his cause in the eastern part of the Empire. The words of Josephus, "Vespasian, you put me in bonds to-day; but next year, when you are the emperor, you will release me," were hardly prophetic, as any very sagacious man, well acquainted with the

---

* Let us not forget that the meanings of words change with time, of which our word worship is a remarkable instance. The meaning now understood by it is not that attached to it by the framers of our marriage service, nor by our ancestors who gave the title of worshipful to the chief magistrate of every town.

state of affairs in the Roman world, might have foreseen much without the aid of inspiration; and there was nothing blasphemous in what Josephus said, though it coincided, and perhaps co-operated, with the idea which Romans imbued with eastern notions had conceived; that Vespasian might be the promised ruler under whose boundless and beneficent government all the nations of the world were to be united. It is not surprising that the Romans and other heathens should have misunderstood the Old Testament prophecies, with which they must have been very imperfectly acquainted. Vespasian's friends, whose patriotic devotion to him agreed with their own personal interests, were pagans; and the leaders of popular movements among pagan nations have in all times pretended to supernatural powers. Every nation that Rome had subdued had fought in that spirit; the multitude believing that they were fighting under a demi-god, or at least under the blessing of their ancestral gods. Our own Saxon forefathers believed that they conquered by the help of Odin, a real hero, deified.*

Thus the heathen were brought up from childhood, were trained and excited to superstitious worship; but it was not possible for even a religious-minded heathen to think of his gods, and to enter a place of worship with the same feelings as those with which a Jew and a Christian enter a synagogue and a church.

* "Such were the claims of Athenio in Sicily, of Sartorius in Spain. The Druids in Britain waged a religious war against the Romans. Marcius the Gaul, Aurinia, Ganna, and Veleda, and German professed to direct the people with a spiritual authority."
—*Merivale.*

THE TRIUMPH.

SADNESS AND MIRTH.

" Ye met at the stately feasts of old,
  Where the bright wine foam'd over sculptured gold ;
Sadness and Mirth, ye were mingled there
  With the sound of the lyre in the scented air ;
As the cloud and the lightning are blent on high,
Ye mix'd in the gorgeous revelry.
Ye met when the triumph swept proudly by,
With the Roman Eagles reared on high ;
I know that e'en then, in his hour of pride,
The soul of the mighty within him died ;
That a void in his bosom lay darkly still,
Which the music of victory might never fill.
Thou wert there, O Mirth, swelling on the shout,
Till the temples like echo-caves rang out.
Thine were the garlands, the songs, the wine,
All the rich voices in air were thine,
The incense, the sunshine—but Sadness, thy part,
Deepest of all, was the victor's heart."

FELICIA HEMANS.

VII.

THE TRIUMPH.

BEFORE the end of the war in Judea, Titus had received the gratifying intelligence that his father had been enthusiastically welcomed throughout Italy, and especially in Rome. The Senate, who remembered the calamities they had endured through the changes of their princes, were glad to receive an emperor whose age, reputation, and military skill inspired them with confidence: and all classes of the people having suffered from the intestine broils were longing for a ruler powerful enough to maintain the imperial sway, and thus to give security and peace.

More especially did the soldiers rejoice in Vespasian's elevation, for they best knew the magnitude of the wars which he had brought to a successful conclusion, and they had prayed that he who alone could ensure their safety and add lustre to their arms might be granted to them.* Since the battle of Actium, B.C. 31, the aristocracy had held nearly complete control. When, in A.D. 69, the popular party under Vespasian had come into power, shared by Mucianus, as leader of the moderate conservatives, the Senate was reconstructed, so as to represent more liberal ideas, and thus a stop was put to persecution on account of religious opinions.

* Josephus.

A rebellion broke out in Germany and Gaul, in quelling which, Vespasian's son Domitian, though young, greatly distinguished himself. With pagan military pride Titus honoured his brother by giving a triumphal feast at Cæsarea on Domitian's birthday, when more than two thousands Jews were "butchered to make a Roman holiday."

Thence Titus went to Berytus (now Beyrout), where he spent some time. There Agrippa and Bernice were residing in a superb newly erected palace.

Breaking up from thence, Titus passed through several Syrian cities; everywhere sumptuous shows were exhibited, in which the captive Jews were made to display their own ruin. To us it seems astonishing that Titus should have so deeply stained himself with the blood-thirsty sins of the age. We can only say that he was a pagan, and that he had been greatly exasperated by the obstinate resistance of the Jews, by their contemptuous rejection of his clemency, and by the destruction of the Temple, which he had determined to preserve as a standing memorial of his great victory. At Antioch he received an embassy from the king of the Parthians, who presented him with a crown of gold on his conquest of Judea.

The inhabitants of Antioch wished him to expel all the Jews residing in their city, but this Titus refused to do. Failing in this request, the people of Antioch proferred a second, soliciting him to remove the brass tablets on which the privileges of the Jews were inscribed. This also Titus negatived. As these Jews had never positively resisted his will, he retained some sense of justice with regard to them. Leaving to the Jews of Antioch everything they had previously enjoyed in that city and country, he set out for Egypt. In the course of the journey he passed through Jerusalem. Of the vast wealth of the town no small portions still continued to be found among the ruins. Much of it was dug up by the Romans, the greater part was brought to light through information given by the captives. Gold and silver, and other valuables were discovered, which the owners had stored underground against the doubtful fortune of war.* The exact fulfilment of prophetic words now came to pass through the diligent search made for hidden treasures.†

Titus proceeded on his intended journey to Egypt, and having as quickly as possible crossed the desert, he reached Alexandria. When he had determined on sailing for Italy, he sent back to their former stations the two legions that had accompanied him, and made arrangements for taking with him to Rome seven hundred captive Jews whom he had selected as remarkable for their stature and the beauty of their persons, and with them their leaders, John and Simon, that they might all be exhibited at the triumph. A favourable voyage brought them speedily over the sea, and Titus was most highly honoured by his father's going forth from Rome to meet him. The citizens crowded to behold the gratifying sight, and were transported with enthusiasm on thus at once seeing their Emperor and his two heroic sons happily united.

Not many days elapsed before it was announced that one common triumph should celebrate the victories, though the Senate had decreed a separate one to each. When the day arrived on which the celebration was to take place, all the people, a countless multitude, issued forth from their houses to see the pageant. Every spot was occupied wherever it was possible to stand, leaving

* Josephus.   † Matt. xxiv. 2 ; Jer. xxvi. 18.

only the space open to the processions which were to be the objects of attraction. Day had not yet dawned when the whole of the military marched out in companies and divisions under their officers, and drew up around the gates of the palace, not the upper palace, but that near the Temple of Isis, for there the imperitors had slept that night, and when daylight was breaking on the following morning, Vespasian and Titus came forth unarmed, arrayed in robes of purple silk, and crowned with laurel. They proceeded to the Octavian Walk, for there the Senate and the chief magistrates, with all of equestrian rank, awaited their arrival. In front of the colonnades a tribune had been erected, which the Emperor and his son ascended, to sit on ivory chairs.

This Portico of Octavia was the most important and graceful structure of its kind. It had been erected by the Emperor Augustus, and named after his beloved sister Octavia, the mother of Marcellus. The portico occupied an oblong space; its colonnades were supported by 270 columns; under them stood sculptures, valuable beyond all price—statues and other works of Greek art by the first masters, Phidias, Praxiteles, and Lysippus, famous for his equestrian statues. Within the spacious area of the Octavian Portico were two temples, to Jupiter and Juno, built from the designs of Greek architects.*

In the pleasure ground belonging to this fine edifice all the magnates of Rome assembled around the Emperor and the victorious princes, and the multitude crowded densely around them.

As Vespasian and Titus took their seats, loud acclamations of joy burst from the troops; all the companies

* C. I. Hemans. The noble statue of Mars, reposing now in the Ludovisi Villa, is said to have been found there.

were bearing many testimonies to their valour. Vespasian, having acknowledged their welcome, made the signal for silence. Deep and universal stillness prevailing, he rose, and covering his head with his cloak, he offered up the usual prayers, Titus praying also in the same manner.

The prayers ended, Vespasian addressed the general assembly in a short speech, and dismissed the soldiers to the customary repast provided for them by the Emperor. He then retired to the gate, which, in consequence of the triumphal processions always passing through, had received its name *Porta Triumphalis*. Here they first took refreshment, and then, having clothed themselves in the triumphal robes, and sacrificed to the gods, whose statues stood by the gate, they commanded the pageant to move forward, driving through the circus and theatres, that the assembled crowds might have a passing view. Platforms also had been constructed for the spectators, many of them three or four stories high. They were so large, and had been so quickly raised, that the public felt distrustful of their safety. These temporary erections were gay with tapestries interwoven with gold, while gold and ivory ingeniously wrought were affixed round them all, and they were also decorated with large pictures representing incidents that had occurred in all the wars in which Vespasian and his sons had been victorious. The war in Judea was exhibited in numerous representations, divided into different sections, affording an extremely vivid portraiture of its events.

Here was to be seen a happy country devastated; there, entire bodies of hostile armies slaughtered, some again in flight, others led into captivity, fire cast into temples, houses overthrown, and their owners buried under their ruins, and other still more horrible pictures, all so true to life, that to persons unacquainted with the incidents it seemed as if they were actually occurring before their eyes. On each of these platforms was placed the governor of one of the captured cities, in the situation in which he was taken.

All the men who had appointed places in the procession displayed on their dress choice and magnificent ornaments, which attracted great admiration. Many species of animals were led along, all wearing appropriate decorations. The men in charge of them wore purple garments and dresses interwoven with gold. Moreover, in the crowd of captives, not one was to be seen unadorned; the beautiful variety of their dresses concealing from view any unsightliness arising from the wretched condition of their bodies. An extraordinary number of things were carried along in the procession. Various productions of different nations, curious or sumptuous, exhibited the extent and greatness of the Roman Empire on that day. Silver and gold and ivory in profusion, wrought in multitudinous forms, Babylonian tapestries, transparent gems, some set in crowns of gold, others in various fashions, had been collected together, and flowed on like a river. "So vast was the display, that we thence learned," says Josephus, "how erroneously we had supposed any of them to be rare." He tells us that very large images of the gods of conquered people appeared in the show, some of which were of very singular workmanship. Probably these graced the triumph on behalf of Domitian. The spoils in general were borne in confused heaps, but conspicuous above all were the vessels taken in the Temple of Jerusalem. A golden table, many talents in weight, and a candlestick made in like manner of gold, but constructed in a fashion quite different from any in ordinary use, for in the centre, affixed to a pedestal, rose a pillar from which extended slender branches resembling the figure of a trident, and to the top of each of these was attached a brazen lamp. These lamps were seven, indicating the honour paid to that number among the Jews. After these was borne the law of the Jews—last of the spoils.

Then followed men carrying images of victory, all made of ivory or gold. Next came Vespasian in a chariot, then Titus in another, and his brother Domitian riding by his side on a very fine charger.

When the victors arrived at the Capitol, the procession stopped; for there, in accordance with an ancient custom, was offered the solemn sacrifice to Jupiter, which formed the climax to the pomp of an imperial triumph; and there they waited until it was announced that the chief leader of the conquered enemy was no more.* On this occasion, Simon, son of Gioras, was put to death, who had been led in the procession among the captives with a halter round his neck. He was executed at the foot of the Capitoline Hill, while the conquerors were worshipping in the Temple of Jupiter. When the customary sacrifices and prayers were ended, the imperial party returned to the palace, where they entertained all who had not prepared sumptuous banquets at home.

The crowds dispersed, but not until the mob had loudly shouted their insults against Simon, even after death had released him from their malice. John of Giscala was imprisoned for life. In spite of the prejudices of Josephus, the tranquil far-seeing eye and firm hand of History has written the names of the Jewish leaders of that hopeless, desperate war among those of the heroes of all generations, who have sacrificed their lives to a sense of duty to their country.†

* Josephus. † Josephus and C. I. Hemans.

The Emperor, who was in his sixty-second year, was old enough to feel fatigued by the long ceremonial. Dean Merivale remarks: "He was prouder, we may believe, of the distinguished son who had shared his triumph, than of the acclamations with which he was himself greeted. He owned that, as far as he was personally concerned, he cared not for these honours. But on that auspicious day the most experienced and wisest men must have rejoiced in the proclamation that followed the triumph, a solemn announcement of peace throughout the Empire, and the Temple of Janus was closed. It had stood open from the birth of Christ to the overthrow of the Jewish nation; for the Senate had refused to sanction Nero's caprice in closing it on his precarious accommodation with Parthia.*

It was a small bronze temple, containing nothing but a bronze statue of the two-faced god; said to have been erected by Numa, near the south-eastern base of the Capitoline Hill, on the site or close to the spot where had formerly stood the Jannalis, as it was called, which was not a temple, but a gateway leading from primitive Rome, the original beginning of the town on the Palatine Hill, to Saturnia, the little town of the Sabines on the Capitoline Hill. They were nothing more than villages rudely built and fortified.

After the rape of the Sabines, Romulus and Tatius made peace, and concluded a friendly alliance. They then agreed to build a gateway between their towns, and to set up a strong gate which was to be open in time of war, that the allies might readily communicate with each other, but shut in time of peace, to prevent Romans and Sabines from quarrelling, when they were

---

* Merivale. The triumph is thought to have taken place in the summer of A.D. 71.

not occupied with external warfare. Thus had originated the custom of closing the Temple of Janus whenever universal peace was proclaimed.

The *Templum Pacis* was another building, which in all probability stood on the site now occupied by the remains of the grand Basilica of Constantine.*

This temple having been recently destroyed by fire, Vespasian determined to erect in its stead an imposing temple of Peace as a pledge of his policy.

The still substantial ruins, strong walls and magnificent arches which now mark that spot may therefore be looked on with singular but manifold interest. The spot reminds us that in darkest times, when ferocious cruelty prevailed, the most warlike nation of the earth built a temple to Peace. Again, it reminds us that Vespasian and Titus, noble pagan heroes, chosen by God to execute His sentence against Jerusalem, having conquered and triumphed, desired to magnify and adore Peace, and to call down its blessings on themselves and their people; and moreover, Constantine's Basilica speaks of the first emperor who bent the knee before the true Prince of Peace. The Roman's nobly constituted mind was in darkness, until the Light that shineth in darkness" was kindled in his heart.†

Returning to the Flavian period, and to the days of Josephus, we cannot follow a better guide than that historian, who tells us that a great many bands of the captive Jews were set to work under Roman masons. The temple of Peace was quickly completed in a style far beyond anything of the kind that had previously been raised in Rome. The wealth lately acquired supplied the means of embellishing the edifice with works of art, paintings, and ancient statues. In that shrine were

* Parker. † St. John i. 5.

accumulated and stored up all those objects for a sight of which men had wandered over the whole world, anxiously desiring to see them while they lay in different countries. Here Vespasian laid up also the golden candlesticks and vessels from the Temple of Jerusalem, on which he prided himself. The law of the Jews, however, and the purple veils of the sanctuary, he ordered to be deposited and kept in the palace. Thus says Josephus, who was at that time living in Rome. He had accompanied Titus on his journey from Alexandria, and Vespasian had received him kindly, had given him a pension, and placed him in apartments in a house in which he had himself resided before his elevation to the throne. So the Jewish historian had seen the triumph he fully and vividly described. Here he no doubt enjoyed the companionship of men whose works, like his own, have survived to our day. During this reign dissent from heathen theology was permitted, and did not even entail the loss of social standing, if we may judge from the elder Pliny's case.* A prince arriving at power after the disorders of civil war must necessarily be burdened for years with heavy responsibilities and anxious cares. Desiring to limit his own personal expenditure, Vespasian checked the dissipation of the finances in the foolish luxuries that had prevailed to an extravagant degree in the imperial court. With a view to this he ordered the demolition of at least the greater

* Pliny's views of a divine nature accord with monotheistic ones, and contradict the idolatry that had been upheld by the previous emperors and the aristocracy. He considered it an imbecility to enquire for the appearance and form of a god. The belief of marriages among the gods, that some were superannuated and for ever hoary, others always young, some winged, and some lame, arose, he said, from the puerility of persons almost insane.

part of Nero's Golden House. But that emperor had built also a gymnasium for athletic sports and gladiatorial shows in which he delighted, and which had long been popular with the Romans. Cicero in one of his letters remarked, "Magnificent are they indeed, but what pleasure can there be to a cultivated mind in the spectacle of an unarmed man exposed to be torn by a furious beast, or of a noble animal transfixed by darts? Such pastimes had suited Nero's taste, and he was also fond of the more harmless amusement of sham seafights, and to provide for that kind of entertainment he had made a large reservoir, quite an artificial lake, in which vessels with two or three or four rows of oars, like those of the Tyrian and Egyptian fleets, could fight with grand effect.

Julius Cæsar had instituted these sports, but had erected for them only a wooden amphitheatre. Augustus had proposed to build one substantially, but left it to his successors to carry out his plan, which Nero commenced to do by erecting his *gymnasium* and *naumacia*. These Vespasian left standing, and included them in his design for an enormous amphitheatre. Nero had built on ground that had been previously built upon, as some very ancient foundations prove and the long thin bricks used only in his time show a little of Nero's work, included in the Flavian amphitheatre, with that of successive later ages. Thus Vespasian became involved in demolition and extension, and in this pulling down and building up large numbers of the captive Jews were employed. As ship after ship unloaded its hundreds, the government had to find for them shelter, food, and work. Doubtless the provision was wretched and the labour hard, and all was embittered by the loss of home and fatherland,

and by galling slavery, against which the human heart naturally revolts.

The part of Rome which is still the Jewish quarter was that selected for the reception of those who came in like a flood after the fall of Jerusalem; yet not all at once. Judea could not instantly be almost emptied of her people. Travellers by land and sea were subject to hindrances, and dependent on winds and waves; so a long time elapsed before all the bands of these prisoners of war had been brought over. The newly arrived must have felt a little comforted on finding fellow-countrymen quite settled in that district; many of them belonging to families who had resided there ever since the Jews had returned to Rome, not very long after they had all been banished from the city by the Emperor Claudius. We know that Aquila and Priscilla soon went back, Some returned to the *Transtevere*, and others, perhaps chiefly the upper-class Jews, then settled in this quarter of the city, near the Portico of Octavia, the Theatre of Marcellus, and the old fish-market, of which such curious relics are still to be seen—even to the stone slabs on which the fish were laid.

In the absence of certain information on that point, we may suppose that after the triumph of Vespasian and Titus the Jews' quarter acquired the name of the Ghetto, for that name is thought to be derived from *ghat*, a Hebrew word which signifies broken; and in various forms of the verb it has a rather different meaning from the root, as shaven, cut down, cut off, abandoned. (See the Hebrew in Isa. xiv. 12, xv. 2; Jer. xlviii. 25, 37; Zech. xi. 10, 14.)*

We need not imagine the wretched abodes of poor

---

* From "The Ghetto in Rome." By the Rev. Dr. Philip. Claudian Press, Florence, 1875.

Jews encroaching on the public walk and the stately precincts of the magnificent Portico of Octavia. The better sort of Hebrews may have settled there before the fall of Jerusalem, and may have continued to dwell near that attractive centre of fashion; and the poorer sort may have in the course of centuries crept up to that arch.

Now, the ancient people, and their high, quaint, dingy, dilapidated houses, which look about coeval with the neighbouring palace of the Cenci, blending with that ruined Portico of Octavia, form beautiful and most interesting pictures.

Even in times far back, when the Jew was free to choose his place of abode, many of the race had settled in this part of Rome, as well as beyond the river, and outside the city, near the fountain of Egeria. It has lately been ascertained that the classic ground connected by the poets with the memory of Numa is on the estate of the Villa Mattei, on a farm beyond the pleasant garden. There, in a meadow we see the remains of a small temple or grotto built in with the rough brick-work of a farm building, beneath which is a deep well of excellent water. This spot, now said to be the real Egeria, is not near the venerable clump of fir trees, which from generation to generation has been kept up because it was fully believed to be the grove in which Numa conversed with the Nymph: it still exists, and is visible from the Appian Way, lying between the tomb of Cicilia Metella and the city. Byron's description is no doubt true to what he saw, and to the tradition sanctioned by history in his day.*

All the Jews who had been residing in or near Rome before the fall of Jerusalem, continued unmolested if

* "Childe Harold's Pilgrimage," canto iv. 115—118.

they entirely and silently submitted to the government under which they were living; but the humiliation of Judea, and the influx of such large numbers of unfortunate fellow-countrymen, could but be disadvantageous as well as grievous to them. The most prosperous could not feel happy, and, as an old Roman proverb says, "Grief is an unjust valuer of things." *

It was well that in Josephus his brethren had a second Joseph, a powerful advocate, one who possessed the confidence of the Emperor and his sons. By desire of the imperial family, and in token of mutual regard, the name of Flavius had been prefixed to that of Josephus, in accordance with the old and common custom. The historian was now putting together all the information he had gleaned, all his notes and recollections concerning the Jewish war. In his autobiography, which was written later, he says,—

"As a prisoner, I was compelled to attend Vespasian and Titus, at first in bonds, but afterwards, being set free, I accompanied the latter when he advanced from Alexandria to carry on the siege of Jerusalem. During the period of the siege nothing escaped my observation, and as to what occurred under my eye in the Roman camp, I carefully noted it; while it was I alone who understood the reports made by deserters from the city. Afterwards, when enjoying leisure at Rome, and having all my materials in readiness, I engaged the assistance of persons competent in the Greek language, by whose aid I composed my history. Confident of the truth and accuracy of what I had written, I submitted it to Vespasian and Titus, to whom the first copies of the work were presented, and afterwards to many of the Romans who had acted a part in the war." †

* Seneca.
† See "Life of Josephus, and Historical Authority of his Writings," appended to the Rev. R. Traill's "Translation of the Jewish War." Houlston and Wright. 1868.

Twelve thousand Jewish slaves are said to have been employed for five years in building the great amphitheatre, and ten million of Roman scudi expended upon it in the same time. The *scudo* was equal to about four shillings.

Nothing certain has been ascertained as to who was the architect of the Colosseum. An inscription found in the catacomb of St. Agnes, in memory of Gradentius, has suggested the idea that he designed it and directed the work, and that he afterwards suffered as a martyr within its walls. Another sculpture upon a tomb represents the machine used for raising large stones to the top of a high wall. This also leads to the conjecture that some of those who helped to erect the Colosseum perished in it as gladiators or martyrs. The general form of the building is oval, and it had four principal entrances. The one now remaining is thought to have been the entrance for the Emperor and his suite, for it is not numbered, as were the other entrances and seats. The amphitheatre was calculated to hold 87,000 persons, and was admirably adapted for its purpose. There were three principal staircases by which spectators ascended to the higher tiers of seats, and these were so arranged that the different orders could disperse without meeting each other. The numerous places of egress, called vomitaria, and the windows to light the staircases, were contrived with great skill.* Spectators were protected from the heat of the sun by a great awning suspended by cords from masts or poles fixed at the top. Pliny describes an awning which represented a midnight sky spangled with stars.

A letter is still extant, written by a young country lad to his friends at home when he was enjoying his

---

* Parker on the Colosseum.

first visit to Rome. "We saw," he says, "the theatre with interwoven beams rising to heaven, so high as almost to overlook the Tarpeian Rock. The steps are immensely high, and the sloping passages gently descend. What shall I describe further? I saw all kinds of wild beasts, and herds of shapeless animals bearing the name of horses, but deformed; hippopotami, the offspring of the Nile. Oh how often have we trembling seen the arena sinking in parts, and a gulf burst open in the ground, from which wild beasts have emerged!"*

This was comparatively innocent sport; the abominable cruelties committed in that amphitheatre are well known.

Seneca mentions an occasion on which a large number of bodies were exposed to view of men who had fought with beasts, and been unable to defend themselves with their swords and shields. He remarks that the persons who encouraged these combats were as savage as wild beasts. To make an exciting spectacle, criminals were torn to pieces by ferocious animals. Near the amphitheatre stood the gladiators' fountain, in which the survivors washed their wounds and refreshed themselves after the conflict.

Between the Colosseum and the Capitol stands the Arch of Titus, on the road which runs under the Palatine Hill, having that majestic height on the one side, and on the other the excavated *Forum Romanum*, which lies below the level of the present surface of the earth.

The arch was erected by the senate and the people under the Emperor Domitian, after the death of his brother Titus, as the inscription shows.

How singular is the interest which that arch inspires!

* Calpurnius.

How manifold are its points of contact with the heart "that believeth unto righteousness," and with the mind which has received impressions from the Old Testament and the New—from history—from life in bygone ages, so far as we can enter into it—from life in our own day, and from the harmony brought out of it all, in spite of reckless selfishness, of cruel warfare, of which the war cry was extermination! Perhaps already the people of that generation know far better than we do why these things were permitted.

Looking upon that Arch of Titus, one seems to feel that the hand of time has been held back by a mightier Hand, which has carefully guided "the effacing fingers;" so that while they have swept off the gloss, they have left all that makes the venerable beauty of the ancient structure perfect, and have lightly touched most of the sculpture and the yet legible inscriptions over the arch. The bas relief in the interior represents the triumph. Very distinctly we see the silver trumpets, the golden table, and the seven-branched candlestick, upreared before the victors. Photography brings everything out wonderfully.

The sculptors, who patiently worked on, cutting those figures and letters one by one, knew as little about the then undiscovered process as we know about the ways and means whereby things now hidden will be made clear in a future day—the day of manifestation, when light has done its work in darkness—has stamped the features of the lives of men.

Considering the circumstances of the times, it is highly probable that a great many captive Jews were employed in the erection of that arch, but we have no proof that it was entirely built by them. It is said that a Jew would not pass under it, that he would make a long circuit to avoid so doing.* This may have been true with respect to some; they were a strong-willed people, and when under chastisement apt to be "stiff-necked," as Scripture expresses it. But among them there were always faithful hearts trusting in God, believing that their country would one day be restored to them or to their children, and that till Jehovah took them back, He would be with them, as He had been with their ancestors in Babylon. The pious Jew knows his God as the Good Shepherd who watches over every sheep and lamb of his flock, and seeks the lost, and leads the weary to the fountain in the desert. Believing this, he is led on over rough paths, or pathless wilds, to the green meadows and the still waters. He does not fear to pass through the valley of the shadow of death, for under every trial the rod and the staff of his Shepherd comfort him, and will do so until we are all gathered into one fold, under one Shepherd, the Shepherd of Israel.

"With the reduction of Palestine the consolidation of the Roman Empire was completed. From the Mersey to the Dead Sea, no nation remained erect, and the resistance of the last free men on her frontiers had been expiated in their blood.

"The boasted restoration of the Capitoline Temple was a vain attempt to retain hold of the past, to revive the lost or perishing, to re-attach to new conditions of thought a worn-out creed of antiquity."†

The Jews, though subjected to a second captivity and dispersion, were not annihilated, and will return when

---

* This story of the Jews not choosing to pass under the Arch of Titus can be traced no farther back than to Madame de Stael, who does not give her authority. She relates the story, and remarks that it is to be hoped it is true, as great calamities should be long remembered.

† Dean Merivale.

their long day of humiliation is over. As the Arch of Titus stands, bearing witness to the past, pointing forward to the future, so also do existing customs of the Jews, as well as their actual condition.

"To this day the Hebrews in every country of their exile and dispersion have continued to observe the 9th day of the month *Ab* (which corresponds with our 25th day of July) in memorial of both the first and the second destruction of their city and sanctuary; next to the great day of atonement, it is the most strictly kept of all their fasts. Even on the previous day the pious Israelite takes nothing beyond what absolute necessity requires. He seats himself on the ground either at home or in the synagogue, by the dim light of a small candle, and the evening service commences with the 138th Psalm.

"Mournful and penitential psalms are chanted in succession throughout the day, (every Hebrew day begins at sunset.) The lamentations of Jeremiah are revived, because many striking features once fulfilled in the taking of Jerusalem by the Babylonians were still more signally accomplished in its destruction by the Romans. But 'these dry bones shall live.' 'Jerusalem shall be trodden down of the Gentiles, until the times of the Gentiles be fulfilled.'

"The city has been trodden underfoot successively by the Romans, Persians, Saracens, Egyptians, Franks, and Turks, from the days of Simon the son of Gioras and John of Giscala to those of Sir Moses Montefiore and the foundation of a bishopric at Jerusalem by Frederick William IV., King of Prussia, and Queen Victoria." †

* Luke xxi. 24.
† "Israel and the Gentiles." By Dr. Isaac Da Costa, of Amsterdam, a Jew by birth, who gratefully expresses his thanks to

Since the consecration of our Church on Mount Zion, eventful years have elapsed, important events have crowded upon one another so rapidly that we have hardly had time to reflect on their importance and their signification.

May we not now couple with the name of Sir Moses Montefiore that of his friend Benjamin Disraeli, Earl of Beaconsfield? and do not their names encourage us to look for what is to follow after God shall have accomplished to scatter the power of the holy people?

We ought to cherish warm feelings of attachment to their holy land. Is it not the cradle of the Gospel, in which the good tidings were first preached by Jews to Jews, whence it was sent forth on its career of spiritual conquest, to grow up into the fifth great power—a kingdom set up by the God of heaven, which shall never be destroyed, the kingdom of which Christ the Messiah, the Anointed One, is worthy to be both High Priest and King?*

As God, the Creator, and man, made in God's likeness, are triune, such also is the view of God's kingdom given to man in his present state. The Father's kingdom, the Redeemer's kingdom, the spiritual kingdom of the Holy Ghost, are three in one, as presented to our threefold though individual power of perception. Thus, though we cannot perceive it with our bodily senses, we can form conceptions of a spiritual kingdom, on which the Holy Ghost descends, seeking fellowship with the spirits of men. We are capable of believing that the Father of spirits gave His only begotten Son, to be,

---

Almighty God for his conversion to Christianity. The book was published in London by Nisbet, of Berners Street, in 1850.

* Daniel ii. 34, 35, 44; xii. 7.

even while invisible to mortal eyes, with His people alway, even to the end of the world.

In the redeemed earthly kingdom, that same Lord, appointed by the Eternal Father, is King of kings. The One Seed of Abraham. He has been visibly lifted up on the cross, He will visibly sit on the throne, and again the Holy Ghost will descend to confer manifest gifts and blessings.

For the coming of our Father's kingdom we daily pray, in words dictated by our Lord Himself, and written under the inspiration of the Holy Ghost.

Is not faith in the *Unity* of the Eternal Trinity the ground on which the Christian stands? and, standing upon that ground, is he not very near his Hebrew brother? Only the veil divides us, through which the Jew cannot see. The Christian sees through it, though but indistinctly; he sees, because his face is turned towards the light, towards the Sun of his soul.*

Deeply affecting is it to hear a Jew emphatically express his faith in words we reverence—" Hear, O Israel: the Lord our God is one Lord "—words from the book of Deuteronomy, which, according to St. Mark, were exactly quoted by our Lord Jesus Christ Himself.

When a son of Abraham meets us with these words, to us doubly sacred, can we not persuade him that we hold that truth as firmly as he does? can we not draw his attention to everything that proves, or even symbolizes, the Unity of the Trinity?

The books of the New Testament, though not accepted as the word of God, are now read by Jews. Can we not help them to catch sight of the farthest point to which the eye of faith is directed by prophecy? †

---

* 2 Cor. iii. 14—16; Isa. xxv. 7.
† Deut. vi. 4; Mark xii. 29; 1 Cor. xv. 21—29.

UNDER THE YOKE.

"He beheld the city, and wept over it."—LUKE xix. 41.

" Where high the heavenly temple stands,
The house of God, not made with hands,
A great High Priest our nature wears,
The Guardian of mankind appears.

Our fellow-sufferer yet retains
A fellow-feeling of our pains,
And still remembers in the skies,
His tears, His agonies, and cries.

In every pang that rends the heart,
The Man of sorrows had a part;
He sympathizes in our grief,
And to the sufferer sends relief."

MICHAEL BRUCE.

VIII.

UNDER THE YOKE.

"He beheld the city, and wept over it."—LUKE xix. 41.

WITH the utmost pomp those rolls on which the Jewish law was written, wrapped in their own strong and splendid coverings, had been carried in triumph before the Roman conquerors. May we not think that in the midst of the noisy tumult of that day, watchful ears caught the gentle voice of the silver bells attached to the rolls, and that to every listening ear their chime was as a *paraclete*—a helping, strengthening comforter; even to those who did not yet understand that in our Lord Jesus Christ the law had been accomplished, that by Him it had been perfectly fulfilled— "*all the types and shadows finished*"—and therefore now it might be laid to rest? The door of a new temple of peace, and the gates of a glorious palace, were opened to receive the precious relics of the past.

The law was not annihilated; on the contrary, the altered state or condition under which it existed gave it power, and it was more vividly present than ever to the Hebrew mind, and obtained more hold upon the heart. "Their law, in the full sense of the word, was a reality, what no enemy could destroy, or even keep in custody, and this they the better understood when the venerated parchment rolls had been taken from them. Though they were captives or homeless fugitives, they became more equal to their vocation as the sons of Abraham, and bravely bore throughout the Roman world, and beyond it, the commandments delivered from Sinai, and the fortitude, patience, and hope resulting from an earnest faith in the God of their fathers." *

In all the cities of the Empire the Jews were allowed to meet together in their synagogues, and no doubt the wealthy members of the community in Rome provided for the accommodation of the greatly increased numbers. We read of several instances during the war in which Agrippa pleaded successfully for the people; we may therefore suppose that to his life's end he used his influence on their behalf. For years Bernice held great power over Titus; but when he had ascended the throne, he yielded to public opinion, and gave her up, and the Jewish princess returned alone to live on a fine estate that had been assigned to her when the affairs of Judea were settled.

It is very remarkable that the expulsion of the Stoics took place in the year following that in which the destruction of Jerusalem occurred. There was, as we have seen, a strong affinity between Judaism and Stoicism. Long before the Christian era, the Stoics had borrowed from the Jews views of the one God, and of the Divine will, with which the acts of men should accord, and they reasoned on wisdom meaning moral intelligence; consequently their notions of morality were superior to those of other heathens. At this time Demetrius the cynic, and many other teachers of stoic doctrines, discussed continually and publicly subjects which almost distracted some of their hearers.†

What these exciting subjects were, we are not in-

* Dean Milman.   † Dion Cassius

formed ; they may have concerned Rome's destruction and the end of the world, both of which at that date were subjects of popular anxiety. Not that these ideas were new, or confined to the Stoics; they had long been afloat, had been perhaps a little forgotten, but earthquakes and the horrors of war had lately revived them.

Mucianus, agreeing with many who considered the stoic teaching dangerous, persuaded Vespasian to promptly expel those philosophers from Rome. They were permitted to leave quietly, and were not further molested. Those among them who lived up to their ideal of a noble life must have obtained influence for good. "Their teaching was distasteful to the sensualist and the tyrant, its tone rebuked his follies and his vices; it set up a higher standard than the will of Cæsar, and despised servile flattery. It taught men to care very much for a good conscience, for personal dignity and freedom, and to think slightly of short-lived goods, over which the will has no control. Here was a rule that was not without a certain grandeur, however wanting it might be at times in tenderness and sympathy."*

Such was the seed widely sown immediately after the great scattering of the multitudinous seed of Abraham, innumerable as the sand of the seashore.

Josephus had been put into possession of estates in his native country, more productive than the land near Jerusalem which had formerly belonged to him ; but he remained in Rome to finish his seven books on the Jewish War ; and having completed that task, he began "The Jewish Antiquities" in twenty books. In his autobiography he says that he wrote it expressly for the use of his excellent friend Epaphroditus, who may

* W. W. Capes, M.A.

possibly be the fellow-labourer honourably mentioned by St. Paul.*

The patron of Josephus was most highly respected; "a man eager in pursuit of every branch of learning, but especially of history; he himself having been long concerned with affairs of state, and having had personal experience of many changes, under all exhibiting an immovable adherence to what is virtuous and noble." With this valued friend the historian enjoyed familiar intercourse for many years, and occasionally they corresponded.

Josephus wrote "The Antiquities of the Jews" in the hope of doing something towards rescuing his countrymen from the contempt and hatred which they had to encounter. This is manifestly the chief object of the work. Throughout the world the Jew had become not only so unpopular as to be generally distrusted and derided, but he was altogether misunderstood, even by persons well disposed, and well informed on most subjects.

The injustice of Roman historians and other writers was cruelly adding to the force of ill-natured prejudice; and Josephus, keenly feeling this, took up his pen in defence of his own people, and dedicated, or addressed, his work to the learned and influential Epaphroditus.

A strongly exaggerated style of writing was so completely the style of that age, that no historian, scarcely a philosopher, was superior to it. Josephus exaggerated, allowed himself to be unduly influenced by personal considerations and ungenerous prejudices.

Suetonius, who gained the reputation of being impartial, eulogizes Titus; shows him to have been naturally amiable and liberal. Titus did not like to send a petitioner away unsatisfied. "No man," he said,

* Philippians ii. 25.

"ought to leave the prince's presence disappointed." He was the first emperor who gained equally the regard of the nobles and the people, which his father had endeavoured to do with incomplete success. But his career was brief; he reigned only two years alone after Vespasian's death, and that short span was clouded with national calamities. Rome was stricken with fire and pestilence, and the great eruption of Vesuvius occurred, which buried the cities of Herculaneum and Pompeii. In A.D. 80 he opened the Colosseum with a grand ceremony, gorgeous shows, and exciting combats. A battle between cranes and dwarfs was the fanciful novelty on that occasion. At the close of the day, when the trials of strength were ended, Titus was seen shedding tears. Possibly he was unnerved by bodily weakness, for life was fleeting away, though he had not attained his fortieth year.

The high character which all Romans agree in ascribing to Titus has not been contradicted by Christian historians; but by the Jews the memory of the Flavian princes has naturally been held in the greatest abhorrence. They invented the wildest legends to blacken the fame of Titus, and to represent his misfortunes and the sufferings of his last painful illness as special judgments and punishments decreed by Divine justice. Certainly one of those stories, and perhaps more, were admitted into the Talmud.*

Vespasian had proved a wise and beneficent ruler, one who firmly maintained the reputation of Rome and her military power; he had set on foot useful works, and had encouraged literature, though he was not himself capable of appreciating it. When on the imperial throne, he had retained the manners and habits of his

* Salvador quoting the Talmud, *Dom. Rom. en Judée*, ii. 498.

former life more than was consistent with his high position. The manners of his sons were moulded to the fashions of the day, but they both inherited some good natural qualities from the simple, honest Sabine stock whence they had sprung. The deepest foundation-stones of character are innate, and the very earliest impressions which the mind receives cannot be quite obliterated as if they had never been there.

Domitian was able to see the great need of a radical reformation in public morals, and no sense of his own personal vices, no shame on their account, deterred him from vigorously attempting to effect reforms which public scandals had shown to be so necessary that they were called for. The Emperor and his counsellors were extremely severe on the Vestal Virgins. High honours belonged to their office, and they were high-born ladies, but the laxity of manners permitted to prevail generally had long polluted their home and their temple. Two condemned culprits were allowed to kill themselves, but a third was put to death according to the rules of Numa, the founder of the Order. Cornelia, with a loaf of bread, a flask of water, and a lamp, was duly buried alive in a vault prepared to receive her. Numa had decreed that stoning to death was to be the punishment, but Tarquin the Elder had substituted the lingering death which gave time for repentance. This punishment had fallen into disuse, had not been executed for two centuries, when it was revived by Domitian. That emperor next investigated the conduct of singers and dancers at the theatres, and this class furnished guilty persons, who first were condemned to suffer death, and then in a whirl of excitement, greater even than that in which they had lived, they met death dramatically on the arena of the great amphitheatre.

Now and then one had self-possession and strength enough to conquer a lion or a tiger, and in these rare instances the Emperor's pardon was generally granted. The decree aimed against players, singers, and dancers, was accompanied by a proclamation against the *Mathematici*, an awful set, or rather sets, of strange diviners of secrets, believed in, though feared by Roman people, not as high-minded as Cicero, who thus describes and comments on them: "I care nothing for the Marsian augurs, nor for strolling astrologers, nor for the gipsy priests of Isis, nor for the interpreters of dreams; for these possess neither science nor art, but 'are superstitious and impudent impostors. They are either lazy or mad, or act to gain a livelihood. They know not the right path themselves, but pretend to show it to others, that they may by their promises gain a penny."*

These meddlers in the occult sciences, very like the wizards, witches, and seekers of the philosopher's stone, of the middle ages, had been agitating society, high and low, with visions and predictions. It was very difficult to arrest, judge, and convict the evil-doers of this large, heterogeneous, strange class, which included many foreigners; so they were sought for, by means of devices as cunning as those by which they themselves deceived the world, and eluded justice.

It is not surprising that the Romans should have confounded uncompromising, zealous, and fanatical Jews with these *mathematici*. That there were Jews who misdirected their zeal, and fell into fanaticism, the history of the Jewish war undoubtedly proves. Many Romans may have thought with Lucan. "Judea," says that poet, "adores some unknown, undiscovered city." After the destruction of their temple, the Jews' faith,

* Cicero, Divin. i. 58.

and their strong opinions, and the religious hope to which they clung more firmly than ever, must have made them a very mysterious people to the Romans. Juvenal reproaches them with worshipping nothing but the clouds and the sky-god beyond them, while they made a traffic of their superstitious dreams. We have seen how a highly talented and educated son of Abraham made use of his imaginative faculties and quick wit to save his own life, and to obtain a safe and good position. Considering the character of the Jew as it has been marked in every generation, at least since their fall, we see how the baser sort, when contending against degrading poverty and undeserved contempt, made use of their natural gifts as an Oriental race to obtain their livelihood by illicit means and practices; by playing on the credulity and vague superstitious notions of the Roman people. The Emperor and the Senate were right in resolutely determining to inquire into the habits and doings of all branches of the noxious *mathematici;* but the persecution that followed is unjustifiable : we cannot desire to justify it. Domitian was a cruel man; he had been badly brought up in his young days, by those who had charge of him, while his father was far away on military duty.

In Church history this persecution is reckoned as the second of the ten ; both Jews and Christians, whom the Romans still looked upon as a Jewish sect, were involved in it. Every persecution made more apostates than martyrs. If it be true that St. John, the beloved apostle, was summoned to Rome to be tried, and that he stood before Domitian as St. Paul had stood before Nero, he must have been sentenced, not to death, but to banishment. That he wrote the Apocalypse in the island of Patmos, some time between the great fire at Rome and the destruction of Jerusalem, is now, after close investigation, generally considered a settled question. The story of his having been thrown into a caldron of boiling oil has no historical foundation.* We may suspect that the cup of poison from which he brought forth a serpent is also a baseless fabrication.

We hear of two other men who were brought before Domitian: their story has been so pleasantly related, that we will take it exactly as it is written for us.

"Two young men were brought into the basilica, and dragged forward; who could have shown their father's name in the great census of Augustus, as a son of David at Bethlehem; and had not their father been one of those twelve who had chiefly preached that strange new error? The two men stood before the Emperor, they said they were sons of Judas, son of Cleopas: their father and two of their uncles had been of the twelve, they had been cousins, called brethren of their Lord; they were like Him, of the old lineage of David, but, for their own part, they sought no earthly thrones for themselves, or any one else; they were hard-working men, and in witness thereof they spread out their hands, horny with the use of the spade, and they owned nothing but a few acres of land.

"'But what is this kingdom?' still asked the Emperor.

"'It is a kingdom,' said the sons of St. Jude, 'a kingdom far away. We look not for it till earth be at an end, and our King cometh to make a new heaven and a new earth.'

"Domitian feared them no longer, but let them depart to their homes, and even became convinced that the Christians meant him no harm." †

These simple-minded men, through a pure faith, working on strong common sense, seem to have escaped the delusions and the confusion of ideas prevailing among both Jews and Christians, which led them into danger of becoming objects of suspicion to the Romans;

* Dean Merivale.
† From "The Exile of Patmos." "The Pupils of St. John the Divine." By C. M. Yonge. Macmillan's "Sunday Library."

because both Jew and Christian, first literally interpreted the prophecies in which they trusted, and then defined their own interpretations more exactly than the Word of God defines its predictions; descending to details not yet given to us, and which perhaps may not be made clear until the second advent of Christ is an accomplished fact. Till He come, it is well to remember a caution which belongs alike to Jew and Christian: "God is in heaven, and thou upon earth, therefore let thy words be few" (Eccles. v. 2).

Forgetting this text, both Jew and Christian entered into full descriptions of their glorious anticipations. Each person, according to the bent of his disposition and the force of his imagination, conceived his own picture of the promised city and its King; and some pure-hearted enthusiasts, and some designing party-leaders, not contented with forming and enjoying their own views, disseminated them, convinced others, and gathered disciples who implicity followed them. Jewish Rabbis spoke and wrote in highly allegorical language, and did not guard the people against puting too literal an interpretation on figures of speech. They said, "In that day there will be corn on the top of the mountains, and the stalks will be like palm trees or pillars; nor will it be any trouble to reap it, for God will send a wind which will blow down the white flour from the ears. A single grape will load a waggon or a ship; and when it is brought to the house, they will draw wine from it, as from a cask. In the days to come, say the Rabbis, God will bring together Sinai and Tabor and Carmel, and set Jerusalem upon them. The city will cover as much ground as a horse can run over from the early morning, till its shadow is below it at noon."*

* "The Life and Words of Christ." By C. Geikie, D.D.

They described in glowing language the beauty and glory of the city, but did not perceive, or at least did not teach the people, the unchangeable truth, that however delightful the next world or the next dispensation may be, still then and there it will be quite as true as it now is here, that not the gratification of the perfected senses, not the exercise of complete sets of faculties, not our love of the world, but our love of the Father, will constitute our happiness. There is a difference between loving gifts and pleasures for the sake of the giver, who is very dear to us, and loving the giver for the sake of what he gives us. Our experience in this world teaches us which is the nobler motive, and it is pointed out in Scripture, especially in the Gospel and Epistles of Saint John, the beloved disciple, the apostle of love, from whose book of Revelation the Christian's brightest anticipations are drawn. Equally vivid are the pictures of Messiah's reign, drawn by the Jews from the books of the Hebrew prophets; but at the period of time we are now considering they searched enthusiastically for every sign that could feed their hopes of rising to worldly pre-eminence, and treading down all other nations of the earth. Jerusalem was to succeed Rome as the mistress of the world, and their minds being filled and satisfied with that view, they missed attaining to the spiritual meaning of their prophecies; they thought only of a triumphal reign of the Son of David, a climax of national pride, grandeur, and terrestrial enjoyment. Thus were their thoughts diverted from Jehovah. Those who do not seek to know the character and attributes of God cannot understand how "Christ in these last days cometh to us from the Father," as is declared at the beginning of the Epistle to the Hebrews, written A.D. 64, shortly before the fall of Jerusalem. "It was to a people infatuated with visions of outward felicity that Jesus Christ came, with His utterly opposite doctrines of the aim and nature of Messiah and His kingdom. Only here and there was there a soul with any higher or purer thoughts than such gross, material, and narrow dreams."*

Consequently, the Jews, as a nation, had rejected the Redeemer, and had been delivered up to the Romans, to be humbled and proved under the conflict of feelings and opinions between the schools of the Rabbis and those of the pagan academies. Every important pagan temple had its academy or college attached to it, on a system very much like that afterwards formed by the Church of Rome for her conventional institutions. We have seen that philosophy which characterized the pagan schools had become a real power, and a very dominant one, because it brought out man's reasoning faculties and his power of self-control, and brought them to bear upon common life, so that where Christian influences were unknown, philosophy was the chief moral teacher of mankind.

These schools had not failed in course of time to propagate ideas which met and in different degrees and various ways affected the ideas of Jews and even of Christians. Shaken together as were these people of different races by the force of extraordinary events, every man who at all believed in Divine omnipotence felt that it had been signally exercised. Many souls were roused to a sense of spiritual truth, but they did not all wake to take the same view; every man, whether heathen, Jew, or Christian, saw according to the heartiness of his faith and the extent of his knowledge.

* "The Life and Words of Christ." By C. Geikie, D.D.

This revival of religious sentiment was, among the Romans, much more profound and energizing than that which had formerly resulted from Augustus Cæsar's endeavours to effect a religious reformation. It was too thorough and too reasonable to be satisfied with worshipping the Emperor; aspiring to the higher adoration of goodness and virtue, it led men to ponder on the great problems of life, and to justify the ways of Providence.

The literary tone which a century before had been worldly, sceptical, and careless, was becoming earnest, and not unfrequently devout; and familiar letters show that religion was with most a matter of serious concern, and a real motive force in action. The numerous inscriptions of this period enshrine many of the most cherished feelings of every social class and race, and the epitaphs attest in every variety of tone the hopes and fears of a life beyond the grave. Yet the popular religion continued polytheistic. Numberless gradations of beings between the infinite God and finite man were thought to exist, and imagination peopled the universe with ghostly visitors, and with an endless hierarchy of supernatural agents.*

There was still, as regards religious belief, a gulf, deep and wide, between the Romans and the Jews. Both Jews and Christians might be branded as impious in the Roman sense; that is, as deniers of the Roman divinities, and as tempting men to withdraw from their service. The sincere Jews, by the innate power of sincerity, seem to have gained influence over many of the Romans; for not a few citizens were

* See chapter on "Revival of Religious Sentiments." Epochs of Roman History. The Early Empire By W. W. Capes, M.A. Longman.

accused of impiety, of having withdrawn from the worship of the gods. This charge was advanced against persons of rank, and combined with those of neglecting the duties of a citizen, and adopting Jewish manners. Whether these culprits were considered guilty of Judaism or of Christianity is not clear. For some time past the imperial household had been a centre of Christianity, the ladies of the court had shown decided leanings towards it.

Dr. Lightfoot, in commenting on the singular reserve maintained by St. Clement throughout his Epistle to the Corinthians, points out that we should bear in mind the close connection of the writer and the bearers of the letter with the Emperor's household. The persecutor and the persecuted met, as it were, face to face. They mixed together in the common affairs of life; they even lived under the same roof. Thus the utmost caution was needed. Clement refers to the sudden and repeated calamities and reverses under which the church in Rome was suffering, but says not a word about the nature of these calamities, nor a word here or elsewhere about their authors, but he mentions the Neronian persecution, and adds, "We are in the same lists, and the same struggle awaits us. The letter therefore was probably written while the church was at the mercy of Domitian's caprice, still uncertain when and where the next blow would fall; but it could hardly have been written before the two most illustrious members of the congregation had suffered, the one death, and the other banishment, on account of their adherence to the Christian faith. Domitian, as he advanced in years, had grown more and more tyrannical. In the fifteenth year of his reign he accused some of his highest nobles, and among them some of his near relations. His first cousin, Flavius Clemens, and his wife Domitella, and the Consul Achilius, were arrested and accused of atheism, which meant refusing to worship the heathen gods, and to this was added the vague charge of withdrawing from the civil and religious duties of a citizen. Achilius, though a man highly respected in Rome, was convicted, and condemned to fight on the arena. He came off victorious in the combat with the beast, and was sent into exile, whence he never returned. Flavius Clemens was executed, his wife Domitella and her two sons were banished. These, and other instances of death or banishment, bravely met by Jews and Christians, constitute what has been called a persecution; but Dean Merivale thinks it has been too hastily dignified by that name

Those were bad times; men gave way to ferocious passions, and bloody scenes were but too common. No greater contrast can be conceived than the spirit of the age and that of St. Clement's letter, which is remarkable for its gentleness and forbearance, and for its lofty moral elevation, so conspicuous in the attitude of these Roman Christians towards their secular rulers, whom at this time they had little cause to love. In the prayer for princes and governors, in the lately recovered close of the epistle, this sentiment finds its noblest expression: " Guide our steps to walk in holiness and righteousness, and singleness of heart, and to do such things as are good and pleasing in Thy sight, and in the sight of our rulers. Give concord and peace to us and to all that dwell on the earth, . . . that we may be saved while we render obedience to Thine Almighty and most excellent Name, and to our rulers and governors upon earth; . . . that we, knowing the glory and honour which Thou hast given them, may submit ourselves unto them, in nothing resisting Thy will. . . . Do Thou, Lord, direct their counsel according to that which is good and well-pleasing in Thy sight, that administering in peace and gentleness, with godliness, the power which Thou hast given them, they may obtain Thy favour." When we remember that this prayer issued from the fiery furnace of persecution, after the experience of a cruel and capricious tyrant like Domitian, it will appear truly sublime—sublime in its utterances, and still more sublime in its silence.*

It seems that many Jews, condemned on different pretexts, or for various offences in the course of years, were by Domitian sentenced, not to death, but to hard labour in mines and quarries in distant provinces of the Empire. Among the quarries of Carrara there are a number not worked now, known as the Roman quarries, and an old chronicle of Carrara informs us that these marble quarries were worked by captive Jews. That Jewish slaves worked on both the Colosseum and the baths of Titus, as their forefathers laboured in Egypt, is a popular idea. Using portions of the Golden House, Vespasian had begun those baths; they were carried on by Titus, and completed by his brother. The enormous ruins on the Esquiline, not far from the Colosseum, bear testimony to their magnificence. Here and there the frescoes are wonderfully preserved especially on the high roof of a long corridor. The guide holds up his torch on a pole to show the delicately painted flowers, griffins, animals, and birds; the most interesting is the eagle copied by the first Napoleon, as his ensign. In one of the nine chambers is the well-known group of Venus with two Cupids, and doves hovering above. These frescoes were supposed to be the most perfect remains of pictorial art in Rome, but they are inferior to those

* "St. Clement of Rome," page 268.

that have been found in the baths of Livia, on the Latin Way. The Laocoon was discovered in the baths of Titus; the ruins are now scarcely distinguishable from those of Nero's "Golden House. Public baths were places of amusement, as well as refreshment. Fellow-citizens met at these institutions, which fill a prominent place in the social life of the Romans; they were, in fact, not unlike the large club houses of our day.

Domitian did not escape the common fate of the tyrant; he died by violence. The successful conspiracy against him spread far and wide, but one hand only gave the fatal stroke—that of a freedman of the late Senator Clemens, who had sworn to avenge his master's death.

The freedmen now constituted a very large class; the offspring of all the conquered people mingled with those of all the most criminal and unfortunate Romans who had fused in the furnace of adversity, from which they had been brought out one by one through many generations. This great body of redeemed men had grown up under influences of gratitude, which have elevating power, but do not make the heart of man less sensitive to subsequent tyranny and unkindness. As the class had gained strength, it had naturally acquired independence of feeling, which had been promoted by the education given to his freemen by many a generous master, who preferred being served by men free and intelligent, to being served entirely by slaves, who saw that it was well to have these men standing between him and his slaves. From small beginnings in every town, and on every large estate in the provinces throughout Rome's wide dominions, the system of redemption was working out results decidedly good, but not unmixed with evil.

The recent war and other circumstances had tended to enlarge the class, and now a considerable number of those who formed that strong bone of the body politic were Jews. Disabilities, unjust and cruel, legal restrictions which closed against them all that were considered the most honourable paths of life, and heavy taxes, kept them in the background; but the number of Jews who became freedmen made the class very different to what it would have been without them. The very lowest grade of free Jews were so dirty, disorderly, and unsettled in their habits, as to annoy their neighbours, and cause disturbances. Domitian repeatedly drove them out of Rome, but they contrived after a while to return. At last he granted them leave to live outside the walls, and many of them paid a small sum for permission to encamp on the ground round the old grotto, long ago erected over the beautiful spring of pure clear water, which for ages was believed to be the fountain of Egeria. Here the lowest Jews lived like gipsies; and being themselves an eastern people, their natural faculties enabled them to live on their strongly imaginative wits, and to encircle themselves with a haze of mystery which kept alive a half-fearful kind of wonder, through which they were looked upon by their equally ignorant and superstitious neighbours, the corresponding class of a western people, among whom they were scattered. Egeria's Grove was stealthily visited by young men and maidens of the city; for there fortune-tellers and all kinds of soothsayers might haply be found. Under trees in the ancient grove, that used to be kept sacred to the memory of Numa and the Nymph, these vagabond Jews passed the night with their families, and in the morning went into Rome to beg, or to sell the most trifling articles, among which matches and bits of old glass are especially mentioned. They were so poor, that many of them possessed nothing but the little basket in which they carried their food, and the bed and pillow stuffed with hay, all of their own manufacture. Some of them kept pigs, not for their own consumption, but obviously because that animal costs little or nothing to keep, and may be profitably sold.

Juvenal has given one pleasing description of the Jews enjoying the rural occupation of haymaking under and around those old trees. In another Satire he vividly pictures an aged Jewess who has crept from her lonely bed to pursue her vocation, and with a trembling voice is accosting a woman of fashion, who, successfully charmed by those few whispered words, crosses the hand of the weird priestess of the tree with a piece of money. The gift is small, for the Jew will sell you any dreams you like for a trifling coin. Probably they traded on the dream or interpretations of Joseph and Daniel, making the Romans believe that the God of the Prophets endowed His people with supernatural insight into the future.

It is not known whether Josephus remained in Rome when a new dynasty sat on the throne. We are assured by his own grateful words that he was treated with respectful kindness by Domitian, as he had been by Vespasian and Titus. He may, like Bernice, have ended his days in his own land, on his ample estate; he may have felt it was the right thing to do, as the absence of Judea's wisest and wealthiest sons could but complete the work of ruin; and Josephus loved his country, although he was not willing to lose his life in the struggle for national independence, which he had done his utmost to prevent, and which he knew to be utterly hopeless. With him the instinct of self-preservation seems to have been strong; he was not a Maccabee or a martyr. He saved his own life, and it was worth saving, for it was not a useless one. His literary work, which cost him years of hard labour, is still valuable, and his personal influence worked for good with both Jews and Romans, between whom he stood as a mediator, privileged to speak with the Emperors, who condescended to treat him as a friend. By means of the dates found in his works it has been ascertained that he was living and in full possession of his intellectual faculties in the year of our Lord 102. He was then in his sixty-fourth year; but even tradition does not attempt to tell us where he was, and beyond that we lose all trace of his existence. If Josephus were living when the "*Histories*" of Tacitus came out, he must have felt indignant and deeply grieved by the manner in which that historian wrote of the Jews. While there were thousands of native Jews and proselytes at Rome, instructed in the history given in the books of Moses, when all the sacred records of the Jews were within his reach, when he could read the works of Philo and Josephus, Tacitus accepted the legends of Greek mythologists and writers of fabulous tales, and drew his information from the hostile Egyptians who came to the Roman camp, and probably from two pretended sages of Alexandria, Manetho and Chæremon, mentioned by Josephus as impostors, who circulated falsehoods about the origin of the Jews. But students of every generation who have read the works of Tacitus must be at a loss to understand what could have induced him to sully his reputation by passages like the following:—

"Before relating the final destruction of this famous city, it will be well to explain its origin. The Judæi, it is reported, fleeing from the island of Crete, alighted on the farthest corner of Libya, at the period when Saturn was driven from his realm by Jupiter. This fact is established from their name: Ida is a famous mountain it Crete, and its people, the Idæi, became denominated with a barbaric extension of the sound Judiæ. Some relate that in the reign of Isis a multitude of people overflowing the limits of Egypt, cast themselves on the neighbouring countries under chiefs named Hierosolymus and Judas. Others again assert that the Jews were a swarm of Ethiopians driven by internal animosities to flee their country in the days of Cepheus. Again it is related that certain wanderers from Assyria in quest of lands occupied a part of Egypt, and quickly possessed themselves of Hebrew towns and territories, and the regions bordering upon Syria. Finally, another tradition assigns them a nobler origin, declaring that their city, Hierosolyma, was built and named by the Solymi the (Lycian) people celebrated by Homer."

Tacitus evidently wished to give the idea that the Jews were properly no nation at all, and consequently entitled to none of the consideration due to the kingdoms of the earth. It was only by establishing their descent from an Homeric people, as Tacitus suggests, that they could claim any right to the protection of international law.

"Most writers agree," he continues, "that a loathsome skin disorder once prevailing in Egypt, King Bocchoris was commanded by the oracle of Hammon to purge his realm of this brood of people, and dismiss them to other lands, as hateful to the gods. Thus brought together and abandoned in the desert, when the rest were overwhelmed with their distress, Moses, one of the exiles, exhorted them to expect no help from gods or men, but to trust in him as a divine leader. . . . They consented, and commenced their journey at random, with no idea whither they were going, or with what object. Nothing so distressed them as the want of water. And now they were reduced to the last extremity, and flung themselves in despair upon the ground, when a herd of wild asses was seen making their way from feeding on a hill covered with wood. Moses followed, expecting them to lead to some grassy spot, and discovered abundant springs under their guidance. Thus refreshed, the fugitives completed a journey of six days, and on the seventh day took possession of lands, driving out their owners, where they founded their city and consecrated their Temple. To make himself a nation for the time to come, Moses appointed them new rites, opposed to those of all mankind besides. Among them everything elsewhere sacred is held profane; all things are lawful which to us are forbidden. . . . Profane, they say, are those who fashion a figure of the Deity with perishable materials, after a human likeness. . . . Accordingly they suffer no such images in their cities, or even in their temples. They concede no such flattery to kings, no such compliments to Cæsars. But because their priests played on pipes and timbrels, and wore ivy garlands, and a golden vine was found in the Temple, some have thought that Father Bacchus, the conqueror of the East, was worshipped by them, though their usage bore little resemblance to his: inasmuch as Bacchus instituted brilliant and joyous rites, but the ceremonial of the Jews is pitiful and sordid." *

"It may be feared," observes Dean Merivale, "that Tacitus was incapable of understanding the burning zeal and solemn enthusiasm which marked the most soul-stirring struggle of all ancient history. . . . . Tacitus commences his review of Roman affairs with the period which succeeds the revolution, after its first and immediate fruits had been reaped, and the benefits, undeniable as they were, which it in the first instance produced, had lost some of their original brightness in his countrymen's memory. The Cæsarean usurpation had run a course of sixty years—years of unexampled prosperity, as Tacitus must himself have acknowledged had he set them fairly before his eyes—when he takes up the thread of events, and devotes the labour of his life to blazoning the disasters which have never ceased (as he pretends) to flow from it. He confines himself to the decline and

---

* Tac. Hist. v. 5: Judæorum mos absurdus sordidusque. Translated by Dean Merivale. (See "Hist. of the Romans under the Empire," vol. vi., page 554, etc.)

fall of the system which had now indeed passed its brief and fallacious prime. He traces the failing fortunes of the republic from the defeat of Varus and the gloom diffused over the city in the last days of Augustus, and closes his gloomy review with the fall of the last of the despots, the mean, the cruel, the jealous Domitian. Thus he embraces precisely the whole period by which the crimes of the Cæsars were chastised: nor will he mar the completeness of this picture by introducing into it the figures of those regenerators of the Empire, whom he himself lived afterwards to see, the records of whose virtue and fortune he reserves for the solace of his old age. . . . We may believe that the author of the *Annals* and the *Histories* regarded the two as a single entire work, and it is possible that he may have contemplated them himself under one title. The unity of their common design, as a lasting record of Cæsarean revolution, traced to its distant consequences, would have been marred by a glowing conclusion on the fame and prosperity of Trajan, nor do we know that Tacitus ever accomplished the labour of love which he anticipated as his crowning work. Perhaps, after all, he felt that the senatorial government of his patron rested on no solid foundations, and shrank at the last moment from glorifying the merits of a constitution which depended on the moderation of its chief alone.*

* This review of the works of Tacitus is abridged from " The History of the Romans under the Empire," by Dean Merivale. (See vol. vi., page 560 ; vol. vii., pages 292, 293.)

FINAL DISPERSION UNDER PATRIARCHAL RULE.

> "Reft of thy sons, amid thy foes forlorn,
> Mourn, widow'd queen, forgotten Zion, mourn.
> Is this thy place and city, this thy throne,
> Where the wild desert rears its craggy stone,
> Where suns unblest their angry lustre fling,
> And wayworn pilgrims seek the scanty spring?
> Where now thy pomp, which kings with envy view'd?
> Where now thy might, which all those kings subdued?"
>
> *"Palestine."* *By Bishop Heber.*

IX.

FINAL DISPERSION UNDER PATRIARCHAL RULE.

AFTER the Temple of Jerusalem had been destroyed, there yet remained on earth one which was modelled after the pattern of that grand national sanctuary, and to which the heart of the Hebrew naturally turned under its feeling of religious destitution. The Temple at Heliopolis in Egypt had been erected by the chief priest Onias, with the sanction of the Ptolemies, during the persecution carried on by Antiochus Epiphanes, king of Syria, against the Jews. Onias, with a few companions, sought refuge in Egypt, and Ptolemy gave him a tract of ground in the prefecture of Heliopolis, on which he built a small town on the model of Jerusalem, with a temple to correspond. The king of Egypt moreover granted an extensive district as a source of revenue to support this Jewish temple and its priests, that there might be a plentiful supply of necessaries for the service of God.

Dispossessed of their ancestral estates, multitudes of the Jews, accepting the doom of national dispersion, had chosen to migrate to those localities within and beyond the Empire, where Jewish colonies already existed. Large numbers transported themselves to Cyprus, Mesopotamia, and Egypt. Among the emigrants were many zealots, who, pretending as usual to a divine mission, inflamed the minds of their countrymen, brought together seditious persons from all accessible places, and roused fanaticism to the pitch of rebellion. They fortified their little town and temple; but the gates were opened at the first summons, and the Roman government, with singular forbearance, only expelled the Jews from the spot, forbidding them to meet there for worship; and every inhabitant was required to make an acknowledgment of submission to the Roman Emperor. On this occasion, such was their firmness, and such their desperation or strength of purpose, whichever we may call it, that it could but excite universal astonishment. Under every bodily torture and suffering devised for this one object, to make them acknowledge Cæsar as their lord, not one complied, nor was shaken for a moment, but submitted to the rack or the flames, as if with bodies insensible, and with souls in them that almost rejoiced in suffering, maintained their resolution. But what most struck the spectators was the courage of the children, not one of whom could be persuaded or forced to call Cæsar lord.*

This inquisition was simply political. Both Jews and Christians were required to express in a prescribed form of words their submission to the Emperor; it was like taking an oath of allegiance. They were called on to do this wherever their numbers made them objects of suspicion or of fear. The Roman government always dreaded political combinations, and by this inquisition and this sacrifice of human life they thought to stamp out insurrection. Yet the religion of the indomitable race was not proscribed; and though the gates of the Temple at Heliopolis, which had been garrisoned as a fortress, were closed, the Jews were

* Josephus.

allowed to worship in their synagogues. This is the last incident of the war, the after-clap of the subsided storm.*

The Jews now quietly dispersed themselves: many of them went to Alexandria, where a Jewish colony had existed ever since the days of Alexander the Great; others went to join their brethren who had settled at Babylon. The nation thus divided into two distinct bodies, the Eastern and the Western Jews; the former inhabited Babylonia, Chaldea, Assyria and Persia, and were governed by a ruler chosen by themselves whom they called the Prince of the Captivity; the latter, who dwelt in Egypt, Palestine, and the European portions of the Roman Empire, were presided over by one who bore the title of Patriarch.

Domitian had died childless, so the race of the Flavii had reigned during only two generations.

The appointment of Nerva to the imperial dignity forms a marked epoch in Roman history. Unlike his predecessors, he was neither a warrior, nor had his family been ennobled by military renown. He was simply a distinguished senator, advanced in years, and the first of a line of Emperors appointed solely by the Senate, but he was liberal enough to abhor every kind of Persecution.

The excellent Nerva had great consideration for the Jews; he relieved them from some of their disabilities and taxes, and even permitted them to rebuild the city of Tiberias as the residence of their Patriarch.

During the great war Tiberias had opened its gates to Vespasian, and its inhabitants had been spared. It stands on the shore of the Sea of Galilee, so often trodden by the Saviour's feet, so frequently mentioned

* Merivale.

in the Gospels. Indeed, in a peculiarly marked way, which we cannot clearly understand, that beautiful district was distinguished. It was watered by the Jordan, overlooked by Mount Tabor—a mountain to which tradition points as that of the Transfiguration, on which the Law, the Prophets, and the Gospel were mysteriously represented. And there Christ more than once appeared after His resurrection.*

Tiberias became the chief seat of Judaism, the centre to which the Hebrews in every part of the world looked for direction and support, as the power of the Patriarch who ruled the Western Jews was superior even to those of the Prince of the Captivity in Babylon, the chief seat of the East. The highest Jewish school was established at Tiberius, which regulated instruction in all places where the Jews resided in any considerable numbers. There, the doctors of the Law interpreted the national Scriptures, and overlaid them with traditions: first with the Commentary of Mishna, and later with that of Gemara; and thus the simple text came to be but imperfectly known by the people, who were led to think more of the commentaries; as in our Saviour's time passages of Scripture were obscured rather than explained by teachers whom He rebuked, exposing the rottenness of all such systems of edification. As time went on, the Jewish mind became more and more blinded by Rabbinism, which has been justly called Jewish popery.

The office of patriarch rose to importance, compassing even a kind of political power, although it was of an exclusively religious character, including no positive temporal authority over the scattered Jewish communities. The Patriarch presided over an assembly

---

* St. Matthew xxviii. 7, 16; St. John xxi. 1.

which bore the name of the Sanhedrim, but we have no evidence that that body had continued its sittings throughout all the troubles of Judea; it seems therefore likely that it was re-constituted at Tiberias. The Jews in Palestine founded schools for expounding the Law, and for preserving scraps of literature which had not fallen into the hands of the enemy, nor been destroyed by fire or other casualties of war and anarchy. These records, many of which were recovered in an injured, imperfect state, were collected together and compiled by the doctors of the Law, who thus ultimately produced the celebrated Talmud of Jerusalem; while similar academies among the eastern Jews produced the Talmud of Babylon.

The reign of the amiable, moderate Nerva was a happy time for the Jews, and we may suppose that it was especially so to those in Rome, on whom the light of his truly venerable countenance fell. It is thought that at this time St. John was set at liberty, and returned to Ephesus, where he lived in peace to the end of his long life. What a special blessing must that dear pastor's presence have been to the church at Ephesus—a little band of Christian people remarkable for their persevering labour and patience and hatred of evil principles, but who had left their first love. By the well-known voice of an exile come back to his home, they were warmly greeted, and then exhorted to turn their hearts back to seek the Lord, and to do their first works, and were subdued and ruled, not by energetic power, nor by strength of mind, for St. John was old and infirm, but by his unfailing love and gentle, steadfast endurance. This Apostle, the last called away of the twelve, attained his hundredth year. He survived the Emperor Nerva, who died rather suddenly, after a reign of little more than sixteen months. Though he reigned so short a time, not one of the Emperors is more vividly characterized in the effigies which remain of him in busts and medals. Among the treasures of antiquity preserved in modern Rome, none surpasses in form and dignity the sitting statue of this Emperor, which attracts all ages in the Rotunda of the Vatican; embodying the highest ideal of the Roman magnate, the finished warrior, statesman, and gentleman. The antiquity of this remarkable statue is acknowledged.*

The death of Nerva left Trajan sole emperor. He had previously been adopted as a son by Nerva, and associated in the government. The defiant attitude of the Prætorian Guards, who demanded the blood of all who had conspired against Domitian, had made the old Emperor feel the need of a colleague.

Trajan was the son of a gallant officer who had taken part in the wars against the Jews and the Parthians. This Emperor in his youthful days had been trained in the camp by his father's side, and had gained the love and confidence of the legions among which he had helped to wage the border warfare of the Empire. Thus he had risen in the army, and at the same time had shown remarkable talent for administration, as well as for war, which led to his holding not only military, but also civil appointments. He was periodically recalled from the camp to become a prætor or a consul.

By the adoption of such a colleague, Nerva silenced all discontent; even the Prætorian Guards were satisfied, and the few remaining months of Nerva's reign were passed in tranquillity. His death was sincerely lamented; for by his character and conduct, not only during the short time he had sat on the throne, but throughout his

* Merivale.

life, he had gained esteem and affection. So perfect was the public peace at the moment of his decease, that Trajan did not find it necessary to hasten to Rome in order to take up the reins. They had devised a system of government which was working well and quietly. He had won important victories on the Rhine, and was engaged in securing the borderland by the erection of a line of fortifications. This work completed, he commenced in the Black Forest a rampart which was to extend from the Rhine to the Danube. Thus a year elapsed between the death of Nerva and Trajan's triumphal entry into Rome. His demeanour on the occasion, and also that of his wife, was warmly applauded. The Emperor received the greetings of the senators as graciously as he had accepted them when he was going forth to war as a fellow-subject: among them he was distinguished only by the height of his stature and the dignity of his bearing. Plotina, as she was about to ascend the stairs of the palace, seeing the eyes of the multitude fixed on herself, looked round on the people, and spoke to them pleasantly. At that moment the uncertainty of the tenure by which everything in this life is held, was the uppermost thought; it impelled her to aspire to equanimity of mind, and she promised that should fate require her to do so, she would leave the palace as calmly as she was entering it. Trajan voluntarily renewed the oath he had previously made in writing, that he never would harm the person of a senator, and he faithfully observed it. He was very severe on the dilators, gangs of spies, or secret informers, which had greatly increased in numbers and flourished in Domitian's time, as that Emperor did not hold himself above accepting such vile service. This augmented class had grown utterly corrupt, and had worked a great deal of malicious mischief in its own evil way; dilators were very much feared and detested by the people. Nerva had brought some of them to justice; but, being a merciful man, he shrank from the responsibility of punishing them according to the cruel customs of his day, and consequently many had hitherto been allowed to escape. Relations and friends of persons who had been put to death, and others who had themselves suffered under false accusations, through the fabrications or misrepresentations of these dilators, were clamouring for revenge, and among them were senators and patricians, who openly blamed the too lenient Nerva. Trajan had no scruples; he immediately set on foot a strict investigation, and showed no pity to those who were tried and found guilty. Pliny describes an extraordinary scene in the circus, when these condemned malefactors, exhibited in chains, and barbarously insulted, were exposed to the scorn of the people infuriated against them. As well as the law could draw the line, they were divided into two sections, condemned to either banishment or death. Great was the general satisfaction given by the fatal performances on the arena of the amphitheatre, when the wretches, in horrible earnest, ended their untruthful lives in the presence of the densest crowds of spectators.

In no other city of the world was the population made up of such very various elements. The inhabitants, as a mass, comprised people of all races. Three of these —the North African, including Alexandrians, and the Capadocians, and the Jews—had each a distinct quarter in Rome. All the people, having more or less suffered through these tale-bearers and false witnesses, were in a state of violent excitement. The Hebrew in the late season of dire adversity had felt that his voice would touch the heart of no earthly king; he had cried, in the words of the Psalmist, "Surely Thou wilt slay the wicked, O God!" "Let his way be dark and slippery;" "Let his net that he hath hid catch himself; into that very destruction let him fall."

Standing, with light on one side, and darkness on the other, the sons of Abraham saw the shadow of Jehovah's Hand pass by, and it comforted them. Only those Christians, really separated from the multitude by the circumcision of the heart, felt that they must not rejoice over enemies who were meeting the same terrible fate which they had brought upon others.

These gangs of dilators lived by lying, as robbers live by stealing. The best of them had a sense of honour somewhat like that which exists among thieves; they outraged truth for the sake of furthering some object they had in view. Among them were men who had, not a dead, but a perverted conscience; who thought their object right and important, and that the end justified every means by which it might be attained. Other dilators, whose ideas never ascended above the lowest level of thought, simply maintained with perfect self-complacency the virtue of fidelity to those who paid them well. During times when secret conspiracies were frequently formed, this degraded class was active under the guidance of conspirators, or of those who suspected and were tracking them. Trajan did his utmost to discover both those employed in the nefarious work, and their employers; for he justly considered the latter as the more culpable, when by means of false accusations the life or the reputation of the innocent had been sacrificed.

This Emperor's otherwise fine character was debased by cruelty; public executions and popular entertainments, *games* they were called, were conducted by him with atrocious barbarity, and occasionally blended together on the arena of a provincial theatre, or on that of the Roman Coliseum.*

Neither the stern duties of administering justice, nor the flattery of the senate, nor the homage of the people, was as much in accordance with Trajan's taste as were the activity and ambition of the military career. In the fourth year of his reign he gladly quitted Rome to make war on the Dacians, and he conquered them, and added the province that was last annexed to the Roman Empire. Slight as are the political traces left of the great Dacian wars, they are eminently distinguished by their sculptured monument still standing upright in the forum which was constructed under Trajan's direction, and which bears his name. A narrow isthmus separated the city from the Campus Martius, and this neck of higher ground, covered perhaps with the miserable cabins of the poor, was surmounted by the remains of the Servian wall that ran along its summit.

Step by step the earlier emperors had approached to the foot of this obstruction, and Nerva had completed a small forum begun by his predecessor, to which he had given his own name. Trajan undertook to complete the whole of the bold design, and his architect triumphed over all obstacles, sweeping away every building on the site, and levelling a large area, on which he built halls and chambers connected by galleries supported by rows of strong and beautiful columns. The new forum had

---

* According to Dion Cassius, the games after Trajan's victory over the Dacians lasted one hundred and twenty-three *days*. Eleven thousand animals, wild and domestic, were killed in them, and ten thousand men were compelled to fight with beasts : we may conclude that most of them were killed. See "Judaism in Rome," page 292, *note.*

rooms for public use and recreation, and two libraries, one for Greek, the other for Roman volumes, and it was bounded on the west by a fine basilica. This forum, with all its adjuncts, occupied many years in building. The area was adorned with numerous statues. The balustrades and cornices of the whole mass of buildings flamed with gilded images of arms and horses. Here stood the great equestrian statue of the Emperor, and here was the triumphal arch decreed him by the Senate, adorned with sculptures, which two centuries later were transferred by Constantine to his own. The one object in Trajan's forum, to which the eye was principally directed, was the column which rose majestically in the centre to the height of 128 feet, sculptured from the base of the shaft to the summit with the story of the Dacian wars, shining in every volute and moulding, brilliant with gold and pigments, and crowned with the statue of the conqueror.

The most interesting feature of this graceful historic monument is the spiral band of figures which throughout encircles it. To the subjects of Trajan this record of his exploits in bold relief must have given a vivid and sufficient idea of the people, the places, and the actions indicated; even to us, after so many centuries, they furnish a correct type of the arms, the arts, and the costume both of the Romans and barbarians, which we should vainly seek for elsewhere.

Beyond the basilica in Trajan's forum, and within the limits of the Campus Martius, the architect who had raised the buildings in the forum, erected moreover a temple for the worship of Trajan himself; but this work belonged probably to the reign of Trajan's successor.*

* Abridged from Merivale's " History of the Romans under the Empire," vol. vii., pages 243—247.

The subsequent exploits of Trajan were compressed within a short space of time. He launched his victorious legions against the centre of the Parthian power, and broke it. No sooner had he crossed the Tigris, than all the tribes of the far East were fluttering with the fear of his descent upon them. Ctesiphon, the chief city of the Parthians, at once opened its gates; the king made good his escape into Media, but his daughter and his golden throne were captured. The restless ambition of the conqueror was not yet satisfied. Seeing a vessel on the Persian Gulf, laden for India, and about to sail, he exclaimed, "Were I still young, I would not stop till I too had reached the limits of the Macedonian conquest." He knew it not, but even when he spoke those words, Trajan's conquering power had reached its appointed bounds. Reports of insurrectionary movements in different parts of the Empire prevented further advance; he turned back towards Rome, and the homeward march was hindered, not only by difficulties of all sorts, by intense heat, and an extraordinary storm, but also by his own failing health.

It was at this crisis that the great rebellion of the Jews broke out; we may call it another Jewish war, which burst out at once in several quarters. It must have been long impending, and at last began like a movement sympathetic with the death spasms of Armenia and Parthia.*

Several collisions had lately occurred between Jews and Gentiles, or between Jews and the imperial forces, but the scanty records left us throw but little light on the causes of these insurrections. No doubt the prohibition of their national rite most violently excited the

* "History of the Romans under the Empire." By Dean Merivale.

Jews, and this happening at a time when other nations were at war with Rome, they thought it a favourable opportunity for rising simultaneously in Syria, Egypt, Cyrene, and Cyprus. Horrible barbarities were perpetrated on both sides; one indiscriminate massacre being avenged by another.

The reports of these outrages greatly troubled Trajan; he was moving on with the army, but was so ill as to be scarcely equal to the fatigue. His disease, the dropsy, made him very irritable, and he fancied he had been poisoned; but if so, it was by the air and climate, not by the hand of man. He sent Hadrian, his best general, to Cyprus, which was very unfortunate for the Jews, not only for those in the island, but for the whole race, as what Hadrian heard of the Jews, and what he saw of their cruelty, especially to the natives, whom they slaughtered more recklessly than they did the Roman residents, turned his mind so against the Hebrews, that he never got over the impression. After more bloodshed the rebellion in Cyprus was quelled, and all the Jews were banished—forbidden to set foot on the island on pain of death, and this sentence was executed on some who had been driven into the harbour by stress of weather. Most likely this was done by a civil or military officer on the spot, who had reason to hate the Jews, and power to act up to the letter of the law. The widespread rebellion was so well concerted, that it could not be quickly put down. Trajan is accused of having been extremely severe—he was a stern ruler, and now a dying man. He did not reach Rome, could proceed no farther than Selinus in Cilicia, where he expired early in the August of A.D. 117, having reigned not quite twenty years. Like the Great Alexander, he had been cut off in the far East, and had appointed no successor. Before that last bitter Jewish war was over, his ashes reposed in a golden urn at the foot of his column.

Hadrian was elected by both the Senate and the army to succeed Trajan. Platona liked him, and having no son, wished him to succeed; stories are related of her endeavours to aid in the cause, but these are not to be relied on as certainly authentic. He was distantly related to Trajan, the son of a cousin; he had at ten years old lost his father, who left him under the charge of Trajan and another guardian. The boy was sent to Athens for education, and there he not only acquired information on all the branches of learning then taught in the best schools, but also imbibed a taste for argument, and for the investigation of all sorts of subjects that came before him. He received the ordinary training in arms and feats of agility, and when old enough was appointed by his influential guardians to a civil office in Rome.

Hadrian's after-life was remarkably consistent with this bringing-up. He celebrated Trajan's triumph modestly, declining to be the chief recipient of homage. An image of the great conqueror was borne with all customary honours to the temple of Jupiter Capitolinus, crowned with a golden laurel crown, which Hadrian gave to the nation. With the spoils of war he was liberal, and devoted a large sum of money to establishing an institution begun by his predecessor for the maintenance of orphans. We can understand his interest in this good work, for he had been left an orphan boy, and had been kindly and well provided for by Trajan. Then he headed his forces, and took the field against a wild horde of Sarmatian horsemen who were bearing down upon Dacia. After his first successes against those barbarians, he thought it wise to abandon that province, which was not worth the men and money which, if it were retained, must be devoted to it. He therefore entirely withdrew the legions, and broke down the bridge that Trajan had built over the Danube. The troops set free were required in the East, to complete the suppression of the Jewish disturbances. The flames of insurrection which had broken out in so many quarters had been concentrated, and burnt more fiercely than ever in the ancient centre of Jewish nationality.

The contest had, on the side of the Jews, taken the character of a fanatical war. All the Hebrews remaining in Palestine, reinforced by the fugitives who had been elsewhere subdued, and who had fled from scenes of persecution, constituted a formidable number; though again and again their faith had been mocked, their credulity imposed upon, yet still they were ready to follow any leader who proclaimed himself the promised Deliverer. Martius Turbo, who was appointed to the chief command of the Roman army in Palestine, was perfectly amazed at the fanaticism of the Jews. The allegorical autobiography of Rabbi Akiba is a most curious legend. The story ends well; for at last, after innumerable difficulties hinted at in a mystic style, he returned to his wife—his bride, who is no other than Jerusalem itself, and she received him joyfully, and, covered as she was with rags, an outcast and a beggar, he presented her to his astonished followers, for he had brought with him twice twelve thousand disciples. The poetical narrative is somewhat in the style of "The Song of Solomon." Its meaning was dark to the Romans, and is so to us, except as we know the Jews understood it to mean that Akiba was a champion who was to lead them on to glory. In

sober truth, he was one of the most learned men of the age, and had held a high position among the doctors of the Law and other learned men at Tiberias. He was, or pretended to be, one hundred and twenty years old; so he, like Samuel, nominated a new David to be the head of God's people. That was the light in which he put himself. He girded Barchochebas with the sword, and placed the staff of command in his hand.*
As long as he was successful, vast numbers trusted in him; but the fortune of war turned. At the storming of Bethar, Barchochebas was killed on the field, and Akiba was taken prisoner, and most cruelly put to death. Barchochebas had struggled with the frenzy of insanity and the obstinacy of despair. Every excess of cruelty was committed on both sides; for the Roman losses had been so uncommonly great as to make them furious with a feverish thirst for vengeance. "It is well, perhaps," says Merivale, "that the details of this mortal spasm are almost wholly lost to us." The name Barchochebas signifies "son of a star," and was assumed with reference to the prophecy of Balaam. The disappointed Jews, when his defeat and death had proved him to be a deceiver, spoke of him not as Barchochebas, but as Bar Cozibah, "the son of a lie." This Jewish war, which was in fact a series of revolts, with mere lulls between the storms, began before the death of Trajan, and lasted sixteen years. Its final conclusion is a turning-point of history as important as that of A.D. 71. Beyond A.D. 133, the Jews were never again what they had been; they did not rally as they had done from the effects of the blow struck by Titus. Dion Cassius gives the number of Jews slain in battle as 580,000, and adds that the multitudes that perished

* Barchochebas, also called Barcochab.

by famine and pestilence exceed all calculation. Allowing for exaggeration, we must believe that hundreds of thousands perished in these latest combats, and that each of the revolts was followed by wholesale captivity and general banishment. Almost all Judæa's people were sent away as slaves or exiles, and but very few of the most prudent or fortunate, who escaped death and capture, cared to stay; they left the shores of their native country as emigrants, seeking refuge in some foreign country. Whole districts were so depopulated, that the land went out of cultivation, and beasts of prey made their dens in ruined towns and villages. Not until this epoch was the dispersion final and complete. Not until now was Jerusalem occupied by a Roman colony, which received the name of Ælia Capitolina, and the supreme god of pagan mythology was installed on the summits of Moriah and Zion. The fane of Jupiter was erected on the site of the Holy Temple, and a shrine of Venus flaunted on the spot to which tradition points as that on which our Lord's crucifixion took place. But Hadrian had no intention of insulting the disciples of Jesus, and this desecration was probably accidental, if the tradition be true, which is questionable. A Jewish legend relates that the figure of a swine was sculptured over a city gate in mockery of the Jews. With equal scorn they retorted that the effigy of the unclean animal, which represents to their minds every low and bestial appetite, was a fitting emblem of the colony and its founders.[*] In this New Jerusalem no Jew desired, or would have been permitted, to reside.

When the first centenary of the crucifixion came round,

[*] "Romans under the Empire." By Dean Merivale. Vol. vii., pages 397—400.

it found Judea and Jerusalem perishing in this protracted agony—this second and final destruction; but centuries rolled on before the direct and indirect effects of this last rising of the Jews had ceased to agitate world-wide spheres of thought and action, in which they had been felt as much as in the land and in the city. The generation which witnessed this crisis, witnessed also the last days of stoicism. Some persons already in its ranks retained their allegiance, but no one born during or after the Jewish war under Hadrian is known to history as a stoic. Many stoics embraced Christianity: at the same time the final separation of the Christians from the Jews took place.*

All things had conspired to make the Christians wish to be no longer confounded with the Jews in the Roman mind. The Emperor Hadrian showed some leaning towards Christianity, or at least a wish to judge of it himself; for he allowed Christians, as well as other sectarians, to expound their doctrines and to defend their customs in his presence. There is not the least evidence that he was in any degree converted, but he listened, and so far respected and favoured the Christians as to give them a formal acknowledgment of his recognition of their perfect independence of the Jews. This was made so clear by imperial decree, that henceforth the Christians could not as heretofore stand in the same category with the Jews. A proclamation or decree aimed against the one body would no longer affect the other, and the man who could prove himself to be a Christian was no longer in the eye of Roman law a Jew, even if he were by birth a son of Abraham. This final cutting of the cord was not done painlessly, without exciting mutual rancour. Henceforward they were

* "Judaism in Rome."

not to be companions in adversity; and there is reason to fear that too often the baser members of each community cherished malignant thoughts, which made them active, though generally secret enemies, and thus the gulf between them widened and deepened. The earnest Christian cannot altogether forget his Lord's injunction, "Love your enemies," but this can hardly be expected from even a guileless Israelite, who has not yet seen Jesus, although he is well known and loved by his Messiah, the Son of God, the King of Israel.*

That Jewish war in the days of Trajan and Hadrian stamped itself in unmistakable characters on the mental and social history of the second century, as one of the most noteworthy contests in the world's history. After its termination the influence of the Jews in Europe was at an end. Thenceforward they were an *isolated* people, unappreciated, too often calumniated or maltreated, whilst, no doubt, they suffered in character and culture from the position in which they were placed.†

Hadrian did not aspire to further conquests, did not glory in the extent of his dominions, but he had resolved to make himself personally acquainted with all his provinces.

He set out on his travels, and from that period the only history of Hadrian and his times is the confused and imperfect record of his journeys through every province of his empire, broken only by occasional sojourns at his provincial capitals, till he settled finally for his last few years in Rome.

It was his object, partly from policy, and partly from a love of acquiring positive information by means of his own observation, to inspect every corner of his dominions, to examine into its state and resources, and

* St. John i. 45—49.   † "Judaism in Rome," page 15.

to make himself acquainted with its wants and capabilities. Curious also about the character of men, he studied on the spot the temper, abilities, views, and feelings of the multitude of officials with whom he had ordinarily to correspond at a distance. There is something sublime in the magnitude of the task he imposed on himself, and in which he persevered.*

Hadrian, as we have seen, had enquired into the doctrines of the Christians closely enough to excite a hope in their minds that he might become a convert. He had also studied the Old Testament and the laws and customs of the Jews; and these excited his curiosity. He could have obtained but a very imperfect knowledge of the Jewish Scriptures and their law, his mind being occupied with so many subjects, though it was more than commonly capacious, and his memory was excellent.

We are now endeavouring to form a just idea of the treatment which the Jews were receiving in Rome. In the absence of positive information we surely cannot do better than to look to the ruling power at Rome. Hadrian's commanding mind, which cared more for grasping correct knowledge of the world, than for grasping territory, influenced the state of things in the metropolis of his empire, even when he was far away. He was deeply prejudiced against the Jews as a race; what he had seen and heard in Cyprus had rendered this prejudice indelible. He thought them a rebellious people, who had been abandoned by their own God, as their own sacred writings had threatened would be the result of disobedience. But his knowledge of character can scarcely have failed to convince him that the stubbornness of the Jew, which made it impossible to

---

* "History of the Romans under the Empire." By Charles Merivale, D.D. Vol. vii., page 427.

subjugate his spirit, might prove a valuable quality in a well-disciplined and liberally cultivated mind. We do not hear that he abridged such privileges as they had been enjoying since Nerva relieved them from some of the disabilities and imposts which had heavily oppressed them. Hadrian was not likely to emancipate Jewish slaves, or in any way to favour the turbulent lower classes, whose increase in number he could not desire, but rather their extermination. Yet, with the educated Jew, this emperor was capable of sympathizing, and such he may have upheld, while, as a people, the Jews were rapidly sinking into contempt and poverty. They still manifested an immense deal of party spirit: of the several parties holding different views of their condition, duties, and prospects, the Zealots and the Moderates were still the chief. Josephus had belonged to the latter. He had passed away, but those who were living in the capital as inoffensively as he had done were probably better off than they would have been in any other city of the Empire. That peaceful class had congregated in Rome in large numbers, partly for security's sake, taking refuge from their own fellow-countrymen, the Zealots and Sicarii, those dangerous political enthusiasts who would postpone every desperate scheme for national resuscitation, to get vengeance on their own brethren, the Moderates or Herodians. Consequently, the Moderates were a numerous body, which had taken root in the midst of Roman society, and formed a respectable, quietly conducted portion of the population, who strongly supported one another.

With the exception of an occasional return to Rome, and a short sojourn there, Hadrian lived the life of an imperial traveller, until the infirmities of declining years checked his energy, and his wanderings ceased. Already, at his command, noble structures had arisen in almost every quarter of Rome, the most magnificent of which was the Temple of Rome and Venus with its double cells placed fantastically back to back. It was raised upon an embankment on the high ground between the *Forum Romanum* and the Amphitheatre, immediately overlooking the colossal edifice. Hadrian, having again taken up his residence in his capital, occupied himself very much with building, first a university, to which he gave the name of Athenæum, in memory of the city, always dear to him, in which he had received his own education; and having finished that, he built his own tomb. The mausoleum of Augustus was full; there were in it no more vacant sepulchral chambers. Nero's remains had been removed from the Pincian by Vespasian; Nero was the last emperor buried there; since his interment it had been closed, and now another mausoleum appeared, almost confronting it, on the further bank of the Tiber.

Procopius describes the tomb of Hadrian as built of large blocks of Parian marble, closely fitted together without cement, or clamps to bind them; he says, "The four sides of the basement are equal, each about a stone's throw in length, and the height is greater than that of the walls of the city. On the summit are admirable statues of men and horses of the same material; and as this tomb formed a defence to the city, thrown out beyond the walls, it was joined to them, by the ancients, by two arms built out to it, so that it seemed to rise out of them like a lofty turret."* Few are the buildings which have passed through such strange vicissitudes as has the tomb of Hadrian, which we see as the Castle of St. Angelo. Its founder threw a bridge across the river,

---

* Translated by Story. See " Castle of St. Angelo," chap. i., page 6. Published by Chapman and Hall.

to make a suitable approach to this place of interment, which, according to Procopius, seems to have been from the first intended also to serve the purpose of a military defence, thrown out with that intention beyond the city walls, yet connected with them.

In the last years of his life, Hadrian often retired from the city to enjoy comparative seclusion and the lovely scenery around his villa at Tivoli, among the ruins of which have been found some of the most beautiful works of art now exhibited in Rome. Yet those last days were terribly trying; he was tormented by a painful disorder which caused excessive irritation, under which, from caprice and vexation, he even put innocent persons to death, though his adopted son and heir, the gentle Antoninus, remained with him, and did all he could to subdue these bursts of temper, to which the Emperor gave way under the wearisome pressure of maladies beyond the reach of medicine.

"On the whole," says Dean Merivale, "I am disposed to regard the reign of Hadrian as the best of the imperial series, notwithstanding the ebullitions of passion which clouded his closing career. His defects and vices are those of his time, and he was indeed altogether the fullest representative of his time, the complete and crowning product, as far as we can judge, of the crowning age of Roman civilization. . . . Hadrian reconciled with eminent success things hitherto found irreconcilable—a contented army and a peaceful frontier, an abundant treasure and a lavish expenditure, a free senate and a stable monarchy—and all this without the lustre of a great military reputation, the foil of an odious predecessor, or disgust at recent civil commotions."

Perhaps Hadrian would not have been quite the man he was, if he had never read the Old Testament

Scriptures, and listened to the arguments of chief Rabbis, and of eminent theologians of the Church, though he disappointed both Jews and Christians, as he turned neither to Judaism nor to Christianity; and so in his own unaided strength, or rather in his own mortal weakness, he met the king of terrors, passed through the last and greatest trial, the dissolution of the body, without sustaining faith and tranquilizing peace. The decay of nature under protracted disease may expose the soul to temptations as many and as great as those which beset the martyr. Hadrian's edict, forbidding circumcision, remained in force after his death. The Jews again took up arms, and the restoration of the national rite was the avowed object of the revolt. Antoninus Pius repealed the arbitrary law, and he then easily suppressed the insurrection. Antoninus, who was a humane man, showed clemency and favour to the Jews in other ways. Humanity had lately made decided progress among all classes, and under the rule of the first Antoninus procurators were especially directed to exercise moderation, to spare the needy, to indulge the unfortunate, to listen to every complaint against the tyranny of the powerful, and as far as possible to redress real grievances. Antoninus was fond of quoting Scipio's noble sentiment, "I prefer the life and preservation of one citizen to the death of a hundred enemies."

Although Antoninus had restored to the Jews the right to circumcise their own children, yet he strictly forbade them to make proselytes. This Emperor continued the improvements in Rome; he completed Hadrian's mausoleum, and erected a graceful column, though inferior in height to Trajan's Pillar. The attainment of power had wrought a marked change in almost all the earlier Cæsars, in some for the better, but generally for the worse. In Antoninus it made no change at all. Such as he had been, kind, modest, and dignified, as a senator, such he continued to be as emperor. He bore himself in all respects towards his inferiors as he had formerly wished his superiors to bear themselves towards him. Antoninus had a happy temperament, a cheerful, contented disposition; he was apparently the happiest man of whom heathen history makes mention, and, being both virtuous and happy, he may very likely have done more good than any other.*

It may be well here to mention a civil law, which, when instituted, was doubtless intended to work equally, yet, in process of time, its weight fell unfairly on the Jews. The law obliged all citizens to take upon themselves certain public offices. Those officers appointed to receive public moneys were responsible for the payment; consequently, the citizens tried by all evasions, to escape the unpopular office, and when they could not do so, they defended themselves against loss by forcing the money out of the poor inhabitants by every kind of tyranny. Persons desiring to be free from the heavy duties of the decurionate were permitted to appeal to the Emperor, giving their reasons for wishing to be held independent of the obligation. Thus room was left for injustice and favouritism. Antoninus Pius was a man superior to prejudice and unfair partiality; but Constantine the Great and some of the intervening emperors granted exemptions so easily to Romans, that the Jews were the more heavily burdened with public duty in consequence, and bitter jealousy was excited. This, however, proves that the right of the Jews to Roman citizenship was fully recognized. The Patri-

* "History of the Romans under the Empire." By Dean Merivale.

archs and Rabbins had the same exemption from all civil and military offices, as had the Christian clergy.

The good Antoninus died in A.D. 161, at an advanced age, giving to his guard, as his last watchword—"Equanimity!"

In that philosophic age a thoughtful Roman generally gave a dying word—a word expressing the idea which at that last moment he commended to his survivors.

Antoninus Pius and his successors are combined by historians as the Antonines, as Vespasian and his sons are called the Flavian Emperors.

The gallant Marcus Aurelius repulsed a simultaneous attack of all the races on the northern frontier, Germans, Scythians, and Sarmatians. The war was continued through the winter and summer; they fought on the frozen bosom of the Danube, and through heat more distressing than the cold. The victories gained are commemorated by a graceful column, banded like that of Trajan with spiral sculpture, by which the incidents are recorded. It was crowned with the statue of the Emperor, but that either fell or was removed, and replaced by a figure of St. Paul. This magnificent and interesting monument was erected by the senate; it now stands between the *Corso* and the Parliament House.

The name of Marcus Aurelius is still peculiarly loved and honoured in Rome, is given now and then by parents to a boy, for with many of the citizens he is the favourite emperor. Perhaps the feeling would ere this have died out had it not been kept alive by that grand old bronze statue on the Capitoline height, which stands in the centre of the square in front of the Capitol.

"Of all the Cæsars whose names are enshrined in the pages of history, or whose features are preserved in the repositories of art, one alone seems still to haunt the eternal city in the place and the posture most familiar to him in life. In the equestrian statue of Marcus Aurelius, which crowns the platform of the Campidoglio, imperial Rome lives again. .... We stand face to face with a representative of the Scipios and Cæsars, with a model of the heroes of Tacitus and Livy. Our other Romans are effigies of the closet and the museum, this alone is a man of the streets, the Forum and the Capitol.*

We pay the highest compliment to the memory of Marcus Aurelius, by comparing him with our King Alfred. Were they not both harassed by the invasions of barbarous plundering enemies? Were they not both warriors, legislators, philosophers, authors of works, on a variety of subjects? Were not both fond of learning, and wise enough to see that wisdom is the right application of knowledge, and that of all the different kinds of knowledge, that, after such knowledge of God as man can at present attain, self-knowledge is the most needful, which can only be gained by habitual self-examination? † In one respect their lot was different. "The fortunes of Alfred's country have increased in power and brightness, like the sun ascending to its meridian, whereas the decline of which Aurelius was the melancholy witness was irremediable and final, and his pale solitary star was the last apparent in the Roman firmament." ‡

Again, there is a difference, a contrast even more noteworthy; the one was a pagan, the other a Christian.

* Dean Merivale.
† A Diary kept by Marcus Aurelius shows that he was a sincerely conscientious man.
‡ "History of the Romans under the Empire," vol. vii., pages 597, 598.

From our present point of view, looking on Marcus Aurelius with reference to our subject, the weak and imperfect side of his character must be turned towards us, and all his fine qualities cast in the shade. His bigoted devotion to false religion must be repulsive to us, when we see in him a relentless enemy to both the Jews and the Christians. He was not naturally cruel, not a Nero or a Domitian, quite the reverse; but he was jealous of the honour of his pagan gods; he thought that refusing to bow down to them in their temples was insulting the majesty of the national divinities. The calamities which succeeded each other with awful rapidity—the horrible incidents of warfare with barbarians—famine—earthquakes, and great conflagrations—excited the superstition of the people; they thought their gods were angry, and required to the propitiated by more zealous and frequent worship. Superstitious observances which had become almost obsolete were revived, and new shrines were raised to every deity whose power might temper the air or the water, the sunshine or the moonshine, which was supposed to either breed pestilence, or to bear it away; and many were the sacrifices offered.

Marcus Aurelius, who looked on all his subjects with a more equal comprehensive regard than this predecessors had done, felt that all should unite in this adoration to deprecate the divine wrath; and he saw no excuse for the horror with which Jews and Christians shrank from joining formally in a service which the chief ruler of the state had prescribed, deeming it right and decorous. It vexed and astonished him; he felt, without being aware of it, that this obstinate refusal to conform to his religious edicts showed ill-feeling towards himself personally, and contempt of the imperial authority; and when this idea had taken possession of his mind, Aurelius made nonconformity a crime, which, if persisted in, would be punished with death, as were all kinds of flagrant disobedience to Roman law and the proclamations of the Imperitor.

Justin, always spoken of as Justin the Martyr, was beheaded in Rome; Polycarp was put to death in Smyrna, where the mysterious volcanic force was frightening the inhabitants into an excess of utterly unreasonable superstition; so they lighted such fire as they could command, to consume unbelievers who would not pray with them, and a number of Jews helped them to kindle it. Ignatius had suffered at Antioch, in Trajan's time. These, and others, as strong in the faith, were among the brave leaders of the Lord of hosts' most noble army of martyrs, which includes thousands whose names are unknown to us; surely among them must be those of many heroes of the Hebrew Church, who sacrificed to God their mortal lives; whose names are written in the "Lamb's book of life," "the Lamb slain from the foundation of the world."

"*Before the mountains were brought forth*,"—before Moriah, Zion, and Calvary stood round about the place that was being prepared for a Jerusalem on earth.

From the death of Marcus Aurelius to the accession of Septimus Severus, Rome was in a terribly unsettled state, governed by four emperors in succession, every one of whom was murdered. Pertinax, who reigned but three months, was the only one of the four worthy of esteem.

Didius Julianus, a wealthy senator, actually bought the imperial crown. He gave a sum equal to about £200 of our English money to every soldier of the powerful prætorian guard, which numbered about 12,000 men.

As to the Jews who were living in Rome during this period, we find in trustworthy history nothing about them worth mentioning, and in evil times we gladly remember that truthful saying, "The silence of history is praise." No doubt every Jew sympathized more or less with his brethren in the far East, with those in Palestine who dared not enter the ancient city of their fathers, or rather, that which under a heathen name occupied its site. Yet they had blessings to be thankful for; free liberty of exercising their own worship, with the single restraint that they should not attempt to proselyte others; their Patriarch was permitted to receive tribute, and to appoint to all offices which solely respected themselves; and they chose from among themselves a council for the regulation of their own religious affairs. When Hadrian abandoned the territory lately acquired by Trajan, the Jews in Mesopotamia fell under the power of the Persians, but were made over from the Patriarch of Tiberias to the Prince of the Captivity, and thus still had their own Hebrew chief ruler. Persia rapidly attained dominion, rose to be one of the leading Powers, when the old Roman Empire was splitting into east and west, and when Rome was sinking from her formerly pre-eminent position.

Owing to the larger measure of influence granted to the Jews by the Persian monarchs, the Prince of the Captivity greatly exceeded the Patriarch of Tiberias in splendour. He resided in a magnificent palace, had his cupbearers and other officers of state, and was complimented with valuable presents by all who approached him; and when on occasions of state he visited the

Shah, he was arrayed in cloth of gold, fifty guards marched before him, and all the chief men among the Jews, near enough to join his train, did homage to their own prince, and fell into the procession.*

Although the Patriarch of Tiberias maintained less state, yet he held more power than his brother who ruled in the East, and by their co-operation the nationality of the Hebrews was preserved; and this we should bear in mind when we read general statements describing the degradation of the Jews.

Dean Milman concisely puts before us the four important turning-points of Jewish history in these ages we are now contemplating, that occur between the commencement of the third and the middle of the eighth centuries, which opened views that could not fail to affect, not only the condition, but also in some degree the national character, of the Jew throughout the world.

1st. The restoration of the Magian religion in the East, under the great Persian monarchy, which arose on the ruins of the Parthian Empire.

2nd. The establishment of Christianity as the religion of the Roman Empire.

3rd. The invasion of the Barbarians who destroyed that Empire.

4th. The rise and progress of Mahometanism.

The Patriarchate maintained full power over all the Jews throughout the Roman Empire until about the middle of the third century, when the scattered people had become incorporated into two communities—one under the Papacy, the other under the Caliphate. Then the Patriarchate was shaken, but lasted in a declining state for nearly two centuries before it quite collapsed.

* "History of the Hebrew Nation." By Rev. T. W. Brooks.

In the time of the Antonines and their successors, and even in Constantine's day, it was still efficient. The Jewish people, high and low, rich and poor, concurred in their faithful attachment to their synagogue, and in strict subordination to their religious teachers. Every synagogue was visited in turn by the Patriarch's legate, every year a proclamation was made in every synagogue, by sound of the trumpet, commanding the payment of the tribute. Its final day of settlement was the last day of May. On the return of these legates to Tiberias, they informed the Patriarch of the state of every synagogue, assisted him as counsellors, and held a distinguished rank among the people.*

No doubt there was in Rome a large body of Jews who were satisfied with the basest means of making money, and who, when they were successful in so doing, grew abjectedly mean, covetous, and avaricious, till their Ghetto was avoided by prudent, respectable persons. The poorest among them had managed to hold the ground that Domitian had granted to them, for which they paid a kind of rent. The lovers of poetry had not been able to chase them and their filthy encampment away from Egeria. The vagabonds had contrived to hold a curious sort of freedom there.

But we may well ask, Can a conquered race, hampered and kept down by disabilities, and oppressed with imposts, be expected to stand more firmly upright, maintaining righteousness and dignity more nobly than does the race that conquered it? Let us see how it was with the Jews' fellow-citizens—the great mass of the Roman people.

Dean Merivale plainly tells us that the masses of the free population of Rome were in fact helpless. They

* "History of the Jews." By Dean Milman.

had become detached from the nobles, their natural leaders, by habits of mutual independence and distrust, which their princes had fostered in both classes. Steeped in slothfulness and poverty, they had neither intelligence nor resources. Mingled and confounded with the crowd of enfranchised slaves of foreign origin and ideas, they had lost the traditions of race which had formerly bound the Roman citizens together, and gave them confidence in one another. Disarmed, disorganized, and untrained, it was impossible for them to act against the moral weight of the wealthy and the noble, still more against the sword and the spear of the legionaries and the prætorians. They had now ceased altogether to be counted among the political forces of the Empire. We may dismiss them henceforth from our consideration.*

Moreover, all history convinces us of the importance of feminine influence, though it should be unobtrusive; and when we seek to know Roman women of those times, such as occupied high positions, whose deeds were recorded in their country's annals, we find that we cannot look into their conduct, we must turn away from the revolting ideas it suggests, repugnant to purity, modesty, and humanity. Modern historians cast a veil over it, which we dare not withdraw. Pagans though they were, those women are without excuse; the stories of Lucretia and Cornelia might have taught them better things.

The Antonines were unhappy in their wives. Faustina, the wife of Antoninus Pius, was not worthy of him, and to us it seems well that her death occurred in the early part of his reign. He gave her divine honours which had become a sort of last complimentary homage to the departed who had held high positions in this world.

* "History of the Romans under the Empire," vol. vii.

Antoninus did not take another wife, and he gave Anna Faustina, his only child, in marriage to his adopted son and heir, Marcus Aurelius. She proved as worthless as her mother. Aurelius acted wisely and kindly; he would not believe the evil reports, nor anything that was said to him against his wife; but when he went forth at the head of his army to meet the barbarians, he would not leave her behind. Unaccustomed to the hardships of camp life, which she had not desired to encounter, and which were severely felt, even by strong men during that campaign, Faustina fell sick and died on the way, when they were advancing from Carnuntum. She was numbered among the deities; and when her apotheosis was proclaimed, her widowed husband publicly thanked the gods for having given him "such a wife, so obedient, so affectionate, and so simple." It is possible that Anna Faustina may have been calumniated: a large proportion of the iniquity which made and left its marks on that age was magnified by slanderous tongues.

The graceful ruins of the Temple of Antoninus Pius and Faustina in the Roman Forum have been mixed up with the masonry of mediæval times. Its columns, monoliths of green-veined marble, are still standing, and supporting the inscribed architrave; and on the side walls are beautiful friezes, displaying in finely sculptured relief, griffins, candelabra, and other distinguishable ornamentation. The remains of this ancient temple are built into the walls of a church, and altogether blended with it. The original edifice, raised above the road from which it was approached by twenty-one steps, must have been magnificent.

IN THE AGE OF CONSTANTINE.

"As in an orchard of olives, upon every tree there are left three or four olives; or as when a vineyard is gathered, there are left some clusters for them that diligently seek through the vineyard: even so in those days there shall be three or four left by them that search their houses with the sword. And the earth shall be made waste, and the fields thereof shall wax old, and her ways and all her paths shall grow full of thorns, because no man shall travel therethrough. . . .

"Be of good comfort, O Israel, and be not heavy, thou house of Jacob.

"For the Highest hath you in remembrance, and the Mighty One hath not forgotten you in temptation.

"Now therefore set thine house in order, and reprove thy people; comfort such as be in trouble, and renounce corruption. Let go from thee mortal thoughts, cast away the burdens of man, put off now the weak nature, and set aside the thoughts that are most heavy unto thee, and so haste thee to flee from these times."—2 *Esdras* xvi. 29—32; xii. 46, 47; xiv. 13—16

X.

IN THE AGE OF CONSTANTINE.

THE portion of the Second Book of Esdras, from which these sentences are drawn, is generally supposed to have emanated from a Jewish mind in a season of extraordinary national distress. With regard to the time at which it was produced under this pressure of sorrow, those who have considered the subject are not of unanimous opinion, but it is clear that the author was sorely perplexed and deeply grieved by the wretched condition of the Jewish people when they were completely subjugated and trodden down by the Gentiles. Esdras appears to be an assumed name, and in the book, which was not all written by one person, we find a great many ideas, figures of speech, and expressions borrowed from the Pentateuch, the Psalms, the Prophets, and the Apocalypse. The first two chapters are supposed to have been prefixed later by a Christian. The significant name of Babylon is used to designate the great and proud metropolis, the reigning city. There were strong reasons for avoiding all mention of the real name of the existing mistress of the world, and with regard to everything directly or indirectly referring to Rome, plain words were highly dangerous; there was safety only in symbols and allegories, and language ingeniously enigmatical. The allegory in the eleventh chapter, of the eagle with twelve wings, means, as is explained in the following chapter, the same kingdom as that seen by Daniel in a vision, and twelve of its kings who reigned one after the other. The series might begin with Julius, the first Cæsar, or with Augustus, the first Imperitor.* If we begin the series with Julius, and include Galba, Otho, and Vitellius, it would expire with Domitian, at the close of the first century of the Christian era. If we omit them, it would expire with Hadrian. Frederick Huidekoper points out that there is a difference between eastern and western writers which deserves, but seems to have escaped, attention. Western authors count Galba, Otho, and Vitellius as belonging to the series. Some, at least, of the eastern ones omit them, perhaps because in their quarter of the world these three emperors were regarded rather as unsuccessful aspirants than as emperors. Eusebius and some other early writers place Vespasian as the successor of Nero. If the author of the chief part of the Second Book of Esdras were an Asiatic Jew, or wrote chiefly for Asiatics, the omission would be natural, and the sufferings of the Jews, of which we read in that book, seem consistent with their condition when the great war burst out at the end of Trajan's reign, and during that of Hadrian. Terrible instances of oppression and cruelty occurred in the reign of Domitian, but the whole nation was not then so utterly broken up and cast down. And at that time, according to Juvenal, Judaism at

---

* The length of the second reign seems to mark it as that of Augustus. Also there is a difference between Galba, Otho, and Vitellius. Galba may justly be said to have ruled during the few months that constitute what historians following Suetonius call his reign. He sat down on the throne, and wielded the sceptre. Otho and Vitellius wielded only the power of the sword.

Rome was swelling its ranks with converts.* Not until the latter part of his reign did Domitian become a persecutor.

The harrowing descriptions scattered through this wildly poetical, incoherent book of Esdras are brightened by gleams of faith, dartings forth of strong convictions that chastisements for sin work together with all things for good to those who love God; that the horrible eagle is doomed to perish; that the earth may rest; and that at last the happy time will come when the Most High will openly triumph over evil, and deliver all who have trusted in Him, out of every sorrow and trouble.

There can be no doubt that the work is Jewish, although it no longer exists in the language in which it was originally written, which was most likely Hellenistical Greek. Three translations, in Latin, Ethiopic, and Arabic, are extant. The retranslation in our English Apocrypha is from the Latin. The name of Jesus in chapter vii. 28 is an interpolation unsupported by the Arabic and Ethiopic.†

When Niger and Septimus Severus were contending for the imperial crown, the Samaritans took up arms for Niger, the Jews threw themselves into the party of Severus. That able general soon triumphed over all opposition, and severely punished the partizans of

---

* See "Judaism at Rome," pages 130, 131, 489, 490.

† The translations extant do not completely and entirely agree. The retranslation from the Latin is that which is printed in the Apocrypha of our English Bibles, though with the addition, from some different Latin text, of two chapters at the beginning and two at the end. On the other hand, a passage of some length has been either by accident or design dropped out of the Latin copies. See "Judaism at Rome," page 130, in which the author quotes from an appendix to the fourth volume of Whiston's "Primitive Christianity

his rival. The Samaritans then forfeited their privilege of Roman citizenship, and to the Jews it was confirmed, and they were set free from some of the restrictions to which they had been hitherto subjected. The new laws made by Septimus Severus were lenient to the Jews; they were permitted to have the guardianship of pagans —were allowed to undertake educational work—which opened to them a wide and most important field; and they were exempted from some burdens which had distressed them greatly, as being incompatible with their religious customs and national habits; but they were still forbidden to return to Palestine. The maintenance of that prohibition was not unreasonable, for the Jews in the East were restless; once more they endeavoured to throw off the yoke of Rome, and Judea was invaded by her own sons. The rebellion was quickly put down by Severus, and he treated even those who had risen up against him with moderation; he did not forget that many Jews had fought bravely under his banner, he was capable of seeing something noble in the obstinacy of the race, in its devotion to its own religion, and its love of independence, and he did not despise it in accordance with the popular cry of the degenerated Romans.

Under the protection of this emperor, the Jews residing in Rome lived as prosperously as their fellow-citizens; the tide of Rome's fortune had turned, but her people were perhaps not the less happy because the heaving ocean of their national life was not crested with glory and wealth as heretofore. Yet still they were victorious, and the Roman warriors, with their emperor at their head, were honoured by a triumph, and an arch was built as a lasting memorial of the military achievements of this reign.

As we stand near the Arch of Titus, we can look across the Roman Forum to that of Septimus Severus. Standing on that spot, one is glad to be reminded that God gave the Jews favour in the sight of the heathen, and "a little refreshing in their bondage." *

Knowing the Jews to be good soldiers, this emperor encouraged them to enter the army, by giving them a fair chance of attaining promotion and renown, with its stimulating rewards: Jews must have taken part in the conflicts depicted upon that arch. The relievi on the north side represent an attack on the city of Atris, in Arabia; the taking of Seleucia, on the canal between the Tigris and Euphrates; and the capture of Ctesiphon. Near the highest angle, at the spectator's right, is represented the siege of Babylon. A rudely designed building with a dome is intended for the famous Temple of Belus; and on the south side are represented the campaigns in Mesopotamia; but here the sculptures are so much damaged, that but little can be distinguished. We can discern, however, on the standards, the dragons adopted by the Romans after those successful wars of Septimus Severus. In the scene of the triumph on the frieze we distinguish, among the small figures in low relief, the seated Roma receiving homage from the subject Parthia, who kneels before her.† Thus on the two fronts were represented the campaigns and victories of the honoured Emperor. On the summit was placed the imperial effigy in a bronze chariot drawn by two or four horses.

The sculptures on this Septimian Arch, representing

---

* Ezra ix. 8, 9.
† Abridged from "Historic and Monumental Rome." By Charles Isidore Hemans. Williams and Norgate, 14 Henrietta Street, Covent Garden, London.

the Oriental victories gained in the years 195 to 198, betray an unaccountable and hopeless decline in art, when compared with the beautiful relievi of 125 years earlier date, on the similar monument erected in honour of Titus.*

Septimus Severus, when his strength was failing, went to Britain, explored in wild Caledonia, and died at York. Throughout his long reign the Jews were kindly treated, and his successors did not reverse his decrees in their favour. Down to the accession of Constantine the Great they suffered but little molestation, all the while they did not themselves disturb the public peace by some act of enmity against the Christians which occasionally caused an outrage or a tumult; but generally, when this occurred, the Romans were more disposed to take part with the Jews than with the Christians. The former were decidedly favoured by Elagabalus, the priest of the sun, who, being on his mother's side connected with the imperial family, ventured on asserting a claim to the throne, and was accepted by the Romans as their emperor.† Having come from the east, he naturally sympathized with his subjects of eastern origin, and moreover he had been nursed in his childhood by a Jewess, to whom he was warmly attached, and this attracted him towards her people. He went so far as to endeavour to incorporate the Jewish doctrines and customs into that strange medley of superstition which constituted his ideal religion; he even tried to impose the rite of circumcision upon his Roman subjects, and to forbid the use of pork, but of course this was resisted, and he was obliged to yield. On the other hand, Elagabalus was

* "Historical and Monumental Rome." By C. I. Hemans.
† Or Heliogabalus.

also disappointed by the Jews, as they refused to accept the Emperor's offer of an amalgamation, a compromise between their own religion and that of the Romans. Their refusal threatened to bring serious consequences on them, which were averted by the death of Elagabalus. Alexander Severus was a philosopher, who honoured both Abraham and Jesus Christ. In a private apartment, a sort of temple for contemplation, he set up their statues among a series of those of all the greatest teachers of mankind, and he looked upon them devoutly, as objects which helped to direct meditation. This amiable emperor was not gifted with conspicuous talents; his intellectual faculties were such as impelled him to choose discriminately, and to follow eminent leaders of thought, rather than to take the lead. He read with tranquil interest the writings of poets, orators, and philosophers, and he liked to make himself acquainted with the works of the good and wise wherever they might be found. He favoured the Christians; and their bishops, in their avowed capacity, habitually attended his court. A dispute arose between the Jews and the Christians over a piece of ground in the *Transtevere*, on which the Christians wished to build a church. The matter was referred to the Emperor's judgment, and he decided in favour of the Christians, who consequently were enabled to raise in the district westward of the Tiber, where the Jews were so numerically strong, the first edifice of important aspect and size that was reared in Rome for Christian public worship. The happy reign of Alexander Severus was brought to an abrupt conclusion by a mutiny in the army, headed by an officer named Maxentius. Alexander fell, and this man, by birth a Thracian peasant, was invested with the purple.

The degradation of Rome seemed complete when its chief was a mere illiterate barbarian, ignorant even of the Greek language, the common vehicle of all polished thought for so many centuries; and this usurper was followed by a succession of emperors, during whose brief and feeble reigns the Empire of the Cæsars sank into still deeper weakness and humiliation, until the accession of Diocletian, which marks a new epoch in the history of the Romans.*

Had Diocletian known how to make the most of the advantages of the position he attained, there might have been a revival, if but for a short time, of imperial rule. The Senate had lost the confidence of the nation; it had long been nothing more than the stronghold of old and vain tradition, and had ceased to control the march of affairs. Diocletian had no need to submit to its prejudices, or to buy its favour by ignoble concessions. The nobles of Rome had relinquished all interest in affairs which they could no longer aspire to conduct. All the power left was in the army, and that was not strong enough to maintain order throughout the Empire, which had so far outgrown its strength, and was harassed on all sides by bold invaders. Diocletian was highly esteemed by the legions; he exhibited great talent in the field; and he more justly appreciated the needs of the commonwealth than his predecessors for many generations had done.†

But the oriental character of his administration, his abandonment of Rome, his partition of the government into separate satrapies, with divided interests, each having its own jurisdiction, tended to hasten on rather than to retard the dissolution of the Empire. He maintained magnificent state at Nicomedia; it is doubtful

* Merivale. † Ibid.

whether he ever visited Rome until his triumph, in the twentieth year of his reign; and on that occasion he stayed only two months. He did not care to reside in the old capital, as it was his policy to lessen the authority of the Senate and the power of the ancient Roman families.

During this reign the tenth and last persecution of the Christians took place. They had become a numerous and influential body. Church building had progressed with wonderful rapidity. About eighty years after the erection of the first large church in the *Transtevere*, forty churches existed in Rome.

Some of these edifices displayed a degree of architectural splendour, and were furnished with chalices, lamps, and chandeliers of gold and silver. Christians were found in the highest ranks of society, and the highest offices of the army and the state. At this crisis of rapidly attained worldly prosperity, it pleased God to test their hearts, to throw His gold into the fire, to separate pure metal from dross. He chose to prove and to purify the best from its earthly alloy. The persecution seems to have arisen out of the grief and anger which Diocletian and his son-in-law felt on account of the conversion of their wives. The Empress Prisca joined the Christians at first secretly, afterwards in open opposition to Diocletian's will; and their daughter Valeria, the wife of Cæsar Galerius, who was associated in the government of the eastern part of the Empire, followed her mother's example. Galerius, who had always bitterly opposed Christianity, was terribly enraged, and he persuaded Diocletian to issue a series of edicts. The first decreed that all who refused to sacrifice to the gods of the Empire should lose their offices, rank, property, and civil privileges; that the Christian churches should be razed to the ground, their sacred books destroyed, and endowments confiscated. Other edicts followed; none of them expressly enacted the punishment of death, but it often resulted from torture, and in many cases it was inflicted, as on Alban, the first martyr of the British Church. Thousands were tortured, imprisoned, or sent to the mines.

The Jews were not at all involved in this persecution, excepting in so far as there seems reason to suppose that the basest individuals among them sided, not with the sufferers, but with the persecutors.

Diocletian set up two pillars in Spain, on which were inscriptions declaring that he had extended the Roman Empire from east to west, and abolished the superstition of Christ, and extended the worship of the gods. He died about ten years after he had erected those pillars, but he had lived long enough to hear of the edict which at last guaranteed to the Christians an established position in the commonwealth.

Diocletian's last years were miserable, all the more so, as he had ruled ably, with judgment and prudence. But persecuted by relentless enemies, chiefly those of his own family, or men whom he had raised, he was, as he advanced in years, so much harassed, that he abdicated the throne; and then the competition for the imperial power caused great confusion. Diocletian would fain have returned to the helm, but his relations and old associates repeatedly drove him from it. Constantinus, the ruler of the Gaulish provinces, was much beloved both in the army and by the people. On his death, which occurred at York, his son Constantine was proclaimed in that city, Emperor of Rome; but for six years he confined himself to the administration of the northern provinces, and carried out his father's conciliatory policy. He married Fausta, a daughter of the ex-Emperor. However politic this union may have been, it produced for Diocletian only an increase of trouble in his family; and at last the aged man put an end to his own life, by the desire of his daughter's husband, the reigning Emperor.

In A.D. 312, Constantine, having gained a series of brilliant victories over his rival, Maxentius, entered Rome, and was acknowledged chief ruler of the whole Empire. Maxentius, when attempting to escape, had been drowned in the Tiber; other adversaries made peace, and Constantine reigned alone. In the year after that of his accession he issued from Milan the famous edict which gave the imperial sanction to the religion of the Christians, and assured them of his favour as well as his protection. He was at heart a Christian, and very zealous in the cause of Christianity; but, as regards its fundamental principles, he was ignorant, and therefore misapprehended the doctrines to which he listened with reverence. His thoughts about the holy sacraments were so darkened by superstitious fears, that he could not be persuaded to be baptized until he lay on his deathbed, knowing that he was departing this life; and through that same ignorance he could but dimly see the meaning of our Saviour's precepts, although he believed in the glad tidings of salvation, and declared that, when on his march from Gaul, he had beheld the vision of a brilliant cross in the sky, inscribed with the legend, "Conquer in this."

Merivale remarks: "It is not necessary to believe that this was either a miracle or an imposture. Constantine was a man of strong imagination, exalted by wonderful successes."

We should always remember that with God all things

are possible. It is as easy for Him to work by miracle as by means. To us, at present, the miracle seems the more wonderful and glorious; but by-and-by, if we should be permitted to see how God has worked by means of His own laws—how He has done to exact perfection the most complicated work, in and for every race and nation, and every individual soul, it may then seem to us most stupendously wonderful and glorious, where we see that it has been carried through from beginning to end, without breaking one of the least of the code of laws to which He subjected Nature, or one of the ordinances of divine grace on which both the old and the new covenant are founded.

Certainly Constantine won a victory that seated him securely on the imperial throne, and he always affirmed solemnly that he had gained it under the power signified by the luminous cross which at mid-day had appeared in the heavens, shining over him and his army. He had the famous standard made, consisting of a cross and the letters XP surrounded by a garland. New religious ideas did not diminish the worldly ambition of this prince, whose object was the unity of the Empire, and through everything he pursued this aim till he had attained it.

The triumphal arch which he erected in Rome, in honour of his victory, still remains. This magnificent relic of antiquity is most valuable to the archæologist, as the bas-relief which represents the triumph shows the Roman Forum as it was in the days of Constantine. From the epigram on the arch we may infer that a senate, still chiefly heathen, agreed that the record chiselled on the marble monument should be so carefully worded as to be consistent with the Emperor's declaration to satisfy Constantine, and gratify the Christians, without offending the pagans. The phrase, "*instinctu Divinitatis*," is so singular, that archæologists long assumed it to be a substitute for some other words originally inscribed. But Chev. de Rossi has ascertained, through minute inspection, that no alteration has been made.* Magnificent as is the Arch of Constantine, it nevertheless speaks of the decline of art, as it was not in the first instance decorated with entirely new sculpture. It seems that the Arch of Trajan had fallen into a dilapidated state, and instead of being restored, it was destroyed, and some of its sculptures used to ornament that raised in honour of the reigning Emperor.

That arch has stood through nearly sixteen centuries. The name of Constantine, the first Christian Emperor, which was revered by Christian barbarians, seems to have defended it against the rude treatment which injured or destroyed most of the grand monuments of Rome. Groups of fine trees stand near it, and a shady avenue leads from the Arch up the Via di S. Gregorio. In the tranquillity of night the scene is solemnly beautiful, when the full moon shines on the Colosseum, the ruin of the Gladiator's fountain, and the Arch of Constantine.

The establishment of Christianity necessarily affected the condition of the Jews. Those among them who were maliciously disposed towards the Christians had no longer the opportunity of procuring their punishment by accusing them on account of their religion, before the Roman tribunes. Under this Emperor and his immediate successors the Jews were deprived of some privileges they had enjoyed under the late pagan emperors, and laws and edicts were promulgated, the special object of which was

* "Historical and Monumental Rome." By C. I. Hemans.

to humble the Hebrew community. The first of these laws enacted that if a Jew should kill or endanger the life of a Christian convert, he should be burnt to death. Another statute prohibited the Jews from proselytising; they were to make no converts. A third decree made it unlawful for a Jew to possess Christian slaves. This was a necessary legal act, as many wealthy Jews had purchased slaves, and had abused their power even to forcing circumcision upon them. The rapid growth of Christianity had tended to strengthen the influence of the rulers of the synagogues, by constantly keeping alive the vigilance and inflaming the zeal of the more steadfast adherents of the old law. Thus the enmity between Jew and Christian had been kept up to a high degree of malice, and the contest between them had been, on the whole, a not unequal one, until an Emperor of Rome threw the weight of his power entirely on the side of the Christians. The Jews, to whom this great change was an unexpected stroke of adversity, could not rejoice over the prospects of a speedy abolition of idolatry by that means, and they regarded the triumph of the Christians with emotions of mingled envy, anger, and astonishment. The early Christians accuse the rulers of the synagogues of having sent messages to every part of the world for the purpose of anathematizing them in all the synagogues, and uttering a solemn curse upon the name of Jesus Christ. It is by no means unlikely that these legates had received instructions to warn all faithful Israelites against this detested innovation, and to counteract by every means in their power, the progress of this new religion.*

Great must have been the dismay of the Jews when

* Milman's " History of the Jews

the edict of Constantine was promulgated, and bitter must have been their grief when another new Jerusalem appeared on the site of their ancient city. Constantine restored its name, destroyed the heathen temples, erected magnificent shines over the sepulchre of our Lord and other holy places. As yet, in a Christian shrine God only was worshipped—only to the eternal Persons of the Godhead were the prayers of the primitive Church addressed.

The eastern Jews, grieved and exasperated beyond endurance by these changes, joined the Magians, massacred their Christian neighbours, and destroyed their churches; but strength was given to Rome, and that rebellion was quickly quelled. It had, however, the effect of making the yoke of the Jew heavier, and increasing his unpopularity. But as a nation, though scattered, they had an innate strength which enabled them to stand against this; it was the kind of strength given by union. Still in every city colonized by Jews there was a synagogue or more than one, according to the number of their people, and each synagogue had its appendant law court, in which lectures were given, and knotty points of the law debated; and though the spirit of independence was gaining influence, they, as yet, all maintained allegiance to the patriarchate. The Jews also had their own market, ruled by their own officers, who regulated the price of every commodity; and the Roman citizens were free to buy in the Jews' market, if they pleased. The Jews were not exclusively and absolutely shut up in their ghetto by an emperor, but by a pope of Rome.*

* Paul the fourth fixed the Jews in their ghetto about A.D. 1555 Then it was ordered that the Jews' gate should be closed at nine o'clock in the winter, and at half-past ten in the summer.

Rome had lived through its springtime of fresh, vigorous energy, when its sap was rising, and all its vital activity at work. It had passed through a glorious summer-tide, and we may call the age of Constantine its golden autumn. As a seed vessel bursts, the territorial part of the Empire, though looking bright, was ready to split, was actually splitting. As, in that metaphorical light, we look upon it, we may at one moment admire the brilliant tints, catching a ray from the sun, and in the next, when a cloud is passing by, we may see it as a withered thing that speaks of death. Let us carry on the simile a little further, and rest our faith on words which have a meaning far wider than the whole compass of the vegetable kingdom: "Fruit whose seed is in itself."

Old Rome's work was nearly done; it had but to scatter its seed on the earth.

Neither Diocletian nor Constantine could have prevented a rupture; it was only theirs to choose in which portion of their dominions the imperial court should chiefly reside. Diocletian, as we have seen, had chosen the east as the division of the Empire which he deemed most worthy of his presence; and perhaps this policy had tended to a temporary restoration of imperial Roman authority, and Constantine had followed it up by spending much time at Nicomedia in Bithynia. Not being perfectly satisfied with that site, his eye had often rested on, and his thoughts had reverted to, Byzantium, on the European shore at the southern mouth of the Bosphorus.

He considered the situation, and decided that it was admirable for defence, and not less so as an administrative centre. He planned a city himself, marked out the ground to be included within the walls, and proceeded to fill the space, which was not inferior to the area of Rome. The Emperor required the nobles of the Empire to erect palaces for their families, and he created for it a new senate and hierarchy of officers, after the model of the ancient capital. The city and senate of Rome remained as before, while those of Constantinople were endued with equal honour and authority; and enjoyed moreover all the advantages of the imperial presence. Two capitals could not long exist on equal terms. Rome sank into a provincial metropolis, such as Alexandria, Antioch, or Treves, and Constantinople became the mistress of the world.*

Constantine died in the May of A.D. 337, seven years after the solemn dedication of his new city. Eusebius, Bishop of Cæsarea, the historian, to whom he was much attached, was with him at the last, and baptized him.

The memory of this distinguished sovereign has been as much injured by the panegyrics of the Christians, as by the unscrupulous detraction of the pagans. Only experienced, thoughtful writers, who are capable of entering into the mental struggles of an age of transition, should attempt to delineate the personal character of Constantine. Undoubtedly, his reign of thirty-one years was glorious, untroubled by such dissensions as had previously prevailed, and his conduct of affairs on every frontier promoted prosperity: although the borderlands suffered from the incursions of the barbarians, after the Roman legions had been removed from the garrisons on the rivers.

Constantine defeated 100,000 Goths, and received into his territories, as his subjects, 300,000 Sarmatians, and gave them land to cultivate. They had been driven from beyond the Danube by their own slaves, who had successfully risen up in rebellion against them.

* Merivale.

All the people beyond the limits of the Empire were called Barbarians, but the name did not then signify what it now does; the word did not convey the ideas which it now suggests to our minds. It meant little, if anything more than *not Roman.* The number of barbarians who were enrolled in Constantine's grand army is incalculable.

Thus by both the sword and the ploughshare, by warfare and by peaceful labour, the miry potter's clay, having been brought into contact with the iron, was being mingled with it; for the fourth great revolution in the history of the world was impending; the agencies that were to accomplish it were already working.

It was long ago since the Romans had first come into collision with the Gauls; they had often harassed the republic, and had proved formidable enemies to Julius and Augustus Cæsar, but in course of time they had not only been overcome by the Romans, but moreover had been in a degree assimilated with them: Gauls and Romans had blended, though not very closely. Gaul was much more extensive than modern France; it included also Belgium, a part of Holland, the Rhine provinces, and the greater part of Switzerland. Rome had subdued the Gauls so completely, that she had Romanized, or Latinized them, as some historians express it. In southern Gaul, Rome had most successfully produced a likeness of herself. The Gauls belong to the great Keltic or Celtic race. The whole human race has been scientifically separated, first into grand primary divisions, each of which in later generations divided again and again, and the divisions and subdivisions cannot yet be positively and clearly defined, because ethnology is a science in its infancy. It has not yet reached the stage at which a science can be taught to the multitude as a positive branch of general knowledge. Botany is an older science; it can be definitely taught on the Linnæan system, and also on that of the Natural Orders; both systems are studied by persons who desire to become well acquainted with that subject. Ethnology, though but a young growing science, has already done good service to those time-honoured sciences, geography and history.

It is now generally thought that Europe was peopled by several migrations, or, as they have been called, waves of population, all flowing from one point in the East. Of these, the two principal were the Kelts and the Germans, both branches of one greater branch or race, supposed to have sprung from Japhet.* The Kelts seem to have made their way into Europe through the districts bordering on the Mediterranean; they spread themselves over all Western Europe. The Germans entered Europe from the shores of the Black Sea, advanced through the centre of the continent, until they came in contact with the Kelts, whom they gradually drove on to the west and south-west. The Germans themselves were urged on westward by a new migration, the Sclavonic, as tribes of Sarmatians were pressing them from behind.†

* "Celt, Roman, and Saxon." By Thomas Wright. Page 1.
According to the system of ethnology set forth in Dr. Latham's "Universal History of the Varieties of Man," the *Lapetidæ*, one of three primary divisions, comprehended among other races the Celts, the Goths, and the Sarmatians. The Goths subdivided very numerously. Their Teutons included the Mœso-Goths and the high and low Germans, which split into many tribes. But not until about the tenth century did the Latin writers upon German affairs begin to use the words Teutonicus and Teutonico—whence our English word Teuton. Previously those nations were known only as Goths, Allmen, or Germans. On this Grimm remarks that "Teuton sounded more learned."

† "Celt, Roman and Saxon." By Thomas Wright.

Readers who desire to learn more about the origin and languages of these nations should study Dr. Prichard's work, "*The Eastern Origin of the Celtic Nations,*" edited by Dr. Latham, who says, "In arguing that the Celts, or Kelts, were of Eastern origin, Dr. Prichard meant this, viz., that they were in the same predicament with certain other nations, to which, by universal consent, or nearly so, an Eastern origin was attributed: these nations being those belonging to the Gothic or German, the Slavonic, the Lithuanic, the Greek, the Latin, and Sanskrit groups. That these formed a class was certain. It was certain, too, as all but universal consent could make it, that they formed a class of Eastern origin. But it was not certain, that to this class the Kelts belonged. Whether they did so or not Dr. Prichard inquired, and, after inquiry, decided the question in the affirmative.*

A fusion of races may produce a valuable compound. The benefit derived from the assimilation of the Kelt with the Roman was not all on one side. The Kelt was naturally gifted with vivid imagination, warm enthusiasm, quick perception of the perfect and the beautiful, with love of simile and all poetical conceptions.† The noble race produced a succession of remarkable persons, who, thanks to Tacitus, shine out with an imperishable light amid the degradation of the world.‡

But in the fourth and fifth centuries, stronger, wilder

---

* "The Eastern Origin of the Celtic Nation." By James Cowles Prichard, M.A., M.D., F.R.S. Edited by R. G. Latham, M.A., M.D., F.R.S. Published by Houlston and Wright, London, 1857. (See page 73.)

† Matthew Arnold.

‡ Montalembert's "Monks of the West."

waves of people poured down on the Roman dominions. First, the Sclavonic Sarmatians, then all the Gothic hosts, including Germans or Allmen, and Franks, as the smaller tribes were called, who gained importance by confederation. No less daring and irresistible were the Mongolic nations—Tartars, Huns, Bulgarians, and the unbrotherly Avars and Turks.

When Romans and barbarians were thus mingled together, wonderfully did the condition of the Empire and the feelings of its mixed population answer to the few prophetic words—"*But, they shall not cleave one to another, even as iron is not mixed with clay.*"*

We often read of Scythians; that word did not signify a race, it meant nomadic people who had become distinguished by the habit of wandering for the sake of pasturage, rather than of pushing on for the sake of conquest; but the word fell into indiscriminate use, and when the general condition of the earth had become more settled, its meaning was obscured.

All these nations, not at once, and in their full force, but in strong representative bodies of brave rude warriors, came down on the Empire, sometimes several of them invaded simultaneously, sometimes in quick succession, on first the western and afterwards on the eastern division of the once enormous dominions. The grand old city fell, was no more what it had been, was not Rome as we have been looking upon it, the metropolis of the whole world. As such it ceased to exist, yet something survived that decease, its better part was not dead, it is still living under altered conditions, in another state of life.

Dean Merivale concisely tells us, that "the Empire of Rome was destined to last for eleven centuries, and

* Daniel ii. 43.

to be continued through a second existence, with its seat transferred to Constantinople, for just eleven centuries more, while no small portion of the ideas which it produced, or which accumulated round it—its laws, its language, its social and civil usages—still exist. The basements of Rome were laid in an antiquity beyond the ken of human intelligence, but we may at least trace them down through a long succession of ages, and discover how they were piled up from era to era, from revolution to revolution, till they formed the soil upon which the historic city was erected, and still continues to stand."†

† "General History of Rome." By Charles Merivale, D.D. Page 1. Longman & Co.

DURING THE BARBARIAN INVASIONS.

>   "But their days,
> Their hours are numbered.   Hark, a yell, a shriek,
> A barbarous outcry, loud, and louder still,
> That echoes from the mountain to the sea!
> And mark, beneath us, like a bursting cloud,
> The battle moving onward! . . . .
>   From the depth
> Of forests, from what none had dared explore,
> Regions of thrilling ice, as tho' in ice
> Engendered, multiplied, they pour along,
> Shaggy and huge!   Host after host, they come,
> The Goth, the Vandal! and again the Goth!"
>
>   ROGERS.

XI.

DURING THE BARBARIAN INVASIONS.

RETURNING to the latter days of the Roman Empire, we find that Constantinus, who succeeded his father, Constantine the Great, showed kindly feeling towards the Jews, until insurrections in Palestine induced him to change his merciful policy, and to deal very severely with the whole scattered nation. They were forbidden under pain of death from possessing Christian slaves, and from marrying Christian women; these prohibitions show that they must have grown wealthy, and also that the animosity between Jew and Christian was less universal than it had been. The interdict of Hadrian, which prohibited their approach to the Holy City, was renewed. Christian pilgrims were crowding into Jerusalem, where the Church of the Holy Sepulchre stood in lofty state on the hill of Calvary, while the hill of Moriah was still desolate, as it had been left by the plough of the conqueror. The Empress Helena, the mother of Constantine the Great, had built the Church over the Sepulchre, and believed she had discovered remains of the true cross, of which an inexhaustible supply of splinters were being disseminated through the Christian world. It is curious that the actual discovery of the cross is ascribed to a Jew.

During the disturbances caused by the Arian controversy in the restless city of Alexandria, the Hebrews joined with the pagans on the side of the Arian bishop, against Athanasius and his followers; frightful excesses were committed, churches burnt, and horrible outrages perpetrated under this perverted religious excitement.

The accession of Julian, whose enmity to the Christians was well known, delighted the Jews, and the Apostate surpassed their most sanguine anticipations; for he immediately rescinded the decrees of Constantine against the Hebrews, relieved them from their burdens, annulled the ban which had so long excluded them from their own land, and invited them to rebuild their Temple on the old site. Never since the commencement of the captivity had such joyful hopes animated the hearts of the sons of Abraham. They thought the Restoration was at hand, and some of them entertained the idea that Julian would prove to be their Messiah. To aid the work in Jerusalem, Jewish money poured in, and bands of strong men of all ranks hastened thither to take part in the labour. The ground was being cleared, and the new foundations laid, when a sudden explosion, caused possibly by fire-damp, occasioned so much alarm and confusion, that the work was interrupted, and soon afterwards finally stopped by the premature death of Julian, in the second year of his reign. Before his accession, he had successfully repulsed an invading troop of the Alemanni, a Teutonic tribe. Jovian reversed all his predecessor's decrees, undid everything that Julian had done; but, fortunately for the Jews, his reign was very short. Valentinian and Valens restored and confirmed their civil rights, which they continued to enjoy under Gratian and Theodosius, notwithstanding the hard, inhuman prejudices entertained against them by Ambrose, Bishop of Milan, who acquired and maintained great power over those two successive emperors.

Gratian, in his boyhood, had been confided by his father to the care of Ambrose, who was considered the great teacher of the day. The youth had learned to understand the baptismal covenant, and was prepared, by God's help, to do his part. Up to this time the Emperors had assumed the title of Sovereign Pontiff, which each had borne until his death, after which he had been deified, and his successor had been invested with that title, as well as with that of Imperitor, or Emperor. When the envoys of the Senate brought the pontifical robes to Gratian, he decidedly refused to wear them. Monuments exist, on which the title of Pontiff follows this Emperor's name, but he did not accept the title, and never wore the vestments attaching to it.

It is sad to read that in after years Gratian, though he always professed Christianity, lost the esteem of his subjects by addicting himself to idle and unworthy pleasures. He was strangely attracted towards Alaric, a brave Goth, to whom he entrusted the protection of his person, and they spent much time in hunting, till it was whispered that the Emperor was becoming a barbarian himself, unlike the descendant of a long line of Roman princes. He was assassinated by a follower of the usurper Maximus. For a moment the power over the Roman world was once more divided among a triumvirate, but the Western Empire was soon restored under Theodosius, who in history is distinguished as Theodosius the Great.

Both in the East and West the Jews were treated as useful loyal subjects, although a calamity occurred, which greatly disturbed both Jews and Romans throughout the Empire. A lawless party of bigoted Christians wantonly burnt a synagogue to the ground. Theodosius issued an edict ordering them to rebuild it, and directed the Bishop of Callinicum, on the Euphrates, to see it done.

Thereupon Ambrose, Bishop of Milan, broke out into the most vehement expressions of indignation; for to him it appeared utterly inconsistent for a Christian sovereign to protect the Jews. Not content with addressing a violent letter on the subject to the Emperor, who was at that time staying in Milan, Ambrose launched out against him from the pulpit. Theodosius yielded to the daring Churchman, the edict was recalled, and the Jews had to do without that one synagogue until nearly the end of this Emperor's life and reign. Then, being removed from under the immediate influence of the Bishop, he ventured to think for himself, and reflection gave him higher views of righteousness and Christianity. Determined to do justice to the Jews, he issued another edict that secured religious liberty to them, and condemned to the severest punishment all persons who should plunder and destroy their synagogues. Although Bishop Ambrose took such narrow, prejudiced views with regard to what was due to the Jews, yet the power he obtained over the mind of Theodosius was generally well exercised. When the Emperor, being greatly provoked by a rebellion that had broken out at Thessalonica, sent a hasty order commanding a general massacre, Ambrose remonstrated with him, and obtained a promise that the cruel order should be revoked. Theodosius, however, allowed it to be executed, and 7,000 persons were slaughtered in cold blood. When the deed was done, and the Emperor's passion had passed off, he was tormented with remorse; and in an agony of self-reproach was about to enter the church at Milan. Ambrose met him in the porch, and sternly forbade him to enter. Theodosius pleaded the example of David. "You have imitated David in his crime, imitate him in his repentance before you presume to enter the house of God," was the reply. The Emperor submitted, and, as the Bishop directed, expressed his contrition publicly for the sin of which he had been guilty.

The penitence of Theodosius became a favourite subject with preachers and painters, and is remarkable as being the first instance of such ecclesiastical authority being exercised over a sovereign prince.

Power was at this time given to the Church, that it might accomplish the destruction of paganism. We well know that often by individual members it has been abused, yet shall we not still be warmly grateful for the loving condescension of the Almighty Father and Ruler of His large family, who permits His children to help in doing His work—weak, foolish, and ignorant though they are?

Bishop Ambrose seems to have been raised up to lead on his fellow-men in the last pitched battle against idolatry. Before that last struggle with paganism, there still existed in Rome 152 heathen temples, and 183 chapels dedicated to different gods and goddesses, and the shrines of Romulus and of the Cæsars, and of Victory, a kind of deified impersonation of Rome herself, of which the people were both proud and fond. The story of the last attack upon the favourite statue in the Forum, the earnestness with which it was defended, and re-erected only to be thrown down again, is touching.

Thirty-eight years elapsed from the baptism and death of Constantine until the pagan altars were overthrown, the temples closed, the sacrifices abolished; and the two men under whose command that iconoclastic victory was gained were Ambrose and Theodosius. Yet how strangely history repeats itself! That zealous Bishop so highly eulogized the martyrs, ascribed to their ashes the power of working miracles, and made them objects of such homage as soon became adoration that expressed itself in a kind of idolatrous worship.

In the year 397, Ambrose rested from his labours. One of his good works, as far as we can judge, the complete abolition of gladiatorial shows, was achieved in A.D. 404; his influence had done it, though he did not live to hear of the legal prohibition which put an end to those horrible exhibitions.

While the power of the bishops of the Church was increasing, that of the Jewish Patriarch was dwindling away. Theodosius had recognized the power of the Patriarch to punish the refractory members of the Jewish community; the prefects were forbidden from interfering with the judicial courts of the Jewish primate.

When disputes arose between Jews and Christians, both parties were expected to appear before the ordinary tribunals. Jews, carried beyond the bounds of reason and prudence by hot indignation against their adversaries, appealed to heathen tribunals, not only to decide their litigations with Christians, but also appealed to the civil authority against the injustice of their own judicial authorities. Such suicidal action could have but one result, that of bringing the Patriarchate under contempt, and hastening its downfall. The formerly revered and potential office, after having exercised authority for nearly three centuries, expired in the person of Gamaliel. Theodosius either divested that Patriarch of the honorary title, and virtually destroyed his authority, or, as some suppose, did away with the office. The offence alleged against the Patriarch was his having built new synagogues in defiance of the law, which required the imperial sanction. Gamaliel may have been permitted to retain the empty title; but at his death no successor was appointed, and this spiritual monarchy of the West was finally dissolved. Its power may be said to have passed into the hands of the chief Rabbis. The Jerusalem Talmud had already been compiled as a new code; it embodied and preserved the learning of the schools in Palestine, which, before the fall of the Patriarchate, had very much deteriorated. The Talmud of Babylon, a later compilation, eclipsed the more obscure and less perfect work of the Jews in Palestine, and became the law and religion of the whole race.*

Ever since the death of Constantine, the Goths had been harassing the old Empire, and during the last thirty years they had made frightful inroads, terribly disturbing the Romans and Romanized Gauls in the provinces; and at last they effected a settlement on the south bank of the Danube. Theodosius, finding that he could not drive them away, made an agreement with them, that they should defend the Danubian frontier; and under his control they might have proved useful dependants on the Empire, but his successors had not his firmness of character and his organizing talents. Before his death, Theodosius divided the Empire between his two sons, making Arcadius, the elder, Emperor of the east, and Honorius, the younger, Emperor of the west: in their time occurred the great Gothic invasion.

Alaric first invaded Italy in the year 400 of the Christian era, and carried off an extraordinary amount of all sorts of plunder. Two years later he returned, but was forced to surrender, and to make a treaty, the conditions of which he immediately broke. Repeatedly he returned, and threatened Rome, and at

* Dean Milman's "History of the Jews."

last actually laid siege to the city, and at the head of his victorious host he entered it on the 24th of August, A.D. 410, exactly 800 years from its conquest by the Gauls under Brennus.

The cowardice of some of the people, and the treachery of slaves, many of whom were related to besieging warriors, helped the enemy to find an easy access to the Salarian Gate, by which they entered; and in the dead of night the blasts of the Gothic trumpets resounding through the streets awoke the inhabitants to such a scene of horror as that generation had never before witnessed. The air was rent with mingled cries of fear and triumph, agony and death. Down every street the helpless and the innocent were rushing at their utmost speed, vainly striving to escape from pursuers who under such excitement were perfect savages.

Happily, their leader, Alaric, was not a heathen barbarian; though ignorant and fierce, he was a Christian. He did not order that the inhabitants should be put to the sword, and the city set on fire; on the contrary, he exhorted his soldiers to spare the lives of the unresisting, and to respect the Christian churches, especially the shrines of the holy Apostles St. Peter and St. Paul. But his greedy barbarians demanded pillage, and for six days Rome was abandoned to them, with only one restriction. By Alaric's command, the churches were to be respected, and all who sought refuge in those sacred edifices, even the pagans, were to be safe, protected from every kind of violence. At that moment, Jews, infidels, heretics, and Christians were densely crowded together in the one fold, and no doubt emotions of real charity were awakened in the hearts of some persons, who, as long as they lived, were the better for that experience.

Often had Rome pillaged other cities, and proudly had she held the spoils of the wide world: gold and jewels, precious fabrics of Eastern looms, massive plate, costly vases from the homes of the patricians, were quickly carried off in baggage waggons; works of art shared the same fate, though they were not appreciated according to sentiments of cultivated taste, but entirely according to their material value. Violence and cruelty could but prevail, resistance provoked further injury; treasures of all kinds were brought to light by threats and tortures, and many were the fathers, sons, and brothers slain in the defence of families and homes. Anecdotes are related of this terrible time, which show that the ignorant superstition of these barbarous enemies in various instances saved their victims from death or dishonour.

Alaric was soon satisfied with his triumph; he left Rome not many days after he had entered it, and did not trouble himself to impose any ruler or any government on the city. His warriors were impatient to get plunder elsewhere, and he led them on through fertile Italy to its southern extremity, allowing them to commit terrible ravages by the way. The rich and beautiful island of Sicily attracted the Goths; the mighty host embarked, but their rude galleys were driven back by a heavy storm; and while they were preparing for a second attempt to cross the Channel, their great chief was taken from them by a stroke of sudden illness. The deep grief of that wild multitude found vent in the ready zeal with which, in obedience to his last command, they diverted the course of a river, and buried him beneath its bed, throwing into the grave heaps of the most precious things which they had brought with them from the sack of Rome. Then they turned the stream back to its ancient course, that its waters might for ever hide and guard the tomb of Alaric.

In this time of anarchy and general distress the Romans and the Jews were very often involved in the same disasters; the Jews had the advantage; they were more free from local atachments of all kinds, more accustomed to be roughly rocked to and fro, and pitched up and down on the waves of life's turbulent ocean; they were more quickly ready for a sudden move, more independent of home comforts. Above all, they were not so dispirited as every patriotic Roman must have been by the melancholy changes affecting the whole Empire, and especially the grand old city; and when the worst of the storm of war had passed off, the Jews could more easily approach the barbarians as friends. They followed the camp of the invaders, and trafficked with them for the spoil. Before the era in which these wild foes came down upon Rome, the Jews had become the great slave dealers of the world. Again they were able to buy Christian slaves for themselves, and might do so thinking they could now treat them as they pleased, for who would check them as several of the Emperors had done? Gibbon says, that sometimes Jews actually took up arms, and joined the barbarians in their attacks upon the Romans, or helped them to defend places already captured.* The family traditions of the Jews about the fall of Jerusalem, and the arbitrary prohibition which had separated them so entirely from their own land, must have made it hardly possible for them to love Rome.

On the death of Alaric, his wife's brother, Ataulphus, was elected chief of the Gothic host. He had lately married Placidia, a daughter of Theodosius the Great.

* "Decline and Fall of the Roman Empire," vol. vii., p. 129.

This princess had been found among the captives, and she pleased Ataulphus. She accepted her fate, which most likely she could only have avoided by putting an end to her own life, and being a Christian, she could not look upon suicide as did the heathen. Perhaps she perceived something in Ataulphus superior to the vulgar barbarian, good traits of character which she might be the means of developing and refining. She was rewarded by finding that under her influence he became impressed with the dignity of the Roman government, and the complexity of the institutions wherewith it sustained the civilization of the age. So deeply did he feel this, that he shrank from quartering upon Italy a swarm of savage conquerors, and refrained from establishing his own camp in Rome. He is reported to have said, "There was a time when I aspired to make the ancient capital of the world my own capital, to convert Romania into a Gothia, to call myself no longer Ataulphus but Cæsar Augustus; but I have discovered that the barbarians can never be subjected to civil institutions. My Goths can never be made Romans. Society shall not perish. I will restore the Roman Empire, and protect but not rule it."*

Ataulphus withdrew from Italy, and established a permanent kingdom on the coast of the Mediterranean, in Southern Gaul; his dominion extended beyond the Pyrenees; he had a royal residence in Spain, but spent more time at Narbo in Gaul: he styled himself King of the Visigoths. Thus Ataulphus nobly surrendered Rome to Honorius, from whom he did not withdraw the allegiance of the conquered Romans. He acknowledged the imperial supremacy over both Romans and Goths. "This kingdom of the Visigoths," says

* Merivale.

Merivale, "rudely foreshadowed the fiefs of the feudal vassals of a later age. It sprang from the same Teutonic soil, and was due, perhaps, to the same cast of political ideas, from which so much of the policy of modern Europe has derived its shape and character."

In that deluge of barbarism, the Goths were but as a wave driven forward by other rollers overtaking it. Next came the Huns, with Atilla at their head—the dreaded foe, not of the Romans only, but also of the Goths, and all the other tribes that had come from the north down upon the old empire, which already they were tearing in pieces before its political life had quite departed and become a thing of the past. These vultures left the prostrate dying prey to attack the living enemy. Visigoths, Burgundians, and the confederation of the Franks joined the Gauls and Romans, and under the command of Aetius they won the victory at Chalon on the Marne, which saved Europe from being overwhelmed by that wildest of wild races, rushing on its way from the great wall of China to the Atlantic Ocean. It belonged to the Turanian or Mongol race, that subdivided into many nations, among which are the Turks and Bulgarians. All that has been said of the Huns agrees exactly with the eloquent description in the book of Joel.* Atilla bore the reputation of being more ferocious and rapacious than any of the chieftains who had preceded him, and in this fame he delighted, for he called himself "The Scourge of God." Though defeated at Chalon, he was not discouraged, and in the following year he led another host into Italy. The marauders sacked and destroyed Aquileia, Padua, Verona, and other towns, and devastated all the beautiful country through which they

* Chapter ii. 2—10.

passed. The terrified people fled before the "Destroyer" and his barbarous warriors, and took refuge among the fishermen's families living in the little islands of the Veneti. From this small and sad beginning arose the most curiously charming of European cities. Persons whose imagination has been at all educated, when, for the first time, they look upon her towers, walls, roofs, and her own venetian shutters, all vividly reflected in the tranquil water, naturally take a momentary glance over her story, from Atilla's day to our own. Ere darting thus through the strong lights and shadows of prosperity and crime, we should be sure the arrow has its proper weight, we should remember that these contrasts of splendour and power, misery and oppression, characterize, not Venice especially, but the times in which she rose. Between us and those mediæval ages lies a halo of romance; we see everything trembling in its glimmer, like the wavering pictures broken by the oars of the dark-robed gondola, that ministers to business and to pleasure, that lulls to rest the weary traveller's conflicting thoughts, till he is conscious of but one idea; that the Queen of the Adriatic is a fascinating city.

Rome, dreading the approach of Atilla, knowing that the day was gone by in which she could refuse to treat with an enemy at her gates, sent ambassadors to the king of the Huns. There was yet one man in Rome, who, more than any other, deserves to be called the last of the Romans; no warrior, no statesmen, but a Christian bishop—Pope Leo the Great. This prelate had contended boldly for the primacy of his native city among the sees of Christendom at the Council of Chalcedon. He now did her better service in accompanying the imperial envoys to the camp of Atilla, and enforcing their persuasions by spiritual exhortations, which exercised no little influence over the minds of the rude heathen. He assured them that Rome was a sacred city, that to attack it would be an act of fatal impiety, and in proof of this reminded them that Alaric had not long survived his sacrilegious exploit.*

The Hun was naturally impulsive, and changeable as the wind; he had become almost devoted to a love of gold, and as yet his religious notions were nothing better than the darkest, wildest superstition. Atilla accepted the promise of a large sum of money, in consideration of which he relinquished his intention of proceeding to Rome. Probably we are but imperfectly acquainted with the circumstances that converged at that crisis; mystery seems to shroud them and the death of Atilla, which quickly followed. He was found dead in his bed, bathed in blood, but it seems to have been admitted that sudden decease was the result of natural causes.

Rome had had a narrow escape, and very short was her reprieve. Valentinian, then upon the throne, was a thoroughly contemptible man. Jealous of the popularity of Aetius, the hero of Chalon, the Emperor stabbed him with his own hand, and he himself fell under the stroke of an assassin not many months later. His murderer proposed to his widow, pleading that it was for love of her that he had taken the life of her husband. In this dilemma the unfortunate Eudoxia sent a messenger to Geneseric, a powerful chief of the Vandals, who acknowledged the supremacy of Rome, begging him, as a loyal prince, to avenge the death of the sovereign Emperor, and to set her free from this painful position. Geneseric accepted the invitation with

* Merivale.

such alacrity, that he arrived before it was thought possible that he could do so. Once more at the head of a long procession of clergy, Pope Leo approached a mighty host of armed barbarians, thirsting for blood and spoil. The Vandal king received him graciously, but would only promise mercy to the unresisting, and that the principal buildings in the city should be protected as much as possible from fire. The Empress went forth to meet her champion, arrayed in imperial robes.

Unfortunately for her, the day of chivalry was not yet dawning ; she was instantly stripped of her splendid dress, her gold and jewels, and her train of silk ; and with her three daughters was transported to Africa. For fourteen days the city was given up to the plundering soldiers, and the Vandals, and the Moors with them, were found to be more cruel and insatiable than the Goths. The treasures of the imperial palace, the gold and silver vessels in the churches ; the statues of pagan divinities and of justly renowned Romans, the gilded roof of the Temple of Jupiter Capitolinus, the plate and ornaments of private individuals, were leisurely conveyed to the Vandal fleet, and shipped to Africa. To this systematic spoliation we must assign the loss of most of the best known monuments of national history and of foreign conquest. Amongst these were the precious records and ornaments of the Capitol,—and there, carefully preserved, as long as Rome could guard them, were found the golden table, the seven-branched candlestick, and the silver trumpets. No grace of art, no charm of historic association, affected the rude minds of the African pirates, who, by a strange mockery of fortune, became masters of all the treasures which during ten centuries of civilized life had been accumulated in the temples and in the marble palaces of the world's metropolis.*

Objects reverenced as connected with Jewish, pagan, or Christian worship shared the same fate; all were shipped for transportation. A terrible tempest rose while the fleet was at sea; ships were wrecked, lives lost, and much of the valuable booty went down to the depths of the ocean. The table and the golden candlestick reached Carthage safely, and sixty thousand captives.† The excellent Deogratius, Bishop of Carthage, did all he could to relieve the distress; he allowed two of the basilica churches to be used as hospitals, and even sold some of the consecrated vessels of gold and silver. Private charity was active, yet the trouble seemed greater than any that had ever been known before: no one could remember such experiences, occurrences that had altered the whole tenor of their lives.

In those calamitous times, when war was raging, and iniquity abounding everywhere, not a few among the peace-loving Christians retired from the haunts of men, under the idea that they might thereby escape both temptation and trouble; and some, who thought that the end was very near, fled from a doomed world, and tried to be alone with God, if by any means they might save each man his own soul in that dread day.‡

In the sweat of his brow the hermit built his hut, worked hard to redeem from some remote wilderness, which hitherto had sheltered only wild beasts, ground

---

* "The Fall of Rome." By J. G. Sheppard, D.C.L. pp. 250, 251.

† The Forum and Temple of Peace, built by Vespasian and Titus, was devastated by fire A.D. 191.

The treasures from Jerusalem are said to have been rescued; but no special mention is made of the Law, which was placed in that Temple of Peace.

‡ The Rev. Charles Kingsley.

enough to produce, by means of continual cultivation and labour, the simple food necessary to sustain his life. When tired nature needed rest, he sat down to read and write. Anchorites generally spent a great deal of time over their manuscripts, perusing again and again the few they possessed or could borrow, and cheered on by the idea that in adding to the existing number they were doing most valuable work. Their compositions naturally partook of the peculiarities engendered by their solitary life. Complete isolation weakens those mental faculties which are given to us to be used in the world, over-strains the nerves, inflames the imagination, and gives it undue ascendency. Very evident are the effects of this on the religious literature of the period.

This movement was begun by individuals who thus separated themselves from society, and devoted their days to prayer and meditation. But the weight upon the spirits proved such as few could bear entirely alone; these recluses gathered round them small fraternities, congregated, first in small, and afterwards in larger bodies; and thus a new agency originated in the Church, and grew and spread irresistibly, over the Roman Empire.

Among the lives of the hermits, that of St. Jerome is one of the most interesting; and, strange to say, it is full of variety. While he lived in the world, he heartily entered into its pleasures, and fell into some of the sins which beset the students of those days, as of these. At the age of twenty he was baptized, and returned home to Aquileia, where he was strongly affected by the preaching of Evagrius, a missionary, who fired the imaginations of the young by his descriptions of Syrian monasticism. Jerome tried the life, enjoyed its charms and blessings, but could scarcely bear its hardships. After three years, his health having suffered from his austerities, and having been annoyed by neighbouring hermits, be returned to the cities, choosing not the least among them, but Antioch, Constantinople, where he was delighted with the preaching of Gregory Nazianzen, and Rome, where the pope appointed him to the important office of his own secretary. He was the foremost priest in Rome, and many looked upon him as the probable successor to the See. But Jerome had retained his love of the ascetic life, and he advocated it so effectually in Rome, that a group of noble Roman ladies embraced it, and put themselves under his direction. After visiting Egypt and Jerusalem, they finally settled at Bethlehem, where Jerome spent the remaining thirty-one or thirty-two years of his life. One of the ladies thus describes the home to a friend in Rome: "Come out of Babylon, and let each one save his soul; so speaks the Scripture. At Rome you have a holy Church, you have the trophies of apostles and martyrs, you have paganism crushed at your feet, and the Christian name daily growing into greater majesty ; but you have ambition, pomp, a huge city, noise, vanity, and pride. Come to Bethlehem, come to Jesus Christ's little city, and see our rural solitude, and share our silence, that nothing but the chanted psalm ever breaks ; where the tiller of the soil sings "Alleluia," as he guides his plough ; where the hot reaper at his rest in the noontide, and the vine dresser, busy with his curved knife among the vines, refresh themselves with verses from the songs of David."

Paula, who wrote this letter, built two monasteries at Bethlehem, one for men, the other for women. Jerome sold his little patrimony, and contributed towards the cost. He lived not far from the Grotto of the Nativity, in a cell in the limestone rock.* Here, being the revered centre of both circles of recluses, he was spared the trials of loneliness, while he enjoyed its advantages, when he needed to be undisturbed; and then his solitude was cheered by a faithful animal—a lion, which he had tamed and trained to be as obedient and companionable as a dog.†

From his home in the rock Jerome carried on an extensive correspondence, and took part energetically in the theological controversies of the day. Here he studied Hebrew, under a Jew; did so stealthily for years, because he feared to offend the prejudices of Christian brothers and sisters. By his aid he accomplished his great work—a Latin translation of the whole of the Old and New Testaments, from the original languages. His version was called the Vulgate; it was, until the Reformation, the authorised version of the entire Western Church, and continues to be used by the Roman Catholics.

When commenting on the prophetical books, Jerome mentions the tribes of Israel: at that time they were believed to be widely dispersed, but not lost; and their restoration was looked forward to as unanimously as was that of the Jews. St. James had addressed his Epistle to the twelve tribes scattered abroad. They were

---

* "Turning-points in Church History." By the Rev. E. L. Cutts, B.A.

† Among the fine pictures in the Vatican, one of the most touching is "St. Jerome's Last Communion," Dominichino's masterpiece. A young priest is holding up the dying man. St. Paula kneeling, kisses one of the emaciated hands. Jerome's still eager eye is fixed on the priest who is about to administer the sacrament. A deacon holds the cup, an attendant the book. The lion, with a look full of grief, droops his head, resting it on his paws, as he lies by the side of his master.

thought to be "scattered among the Parthians, Medes, Indians, and Ethiopians, living in a state of dependence on the barbarous nations there,"* somewhat as the Jews lived dispersed among the more civilized nations. Jerome confirms this view in his notes on Joel and Hosea. Commenting on the third chapter of Joel, he says, "They dwell in the cities and mountains of the Medes to this day."† Media ran round two sides of the Caspian Sea, and joined Armenia, and in an opposite direction stretched away to Assyria. Its boundaries shifted, sometimes encroaching on neighbouring countries. The name first appears in Scripture in connection with the Israelites.‡

The Jews in general considered that the ten tribes, and all who had preferred remaining among the heathen when they might have availed themselves of the edict of Cyrus, had, by failing to return to their inheritance, cut off themselves and their children from its advantages; that nevertheless all the sons of Abraham who continued to acknowledge and worship the one God, still did their part, man by man, according to the measure of his faith, towards accomplishing the word of God. Therefore they were like seed widely sown; faithful Israelites were good seed; the unfaithful, such as gave little or no sign of religious or moral vitality, were the worst portion of the seed, withered, decayed, lost, or rather incorporated in the earth, which was enriched by

---

* Sulpitius Seroms, contemporary with Jerome, lib. ii. c. 26.

† Jerome wrote in the fifth century. The subsequent conquests of the Mahometans disturbed those countries—during the anarchy the Israelites had ample opportunity of retiring to the fastnesses bordering on the Caspian Sea, or of plunging into that vast, imperfectly known territory eastward of that sea. See "History of the Hebrew Nation." By Rev. J. W. Brooks.

‡ 2 Kings xvii. 6, xviii. 11.

its physical properties.* On the other hand, the Jews thought that fragments and individuals of the ten tribes who had returned to the Holy Land with the two, by so doing resumed allegiance to the House of David from which their ancestors had fallen, and were therefore restored and incorporated into the body of the Jewish nation, as it had been called since the return from captivity. Christians as well as Jews considered Josephus to be the great authority on the history of the Hebrew nations (or the twelve tribes descended from Israel). Copies of the works of Josephus, or of portions of them, were treasured in the earliest monasteries and in hermits' cells; and all the few existing manuscripts, which had cost so much careful toilsome writing, were perused by those thoughtful readers again and again with unabated interest.†

Jerome always gladly entertained travellers who happened to pass his secluded abode, and he heard from

---

* Gen. xii. 13, xviii. 18; Jer. xxxi. 27; Ezek. xxxvi. 8—12; Hosea ii. 23; Zech. x. 9.

It was, with few exceptions, the less noble and wealthy families who listened to Zerubbabel, and availed themselves of the edict of Cyrus. The prosperous, who had already spread themselves over the provinces of Babylonia, or who were dwelling at ease in the great, luxurious, yet busy city of Babylon, did not for the most part desire to return to Judea, and did not embrace this opportunity for so doing. As time went on, a great many Israelitish families grew rich and very numerous, which induced them to emigrate for commercial purposes. Colonies from Babylonia founded cities on distant shores, several on the coasts of Spain, which were flourishing in early Christian times. See "Israel and the Gentiles." By Dr. Isaac Da Costa.

† Josephus says, "There are but two tribes in Europe and Asia subject to the Romans, while the ten tribes are beyond the Euphrates till now, and are an immense multitude that cannot be reckoned by numbers."—*Antiquities* I. xi. c. v.

them a little news of the world he had renounced. He says that he often took in Roman wayfarers, men well born, well educated, and once wealthy, reduced to such a state of destitution that they thankfully accepted alms. Romans begged their bread in Judea!

Probably most of them were Christian Romans who had come to see the Saviour's birthplace. What else could have attracted them to that spot?

The custom of making pilgrimages to holy places was beginning to prevail, and with it a childlike faith which gave a new kind of life to the wearied heart, refreshment to the unfortunate. They believed in a special providence guarding the pilgrim, and that all he needed by the way God would provide. On this happy enthusiasm the Jew looked with amazement, for Roman and Jew had been bound together for a moment by the strong tie of fellow-suffering, and the earnest Jew as well as the Christian had enthusiastic faith. Both overtaken by the storm, each fixed his anchor on the selfsame Rock. This in the blinding darkness they could not see, but sure and safe was the anchorage afforded by the Rock. Jew and Christian understood that figure which occurs in the Old Testament Scriptures as often as in the New.

The Jews of all ranks who had been settled in Rome had shared in all the calamities that had befallen the Romans, and had also lost all their possessions. We have already seen that Jews and Christians had, in a visionary kind of way, looked forward to the destruction of the city of Rome, as they both had prophecies in their sacred books which pointed to the destruction of a sinful city, that had defiled itself by all kinds of wickedness, especially cruelty and oppression, and had shed the blood of martyrs. All the Eastern Jews had clung firmly to this old persistent faith: those living prosperously in Rome had cast the subject off their minds, but the troubles caused by barbarian invasion revived it.

Yes! every generation has to learn by heart and by experience that "one day is with the Lord as a thousand years, and a thousand years as one day," and learning this, while it exercises patience, confirms faith. We have remarked that the word *day* bears its most limited meaning, or it may signify a generation, a century, a period; the lifetime of a man—of a kingdom—of the world itself.

All that we know of what we call the universe convinces us that its Creator and Upholder forms circle within circle, sphere within sphere, wheel within wheel; and the Christian knows that of all the life-spans that have run their course in fleeting days and years, and left their mark, never to be obliterated, that day of thirty-three years, the life of the Redeemer on earth, has pre-eminent undying power, though, while those years were running on, outside spans looked more important. The day of the Roman Empire had begun before Augustus Cæsar unconsciously aided in the fulfilment of prophecy by issuing a decree that all the world should be taxed; and, having run its course, its sun went down behind those terrible storm-clouds that gathered blackness, one over the other, and burst in that extraordinary flood, when the cultivated earth was deluged with races of men, half-civilized, or savage as the Huns;—hordes driven onwards from far countries, whose features and languages and manners were all strange in the old Roman world.

WHEN IMPERIAL POWER FELL, AND PAPAL POWER ROSE.

"That the world—such, at least, as they saw it then—was doomed, Scripture and their own reason taught them. That they were correct in their judgment of the world about them, contemporary history proves abundantly. That they were correct, likewise, in believing that some fearful judgment was about to fall on man is proved by the fact that it did fall; that the first half of the fifth century saw, not only the sack of Rome, but the conquest and desolation of the greater part of the civilized world, amid bloodshed, misery, and misrule, which seemed to turn Europe into a chaos—which would have turned it into a chaos, had there not been a few men left, who still felt it possible and necessary to believe in God, and to work righteousness." REV. CHARLES KINGSLEY.

XII.

WHEN IMPERIAL POWER FELL, AND PAPAL POWER ROSE.

WE have seen how the flood of barbarian invasion overwhelmed one half of the ancient provinces of Rome; these conquests, both by their effect and their example, threatened the speedy downfall of the rest. At the beginning of the sixth century of the Christian era the Empire of Constantinople, in like manner attacked by enemies, and showing symptoms of decay, seemed very near its end, but the genius of one man averted dangers, and corrected defects; the tottering empire was upheld, and the emperors were enabled for a time to resume their former ascendency, and to wrest from the hands of the barbarians their most important possessions. This saviour was Belisarius, whose name in his native Illyrian (or Sclavonic) language signifies the *White Prince*, as Belgrade or Beligrad means the *White City*.

Belisarius rose into notice in the reign of Justin the First, when that emperor, having survived the military prowess to which he owed his reputation, and his elevation to the imperial throne, was sinking into the dotage of his faculties. His death left Justinian sole sovereign in fact as well as in name.*

Then there were three very remarkable contemporary

* "The Life of Belisarius." By Lord Mahon, afterwards Earl Stanhope.

sovereigns reigning over the world. Nushirvam, whom the eastern historians celebrate as the greatest and most glorious of Persian monarchs. Theodoric, the Gothic king of Italy, who extended his dominions, and governed with extraordinary vigour and ability; and Justinian, Emperor of the East.

The first named of these reigned in a sphere beyond the limits of our subject. Theodoric humanely protected the Jews all over Italy, and repressed the violent measures against them to which his fanatical Christian subjects were too much disposed to resort. For this impartial justice, often denied to them, the Jews were sincerely grateful, as they soon had full opportunity of showing; they defended the Gothic monarchy with the same indomitable stubborn firmness with which they had defended their own country: none of the king's subjects were more ready to contribute money, to shed their blood, and to give their lives to the cause of their protectors. Theodoric was an Arian, and the Jews before his time, ever since Arius had first preached his heretical doctrines in Alexandria, had sided with that powerful sect, against which every kind of war was waged by orthodox Christians.*

After the conquest of Italy by the barbarians, it might have been expected that the subjects of Constantinople would no longer call themselves Romans. but this title was too glorious to be so easily relinquished. In every succeeding age the rabble of Greek armies still boasted of their kindred with the ancient legions, and the name of Romania was applied to the varying limits of Byzantine territory, until it settled on Thrace, to which they were latterly confined. At the accession of Justinian, however, the boundaries of

---

* A natural combination. Arians denied the doctrine of Christ.

his empire were nearly the same as those of the Ottoman at present. In comparing Justinian with his contemporaries at Ctesiphon and Ravenna, it may be remarked that their very unequal merit has been almost equally rewarded by fame. Nushirvam's name has not lost its lustre, Theodoric yet lives in the rustic songs and legends of his countrymen, and Justinian's name is adored by civil lawyers. By their absolute power and the length of their reigns all three possessed the means for effecting their plans of conquest or reform. Yet, while the kings of Persia and Italy are indebted to their own achievements for renown, the Emperor only shines as a general or a legislator through the borrowed light of Tribonian and Belisarus.*

The former, after obtaining high reputation at the bar, rose through a succession of state offices to those of prefect and consul. The Emperor intrusted to him the responsible office of superintending the formation of a new code of laws. His labours resulted in the production of the celebrated Digest and Pandects which procured for Justinian the reputation of being the greatest of lawgivers, the reformer of Roman jurisprudence.

Most interesting is the career of Belisarius, for he was a great and good man, as well as a wonderful military genius, a prescient general, and when surrounded by his soldiers, whom he looked on as his comrades, though he kept them under discipline, he was the bravest of the brave.

When Justinian was meditating on an expedition to Africa, all the generals of the so-called Roman army shared so strongly in the public panic, that even ambition yielded to alarm, and they shrank from the command of the intended expedition. Belisarius accepted

* Lord Mahon (Earl Stanhope).

the responsibility, and the designation, "General of the East." The mariners of the fleet set their sails and plied their oars so well, that, in spite of boisterous gales, the landing was soon effected at Grasse, fifty miles from Carthage. Here the invaders met with so little resistance, that they had leisure to admire and enjoy the beautiful country palace of King Gelimer, surrounded by a delightful garden. It was called Paradise, and seems to have been as worthy of the name as a pleasure ground on earth can be.

But now those who had loved this pleasant home, looking upon it as their own, had to learn how uncertain is the tenure by which all earthly things are held. Procopius describes the sparkling fountains, the groves and flowers, and tells us that although the soldiers helped themselves to as much fruit as they could eat, yet so great was the abundance, that it was hardly missed. Belisarius strictly restrained his men from plundering the country or the private citizens. The moderation of his army, so different to the conduct of the barbarians, and his own courteous, friendly behaviour, gained the confidence and good-will of the Africans, who crowded to the camp, and brought provisions for sale, which were fairly paid for.

Gelimer was absent from Carthage. He was a usurper, having dethroned the aged and infirm Hilderic, who had become imbecile. Justinian had espoused the cause of Hilderic, and it served as the pretext for this attack on Carthage.

When Gelimer received intelligence of the landing and progress of the Romans, he was greatly enraged, and immediately gave orders that the captive Hilderic should be put to death; a crime committed in the passion of the moment, which was as impolitic as cruel.

The Vandals were totally defeated in a great battle which took place ten miles from Carthage; then all idea of resistance was abandoned, the gates of the city were thrown open, and the chains across the entrance to the harbour removed. Citizens who had maintained allegiance to the poor old King Hilderic welcomed the Romans with bonfires and illuminations; the partizans of Gelimer sought the sanctuary of churches. Belisarius, before he entered the city, made a fine speech to the troops. He reminded them that the Africans had formerly been, like them, subjects and citizens of Rome, and that their allegiance was transferred to the Vandals, not through any voluntary rebellion, but through a foreign conquest, from which none had suffered so severely as themselves. "It was," added Belisarius, "the knowledge of these sufferings which impelled the Emperor to send forth this expedition, and it would be as absurd as criminal for the Roman soldiers to treat with outrage or oppression the very people for whose deliverance they were sent here." The army then entered Carthage, and Belisarius gave a grand banquet in the palace; he seized for his sovereign, the royal treasure, but forbade his soldiers to pillage the city; this, however, he found it impossible to prevent, and after making a vain attempt to restore discipline, he passed the night of his victory with all the anxiety and alarm of a defeat. Conquest was not yet assured, and Gelimer was undaunted; he assembled all the troops he could command, and some friendly Moors joined his standard. Although the Vandal king had in a moment of great excitement committed a horrible crime in putting to death the aged Hilderic, the consequences of which had so quickly recoiled on himself, yet he was not habitually cruel, and he had generally acted with good judgment, and had shown great military skill. He intrenched himself in the mountain of Papua, near Hippo-Regius. The steep and craggy sides of this height presented an insurmountable barrier to the assailants, and it was inhabited by a wild tribe of Moors, who readily afforded refuge to the king. Against a place thus fortified by nature, force was useless; Belisarius could but blockade, and, pressed by famine, Gelimer at last surrendered, and was taken back to Carthage as a prisoner. With the capitulation of Gelimer, the Vandal war was at an end. Belisarius only remained for a short time to make such arrangements as might render the acquired territory permanently useful to the Empire; but while he was thus serving his country, enemies were intriguing against him at Constantinople, poisoning Justinian's mind with vague suspicions that he was lingering on in Africa in the hope of gaining such popularity as might help him to acquire undue power. It was well known that the soldiers he commanded were devotedly attached to him, and it was remembered that one half of the emperors since the time of Augustus had been raised by the army to the imperial throne. Informed by friends of these machinations, Belisarius with a heavy heart left the city he had conquered, with the captives and the spoil. He had the honour of bearing away the golden table and the seven-branched candlestick, which graced a second triumph. A change worthy of observation had altered some of the customs pertaining to a triumph. The conqueror, instead of sitting in a grand chariot of war, drawn perhaps by elephants, if he had reaped his laurels from lands but lately reclaimed from their ancient forests, now marched on foot at the head of his companions in arms. Immediately after the Vandal spoils, above which were upheld those redeemed treasures, so deeply significant, so wonderfully real, came Gelimer, still wearing the royal purple, and maintaining the dignity of a king. Marching slowly through Constantinople at the head of the captives, he continued to repeat in a loud voice, "Vanity of vanities! all is vanity!"

May we not ascribe the modification of ancient usages to the profession of national Christianity? On reaching the Hippodrome, Gelimer was commanded to prostrate himself before Justinian. Scarcely had he risen, when, acting on a generous impulse, Belisarius did homage in the same manner, to show the Vandal king that he had merely made such tokens of submission as Romans were in the habit of making to their Emperor. Justinian assigned to the Vandal monarch an extensive estate in Galatia and to this peaceful secluded abode he retired.

Those words of Solomon applied more forcibly and exactly to the fate of the victor than to that of the vanquished, for although for a time Belisarius was loaded with honours, thanked and praised, and liberally rewarded, yet in the end his enemies prevailed, and certainly he experienced the extremes of prosperity and adversity, although it may be doubted whether the story that his eyes were put out, and that the blind old hero begged his bread, be literally true. There is no ground for believing that he was in any way a party to the conspiracy against Justinian's life, of which he was accused, and for which he was condemned. He was ruined by jealousy. Justinian, quite unconsciously to himself, was jealous of the man to whom the military glory of his reign was really attributable. From the same cause Tribonian suffered, though in a less degree, and he in some measure deserved his fall, as his ambition appears to have been of a selfish character; yet, as he, being a quick-sighted and experienced lawyer, had done much towards the formation of that code which commands the admiration of the world, his disgrace left a stain on Justinian's memory; all generations have since perceived that his suspicious jealousy encouraged and empowered that of baser-minded men than himself. For Justinian, in spite of some weakness of character, was, on the whole, a man of superior abilities, who had risen from an obscure family chiefly by the force of his own talents, which were of no common character. The desire to reform Roman jurisprudence, and the resolution to do so, originated in his own mind, as, no doubt, did also most of the wise conceptions of justice and prudence which lie at the foundation of that important science. He was gifted with extraordinary genius for organization, which led him sometimes into the error of carrying reliance on rules and regulations too far, and thus too much restricting the liberty of, not only the Jews, but, in a less degree, of all his subjects. In approaching Justinian as we have done, through the Jews, and Belisarius, and Tribonian, we have seen quite the worst side of his character. He was a conscientious man, his religious opinions were strong, and generally he acted upon them consistently, even when they ran counter to his desires. He wished to keep the golden table and the candlestick in his own palace, but a zealous Jew convinced him that it could not be their proper place, yet his feelings as a Christian sovereign prevented him from returning them to the Hebrews. On mature consideration, he arrived at the conclusion that they belonged to the Church of Christ; he entrusted them to the Bishop of Jerusalem, and sent them back to that city, to be placed in the principal church, and some other smaller sacred vessels were distributed among the other churches in that venerable city, where they remained until they were, for the third time, carrried away among the spoils of war, when Chosroes the Second, King of Persia, captured Jerusalem in A.D. 614.*

They were taken to Persia, and beyond that we have no trace of them; and now it seems remarkable that the country in which the branched candlestick—that Old Testament type of God's ancient Church—was lost sight of, the Jews of our own generation are calling to the Christian Church, expressing their unwillingness to receive the Gospel. A touching appeal from forty leading Jews of Hamadam, the old Ecbatina, requesting that Christian teachers might be sent to them, has recently been made.†

The strength and the civilization of Italy had completely centred in Rome to an unhealthy degree. The heart of the Empire did not so act as to do its duty to the great body of the nation. Both numerically and intellectually the people of Italy were in a weak, poor, neglected condition; for the cream of the population had for centuries gone to or near Rome. Consequently, the so-called barbarian leaders were more civilized

* "Historical and Monumental Rome." By C. I. Hemans. pp. 442, 443, etc.

† For a long time past, the ground has been under preparation, and the blessed seed has been taking root and developing. Sixteen years ago, a missionary, named Brühl, who was then at Bagdad, wrote—"Hitherto we have had to beg the Jews to accept a New Testament, and to read and examine into its precious truths, but now many come of themselves to ask for it, and when they obtain it, read it diligently and earnestly."

This accounts for the present movement in Persia, for the application now made by the Jews in Hamadam, who tell us that if they become Christians, all the Jews in Persia will follow their example. See "The Untended Flock." By W. Harden, B.A., clerical secretary of the Society for Promoting Christianity among the Jews.

than their Italian subjects. Odoacer, who compelled Augustus, the last Emperor of the West, to abdicate, ruled the country wisely and beneficently, until, in his turn, he was defeated and deposed by Theodoric. This king, though a Goth, deserves the surname of Great better than do many sovereigns to whose names the proud title is appended. We have seen how the schools of Greece cultivated the Roman mind; in Theodoric we see what they did for a Goth, who in early life had lived in the midst of Greek culture. Under his government Italy recovered prosperity, agriculture and industry revived, literature and the fine arts were encouraged, throughout the land improvements were carried on, and new monuments erected; yet his life was one continued struggle; very stormy was the glory of his reign. Disagreements occurred among the Goths themselves, and also between Goths and Romans, and between the reigning sovereigns.

This clashing of interests inspired Justinian with ambitious views; he anticipated a reunion of the great old Roman power of the past. Under the influence of this hope, and under this condition of affairs and feelings, antagonism was naturally engendered, which soon broke out into open war. Belisarius was appointed to head the troops that with hostile intentions were ordered to Rome.

We can better imagine than define the feelings with which, under such circumstances, Belisarius, Procopius, and other noble-minded, educated men, whose ancestors were Romans, who called themselves Romans, approached the Eternal city, after it had been for sixty years under the dominion of the Vandals and Goths. During that time Rome had enjoyed the blessings of peace and prosperity, it had been an object of peculiar care attention, and munificence, and had received the respect and honours due to the ancient mistress of the world.*

The Jews of Rome and Naples sided with the Goths, by whom they had been uniformly well treated. The Vandals had left them free to exercise their religion, and by Theodoric they had been decidedly favoured.

Justinian, on the contrary, had treated the Jews in his dominions very harshly; had deprived them of all political privileges, and excluded them from every office of dignity and emolument. Many of Justinian's enactments were particularly vexatious to the Jews, as they dealt with things appertaining to their own religious usages among themselves, regulating their calendar and the worship of their synagogues, and even prescribing the use of the Greek instead of the Hebrew Scriptures. To such tyranny the Jews were unaccustomed; for in the more vigorous days of the Roman Empire they had been recognized simply as followers of another religion, and they had never been persecuted on merely religious grounds.† They were accused sometimes falsely, but it was always on political grounds.

The conduct of the Jews during the war between the eastern Romans of Constantinople, and the Goths who held old Rome, claims our admiration; for they warmly espoused the cause of those who had befriended them, and under whose government they had enjoyed justice and security. The Jews very bravely defended one quarter of Naples; but the town was taken, and every Jew was put to the sword, irrespective of age or sex. Belisarius had no sooner secured the fortune, than he strove to restrain the bloodshed of that day; but his

---

* "Belisarius." By Lord Mahon (Earl Stanhope). Page 184.

† "History of the Jews." By E. H. Palmer, M.A. Pages 214, 215. Published by the Society for Promoting Christian Knowledge.

men had been brought up under the most cruel prejudices against the Hebrews, and had been maddened by their enthusiastic resistance and by their firm loyalty to the Goths.

From Naples the victorious army proceeded to Rome. The feelings with which Belisarius and many of those who were with him looked upon the venerable birthplace of the Empire induced a brotherly feeling towards the inhabitants of the city, and not a few of them felt something akin to this when they saw the army of the Roman Empire preparing to invest and blockade Rome. There was also religious sympathy between them, such as could not exist between Romans, who now for generations had professed the faith of the Christian Church, and Goths, who were Arians.

Unable to withstand the evident inclinations of the Roman people, and to sustain a siege without their co-operation, the Gothic garrison marched out of the Flaminian gate, now Porta del Popolo, and Belisarius entered by one on the other side of the city. The Gothic general refused to join in even a necessary flight: with noble firmness he would not quit his post, and was taken prisoner. Belisarius sent him to Justinian with the keys of the city. He immediately began to repair and fortify the walls, as he foresaw a strong probability that they would soon have to sustain a siege.

Rome was fiercely assailed by the Goths, who were now commanded by Vitiges. Hordes of Franks and Germans flocked to his standard; he promised them the city of Milan, if they could take it. After a dreadful siege, during which multitudes died of famine and disease, Milan fell, and its inhabitants were mercilessly slaughtered. Belisarius was shut up for more than a year within the walls of Rome by Vitiges, but the arrival of reinforcements from Greece changed the fortune of war. The barbarian, as the Greeks and Romans still called him, was forced back into Ravenna, his own capital, the last stronghold of his power. It was taken after a stout resistance by the troops of the Empire, and with it fell the kingdom of the Ostrogoths. The achievement was wonderful, for it was performed by Belisarius at the head of an army which scarcely ever exceeded 20,000 men.

This event made a sad change for the Jews in Rome. All the noblest and best men of that people had borne arms against the Empire, many were put to death or banished, and those who remained were treated with the greatest rigour, were disqualified from holding civil or military offices under the state, and inhibited and shackled in many other respects; indeed, the Jews living under the dominion of Rome had become very much less independent and happy than those who had scattered themselves beyond its now circumscribed limits.

Before the irruption of the northern barbarians, there were a great many Jews in Belgium, all along the course of the Rhine, and in such parts of Germany as were at all civilized; and also in Gaul, Italy, and Spain. Of their original progress into these countries history takes no notice, for they did not migrate in swarms, or settle in large bodies, but sometimes as slaves following the fortune of their masters, sometimes as single enterprising traders, they had travelled on, and advanced as profit or convenience tempted, till they reached the verge of civilization. On them the successive inroads and conquests of the barbarians fell much more lightly than on the native inhabitants. Attached to no fixed residence, with little interest in the laws and usages of the different provinces of the Empire, rarely encumbered with landed property, or with effects that could not easily be moved, sojourners, not settlers, denizens, rather than citizens, they could retreat before the cloud burst, to the more secure dwelling-places of their brethren, and bear away with them the most valuable portion of their goods. Without much difficulty they shifted their quarters, and found new channels for their trade, as fast as the old ones were closed.*

The period of European history which intervened between the fall of Rome and the coronation of Charlemagne, A.D. 800, may be called the pushing period; for all the now half-civilized nations were struggling together, and driving one another into the positions in which they finally settled. Among the Teutonic tribes in the central and northern parts of the continent there was continual agitation. The Burgundians and the Franks were driving the Gauls, and in our own island the Saxons were pushing the Kelts westward, and founding the kingdoms of the Heptarchy, which finally were united by Egbert, the contemporary of Charlemagne; and these are but examples of what was occurring everywhere. The young kingdoms of modern Europe were all fighting for the ground they were to occupy, on which they afterwards settled and spread. Meanwhile, commotion was universal and incessant; peace seemed to have departed from the earth.

Through burning towns and ravaged fields the Jew travelled, less grieved than most people by surrounding misery which enveloped those with whom he had no strong tie of attachment. If splendid cities became a prey to the flames, or magnificent churches lay in ashes, his meaner dwelling was abandoned without much regret, and with no serious loss, and even his

* "History of the Jews." By Dean Milman.

synagogue might perish in the common ruin, without either deeply wounding the religious feelings of the worshippers, who had no particular local attachments, and the humble edifice could be restored at no great expense.

Where battles were fought, and immense plunder fell into the power of the wandering barbarians, the Jews were at hand to traffic the worthless and glittering baubles with which ignorant savages are delighted, or the more useful, but comparatively cheap, instruments and weapons of iron and brass, for the more valuable commodities of which they knew not the price or the use. These, by the secret correspondence which the Jews had already established with their brethren in every quarter of the world, were transported into more peaceful regions, which still afforded a market for the luxuries of life. As to the particulars of this commerce, we have no certain information, but if it existed to the extent we have reason to believe it did, it must have been highly lucrative, when the sellers were ignorant barbarians, and the purchasers intelligent and perhaps not over-scrupulous traders. Perhaps by keeping alive the spirit of commerce the Jews were really the means of promoting the civilization of these wild hordes.*

But the branch of commerce which the Jews contrived to monopolise was the trade in slaves, which they carried on throughout Europe, reaping enormous profits by this inhuman traffic. The Jew not only drove his gangs of slaves to the different markets, wherever he could get the best price, but he moreover bought, in perhaps a somewhat more private way, those among the unfortunate who were of gentle birth—fine youths and fair young maidens, whom he either kept

* Abridged from Dean Milman's "History of the Jews."

for his own domestic use, or passed on into the hands of strangers with whom he could make the best bargains. Yet this slave dealing, revolting as it is to look back upon, had, in those cruel times, some good effect towards mitigating the atrocities of war. Slavery was a great evil, but it prevented massacre. Those savage warriors could not make use of all the captives they took; they had no respect for human life; they valued a slave only according to the price at which he might be sold. Dean Milman remarks: "This state of things must have inspired a kind of revengeful satisfaction in the mind of the zealous Israelite. While his former masters, or at least his rulers, the Christians, were wailing over their desolate fields, ruined churches, pillaged monasteries, and violated convents, he was growing rich amid the general ruin.

Certainly, under this kind of commercial prosperity, the character of the Hebrew must have rapidly and terribly degenerated, and the gulf between the Jew and the Christian must have deepened and widened.

When we remember that this slave trade was a very different one from that against which Wilberforce contended, that it dealt not only with the lowest classes and races of men, women, and children, but with all classes of the unfortunate—that the detestable trade was covetously grasped by the Jew—that he grew rich, or was always supposed to have grown rich upon it— we can better understand why he was hated and despised. It accounts for the fact that the Hebrew race was more crushed in Christendom than it had ever been in the pagan world; so that when the popes had gained ascendency, they were generally more at enmity with the Jews, than the emperors (with a few exceptions) had been. It also gives a clue to one reason why a

Jew often hid his gold, and deceived the world as to the amount of his wealth. It became generally known that a great deal of money was hoarded up among the Jews, and this was really the secret incentive to many of those persecutions under which they suffered. Long ago they had been warned by the prophet Isaiah that for the iniquity of covetousness the Lord would smite His people.*

While Jews were growing passionately fond of money, churchmen, not only bishops, but also priests, monks, and hermits, were growing as ardently fond of power; and falling into this excess, many Christian men and women grasped authority in a spirit that undermined the foundations of Christian character. Often pride rather than humility was the governing principle, and self-denial, though ostentatiously practised, did not go so far as to curb self-will, and to restrain the temper that will not brook contradiction. Thus bigotry became engendered, around which all the follies and cruelties of superstition are sure to germinate and to grow rampant, and to hide the ground of the truth in which both the Hebrew and the Christian Church was planted— the simple truth that by the law of nature and the law of grace God demands of man self-sacrifice. Self-confidence and self-assertion deluded Augustine, the Archbishop of Canterbury, and Jerome, the monk of Bethlehem, and many other good men, into making great mistakes. Jerome felt the need of a Hebrew teacher, but had not truthfulness and courage enough to acknowledge it; he did not see that the Church needs "not mere Hebrew scholars, but Hebrew spirits —Hebrew men, who can see all heaven and earth with the eyes of Abraham, David, and St Paul." †

* Isaiah lvii. 17.
† " I would therefore entreat you and every other converted Jew

The Bishops of Rome were distingushed by the title of Pope, which as yet meant little more than father, a word signifying the union of reverence with affection; but the papal power, as that expression is now understood, did not then exist.*

It was the result of a struggle; claims were made, and for some time were strongly resisted.† When John, Bishop of Constantinople, asserted the supremacy of that see, Gregory, Bishop of Rome, declared that in his opinion the title of Universal Bishop was contrary to the spirit of the Gospel, and injurious to the Church. Pope Gregory wrote, "Whosoever designates himself Universal Priest, or in the pride of his heart consents to be so named, he is the forerunner of Antichrist."‡

Gregory the First had a keen perception of right and wrong, and when he felt convinced that any course of action was right, nothing diverted him from his purpose. This characteristic is illustrated by the well-known story connected with the conversion of the Anglo-Saxons. The fair boys from Britain, whom he admired and pitied, were most likely exposed for sale in the Forum by a Jewish slave dealer.

The Jews were not only dealers in, and owners of,

not to sink your nationality because you have become a member of the Universal Church, but to believe with the old converts of Jerusalem that you are a true Jew because you are a Christian, that as a Jew you have your special office in the perfecting of the faith and practice of the Church, which no Englishman or other Gentile can perform for you; neither to Germanize nor Scoticise, but try to see all heaven and earth with the eyes of Abraham, David, and St Paul."—*Rev. Charles Kingsley to Adolph Saphir, Esq., then a student in Edinburgh.* (See "Life of Charles Kingsley," vol i., p. 281.)

* See "Lives of the Archbishops of Canterbury." By Dr. Hook.
† Dr. Hook.
‡ See "Eighteen Christian Centuries." By Rev. James White

slaves, many of them had become proprietors or cultivators of land in Italy, and employed large numbers of slaves on their farms. Some of these Hebrew masters were very tyrannical, quite forgetful of the laws and injunctions of Moses, which should have taught them moderation and mercy; moreover instances occurred in which circumcision was forced on Christian slaves.

This evil did not escape the vigilance of Gregory, who consequently effected a reformation in the laws, with a view to protecting Christian slaves against the arbitrary conduct of Jewish masters. He ordained that those who had been long in servitude, and had proved faithful while under the yoke, should be considered as attached to the soil; and that if the Jew resisted this, or in any way abused his seignorial right to transplant the slave from the soil to which he belonged, he should lose his lease of land, as well as his right over the slave. No Jew or heathen who wished to become a Christian was to be retained in slavery. Gregory, who greatly desired the conversion of the Jews, ransomed an immense number of Jewish slaves immediately on their receiving baptism; and he ordained that taxes peculiar to the Jews should be remitted with regard to all who embraced Christianity. Many letters of Pope Gregory on this subject are extant; one to Leo, Bishop of Catania in Sicily, establishes the curious fact that the Samaritans shared this traffic with the Jews. Gregory wrote—

"A circumstance both revolting and contrary to law hath been made known to us. We are informed that certain Samaritans, resident at Catania, buy heathen slaves, whom they are so daring as to circumcise. You must investigate this affair with impartial zeal, and take such slaves under the protection of the Church, and not suffer these men to receive any repayment. Besides this loss, they must be punished to the utmost extremity of the law."

"In all other respects Gregory maintained that tolerance towards the Jews which, with few exceptions, they enjoyed during the period of confusion, and even for some time after the conversion of the barbarians to Christianity. For, during all this time, the Church was sadly occupied in mourning over the ravages which enveloped the clergy and people in common ruin, or, more nobly, in imparting to the fierce conquerors the humanizing and civilizing knowledge of the Gospel. It had not the power, we trust not the will, to persecute. The Church was in adversity, that best school of Christian virtue."*

Many of the barbarian nations had become more settled, and partially civilized; the Lombards were the wildest and most formidable of Pope Gregory's time; and they had embraced the Arian religion. Antharis, their leader, was ambitious enough to dream of playing over again the part of Theodoric, or of perhaps reviving the glories of the ancient Empire; this may fairly be inferred from his adoption of the name of Flavius, which had distinguished imperial princes. He enlarged his dominions, he baffled his Byzantine enemies, he drove back the Franks who had dared to invade his territories, and he carried fire and sword into the dominions of the Church. His brilliant reign was brief, and he left a young widow who was highly esteemed and much beloved by the Lombards.

The chiefs agreed to accept as their king the man on whom Theolinda should bestow her hand. She

---

* "History of the Jews." By Dean Milman.

chose her cousin Agilulf, Duke of Turin. Theolinda, a Bavarian by birth, had been brought up in the orthodox faith, to which she was heartily attached. Of this Gregory took advantage; he addressed to the Lombard queen several letters, which aided Theolinda in converting her husband from the Arian heresy. Agilulf accepted the doctrines of the Church, professed to be a faithful member, restored the treasures he had plundered, and reinstated the bishops whom he had deposed. Whereupon Gregory rewarded him by the gift of the famous Iron Crown, which twelve hundred years later Napoleon claimed as the prize of victory, and which now belongs to the King of United Italy. It is a broad circlet of gold set with precious stones; to the interior is affixed a slender iron circlet, said to be a nail of the true cross beaten out into that form.

Pope Gregory framed the Liturgy and ritual of the Church of Rome, appointing observances for solemn days—Christmas, Holy Week, and Easter; and through the efforts and skill of this energetic bishop, Church music acquired its distinguishing character of solemn harmony.

From the Arch of Constantine, near the Coliseum, a road shaded by an avenue, which under an Italian summer's sky is most delightful, leads to Gregory's old convent and the church that bears his name; it stands on part of the ground formerly occupied by the convent. Montalembert calls this spot the cradle of English Christianity. Referring to its proximity to the Coliseum, he says, "It touches the soil steeped in the blood of thousands of martyrs, and faces Mount Palatine, the cradle of pagan Rome, still covered with the vast remains of the palaces of the Cæsars. Where then is an Englishman, worthy of the name, who can without emotion stand in that little corner of ground, whence came to him faith, the name of Christian, and the Bible of which he is so proud?"*

It is a green corner, a nook in the valley between the Cœlian and the Palatine hills. Left chiefly to nature's guardianship, it looks like a little bit of England, the quietest corner of a village green, or of a wild orchard quite in the country. It may thus strike a traveller resting on the lowest steps of the numerous flight, hoary with age and grey moss, but enlivened by a tiny fern, and by the smallest *Linaria*, which seems to lead such a happy life, basking in the sunshine of to-day, though rooted among the stones that tell of the years that are past. The steps lead up to the church and adjoining convents on the edge of the Cœlian hill; which in earliest times was called "The Hill of Oaks." It extends from St. John Lateran to the site of the ancient Porta Capena, at the commencement of the Appian Way, and from the Fountain of Egeria to St. Gregory's Church and its surroundings. The traveller should ascend the steps, and pass through the cloistered court of the church into the convent garden. There the view obtained is Rome—the ancient, and beyond it the modern city—a view not to be forgotten.

And all the things connected with Gregory's life are more simply real than are most of such things exhibited in Rome. The convent garden is not modernized, and the flowers blooming there are those that must have refreshed and cheered Gregory, through all the changing scenes of life—a life of study, of toil, and anxiety; supported, guided, and sweetened by those old cardinal virtues, Faith, Hope, and Charity. The church has been repeatedly restored; it includes the monastic cell

---

* "Monks of the West." By Montalembert.

that used to be in the convent—the little private chamber in which Gregory slept, and studied, and probably often wrote. The side of the cell formerly occupied by his bed is guarded by an iron grating, through which, by the light of a lamp, is shown a coloured picture of the saint in repose. His chair is more attractive, because it is simply an antiquated seat, and looks really what it is said to be. It is of fine white marble, perhaps from Carrara, semicircular, and is still, from its size and form, a comfortable chair. In the garden Gregory played as a child; for it belonged to his mother Silvia's house, remains of which are existing.

Gregory was well born, and inherited a great deal of property. When he had attained to manhood, he built, close to his mother's house, a convent, which he called St. Andrew's, in which he lived for many years as a monk. In that garden of his childhood's home, three chapels now stand, built in the sixteenth century. That of Ste. Silvia, in which we see a fine statue of Gregory's mother, and over it a fresco by Guido, intended to represent God the Father and a choir of angels. The second chapel of St. Andrew contains two famous rival frescoes by Guido and Domenichino. Guido's is a touching picture: he has put St. Andrew before us as on his way to execution, followed by a Roman crowd. He has just caught his first sight in the distance of the cross on which he is to suffer; he has thrown himself on his knees, and with his eyes on the cross is thanking God, and praying for strength to pass through the last trial. Domenichino's is by many preferred as a painting, but the subject, the saint on the rack, is not pleasing, though well treated. The third chapel, of Ste. Barbara, contains a statue of Gregory, with the dove on his shoulder, according to the legend, and the table at which he daily fed twelve poor men, after he had washed their feet. The Roman breviary relates that on one occasion a thirteenth guest, an angel, sat down as one of the company.

This story, and other more authentic incidents in Gregory's life, are represented in rude frescoes on the walls. Two of the largest pictures are historically interesting. One represents Gregory taking leave of Augustine and the other monks; bestowing, with his blessing, his parting presents.* The companion frescoe, a scene in Canterbury, is amusing, for it shows that the Roman painter understood our Anglo-Saxon ancestors about as well as Tacitus understood the Jews. Ethelbert is graciously receiving the missionaries; he wears a primitive gold crown, but the king and his people are perfect savages, and Queen Bertha does not appear.

Gregory's life in the convent was tranquilly happy; and after his elevation to the papal chair he regretted the seclusion he had felt impelled to quit. One day, Peter the Deacon, the playfellow of his boyhood, and the companion of his studies, to whom he was warmly attached, found him looking very sad, and inquired as to the cause. "My grief," answered the Pope, "is that which oppresses me every day, always old, yet always new, by its daily growth. My poor soul remembers what it was formerly in our monastery. . . . And now, in consequence of my pastoral charge, it has to hear the thousand affairs of men and of the age, and the getting soiled in this dust. I think of all that I have

---

* We hear of only one copy of the Bible, one Testament, and a Psalter. The monks accustomed themselves to commit whole chapters to memory, which they repeated when giving instruction. Gregory afterwards sent them manuscript Gospels; two are still existing, one in the library of Corpus Christi College, Cambridge, and the other in the Bodleian Library at Oxford.

suffered and of all that I have lost. Here I am tossed upon the ocean, all beaten and broken by the tempest. Looking back upon my life is like looking back towards the quiet shore ; and the worst of it is, that being thus driven before the stormy wind I can hardly get a glimpse of the port that I quitted."*

Although Gregory so vehemently objected to the assumption of the title of Universal Bishop, yet certainly he laid the foundation of the temporal power of the popes. Little did he anticipate, indeed he could not foresee, many of the results of that achievement—results which would not have been altogether such as have occurred, had all his successors been men as pure in heart and as noble-minded as himself. Montalembert says—

"By his genius, but above all by the attraction and influence of his virtue, he originated and organized the temporal dominion of the popes ; he developed and regulated their spiritual sovereignty, he founded their paternal supremacy over the new-born kingdoms and nations destined to become the great people of the future, under the names of France, Spain, and England. It may be truly said that he inaugurated the middle age, modern society, and Christian civilization."

With the most benevolent intentions, Gregory spent a great deal of his own private money on the purchase of slaves. We may look on the ground round his mother's house and his own convent, and imagine how, long ago, it was tilled by those young strangers in a foreign land, the lads from Northumberland, and by Jews whom this philanthropist bought because they had been converted to Christianity, and needed to be shielded against the bitter animosity of their relations

* Montalembert's "Monks of the West."

and of all their own people, and also Christian slaves whom he had redeemed to set them free from the power of Jewish masters.

Gregory died A.D. 604, the year in which Mahomet openly proclaimed himself a prophet. In A.D. 606 the Emperor Phocas decreed that the Church of Rome should be the head and mistress of all the Churches, and Pope Boniface the Third assumed the title of Universal Bishop, against which Gregory had so resolutely protested.*

Thus simultaneously arose those two powers, destined to become widely extensive and supremely dominant. By one or other of them every acknowledged nation of the earth was subdued, and by both of them the homeless nation was affected, not only in its condition as a nation, but moreover in the character and pursuits of its scattered people. Portions of the *Transtevere*, and the whole of the Ghetto, are the parts of Rome less altered by time than are all the other districts of the city. Comparing the present aspect of the Ghetto and its inhabitants with the earliest descriptions of it that can be found, the very little alteration that has occurred during the course of the last twelve and a half or thirteen centuries is astonishing.

We see very narrow streets united by crooked lanes, houses so old as to be falling into ruin, yet utter ruin has not abolished the Jews' Ghetto—it has lived on in a perpetual state of decay. Here and there its buildings are supported by huge props of timber, but they are

---

* According to Bishop Newton, a cycle of 1,260 years was clearly marked out as of great prophetical significance. The temporal power of the Popedom was not to be materially diminished until after that term of years had run out. (See Newton on the Prophecies, Dissertation xiv., on the seventh chapter of Daniel.)

full of Hebrew life, lying prostrate at the foot of the majestic height crowned by the Capitol of Rome. Some of the houses have been grand in their day, irregularly built, and mostly with overhanging roofs, but not without pretensions to architecture, as some of the ancient pillars and doorways indicate; and woodwork on which are quaint carvings and devices of beasts and birds, and a few Jewish emblems, all in a worn-out, neglected condition, all in harmony with the surrounding relics of the portico of Octavia, the theatre of Marcellus, the fish market of old Rome, the Flamminian circus, the Jewish ambassador's residence in the Forum Judæorum, and the circus of Balbus. In the open space called Piazza della Scuola, the cleanest part of the Ghetto, stand three synagogues, for German, Spanish, and Italian Jews, all built on the foundations of the large one erected in the reign of Titus. The chief synagogue is adorned with sculpture and gilding. On the external frieze we observe the seven-branched candlestick, Miriam's timbrel, and David's harp. On the interior frieze are representations of Noah's ark, the tabernacle, and the temple, with its surrounding courts; and the sacred furniture and vessels; also the symbols of the twelve tribes, each in gold, on a white banner; and other national emblems; but the Jew in charge of this house of prayer cannot explain them.

Restoration must from time to time have been made, or the Ghetto could not have been thus preserved; but still the aspect presented seems, through all these centuries, to have been consistent with the meaning of its name, "*Broken and Destroyed.*"

European costumes have changed, but everywhere the poor Jew is still conspicuously shabby and dirty; not as picturesque as the ragged Italian, nor does he look as light-hearted. The air in these narrow streets is so revoltingly impure, that one can but expect to see pale and haggard faces. The wonder is, how people can live on, enjoying any degree of health and strength and spirit in such a noxious atmosphere. They look thin, sickly, and miserable; yet here they are, in spite of all the revolutions that have overthrown governments and institutions, political and religious.

The Hebrew Church bestows much teaching and exhortation on its young members before they are admitted to full religious privileges and undertake consequent responsibilities. The higher classes are no doubt carefully instructed, but they do not now live in the Ghetto. Great ignorance exists there; for a missionary now working among them found Jewish women who had not heard of Abraham, and knew nothing about Jerusalem. The men of the lowest classes are taught something; but such ignorance on the part of their mothers, wives, and daughters, shows the education to be superficial, not such as is calculated to touch the heart and to make them acquainted with Jehovah, and their relationship to Him.

As regards spiritual destitution, this Jews' quarter must be very much as it was in those early summer days of A.D. 596, when the prior of St. Andrew's Convent and the chosen band of missionaries—those forty self-denying, devoted men who had undertaken to bear the Gospel to the heathen Saxons of Britain,—were hurrying up and down the streets of Rome, making their preparations for leaving the civilized world.

Though it has no ground of its own to stand upon, the Hebrew race lives on, and is not without internal power which energizes activities that bear witness to the existence of life both natural and political. So singular is this race, that notwithstanding the material difference wrought by time in the amount of knowledge acquired by man, and in the opinions and manners of all the people of the earth, still the Hebrew of to-day is the only type of what he was when Rome, when Greece, when Persia, and when great Babylon were flourishing. Then the Jewish nation had already begun to be that strange people whom we know so cosmopolite, and at the same time so distinct.

The race is certainly one of those most fully endowed by God, for He has given it courage with patience, energy with reticence, impulsive eloquence with delicately clever stratagem, and strong reasoning power.

"In present as in ancient times, but much more now than then, Jewish sects multiply, and religious opinions are deep. Their intellectual centre, the law, is drowned under commentaries; their ritual centre, the Temple, no longer exists; their hierarchical centre, the high-priesthood, has disappeared. Nevertheless unity subsists, unity of race, not unity of faith; national, not religious unity. Coherent, notwithstanding its dispersion; one, notwithstanding its differences; powerful, in spite of dependence; indestructible, in spite of political annihilation; the Jewish race was neither the least wealthy, nor the least free, nor the least influential of those subjected to the Roman Empire, as to-day it is neither the least wealthy, the least powerful, nor the least independent of those now living in the midst of Christian kingdoms."*

But the Jewish nation had then something which it now has not—religious zeal, springing from an ardent

---

* Translated from "Rome et la Judée." Par M. le Comte de Champagny, de l'Académie Française. Paris, 1876. (See vol. i., chap. iv., pp. 125, 143.)

desire for the conversion of the world, that all the people of the earth might know the God of Israel.

Such was her feeling, because she then had religious hope; she believed in the future restoration of her political life, though it seemed to be extinguished, and in her religious life, which had hitherto been a life, not of perfect fruition, but of expectation. She hoped that this restoration might be near at hand. She had her past glory to look back on, but she thought more about the future. Whatever view she took of coming glory, she dwelt on it more than on that which had existed and was departing, though still she then had her imposing religious ceremonies, her grand solemn forms of worship, her holy city and temple, her hierarchy and her law.* Hers was not yet that "*decapitated religion*" which has lost not only the most brilliant objects of desire that can glitter under our created sun, but also its institutions of the past—even that wreck of a law that cannot be utterly destroyed, because it was given to her by God Himself, when she was a pilgrim nation journeying to her promised land; and she received and held it in faith, expecting completion and perfect accomplishment, though, while her patience was tried by the long waiting for fulfilment and clearer light, she was too apt to deceive herself, and to mistake a shadow for a substance.† "*Blindness in part is happened to Israel, until the fulness of the Gentiles be come in*," wrote Paul, a Hebrew, to the Romans.‡ Under this depressing condition they have lost the old national ardour for winning souls; nevertheless, in the heart of many a son of Abraham it exists in all its purity and fervour. The Jews nationally are no longer propagandists, but they

* "Rome et la Judée," vol. i., p. 144.   † Ibid.
‡ Rom. xi. 25—27.

can sympathize with Christians in the spirit of missionary enterprise, as some did, to a certain extent, when Bishop Armstrong was founding the mission stations in Kaffraria, and no doubt this case is not a solitary instance. The readiness and liberality with which Jews assist in promoting all kinds of useful and benevolent objects is too universally known to need exemplifying.

WHAT THEIR BURIAL PLACES SHOW.

JEWISH VIEWS CONCERNING THE STATE OF THE DECEASED.

From a Manual intended for Young Rabbis.

"Children of the house of Israel! in this life of frailty, where all that i united to us by the strongest bonds to-day, is to-morrow relentlessly torn away, where nothing is permanent except change, nothing constant except instability, it is the greatest comfort to us to have one steadfast pillar, Remembrance. . . . The ancient heathens adorned the graves of their beloved ones with flowers and wreaths, for they thought that the souls of their beloved were laid in the tomb; they materialised the soul, they were only heathens. But the Jewish religion, which also makes use of symbols, yet not to materialise the spiritual, but to spiritualise the material, teaches us to seek the souls of the departed, not in the grave, but in heaven, in the bosom of God, the Father of Love. Therefore, on the recurrence of such commemorations, Israelites do not strew earthly flowers on the grave, but offer spiritual wreaths to heaven; they offer prayers to God for the blessedness of the departed. . . . Let every Israelite join in the heart-affecting prayer, 'May God remember the soul of my father, of my Lord N., of the son of M., who is gone to his everlasting home, because I offer here a charity for him; for the reward of this may his soul be bound up in the bundle of life, together with the souls of Abraham, Isaac, and Jacob, Rebekah, Rachel, and Leah, and others, male and female, who are in Paradise.'"—Dr. S. M. SCHILLER-SZINESSY. See "After Death," pages 57, 58. By H. M. Luckock, D.D. Rivingtons. 1882.

XIII.

WHAT THEIR BURIAL PLACES SHOW.

THE oldest Jewish cemetery is that near the Porta Portese, which was situated conveniently for the colony in the Transtevere. There is also an extensive one not far from St. Gregory's Church, on a ridge in the valley of the Aventine. Among the emblems sculptured on the tombs, the nationally characteristic are the Star, the Lion of Judah, and the seven-branched candlestick—the cedar of Lebanon, and vines and olive branches variously arranged.

Among the simply suggestive emblems, the flight of time is represented by the hour-glass, with or without wings. We see the shock of corn, and the sickle that cuts it down: inverted torches are numerous, and over one a butterfly disporting in the sunshine betokens faith in the new life of the liberated soul. Many tombs are sculptured with funereal urns, flowers, wreaths, palm branches, and crowns of victory. A strong tower, often in connection with the lion, is a favourite device. In another Hebrew cemetery, the secretary-bird, carrying away the serpent, beautifully sculptured, points forward to the triumph of all that is good, and the destruction of evil.

On several of the tombs in the Aventine cemetery we see three poppy heads bound together. Poppy seed is the emblem of sleep, and may here signify sleep "until the day break, and the shadows flee away." A small oblong citron, called in Hebrew the *ethrog*, is a favourite emblem. This pretty golden fruit is used for decorating the tents for the feast of Tabernacles, and we find it sculptured on gravestones. Jewish tradition says it is the forbidden fruit of the garden of Eden.

The pomegranate, which often appears, is an admirable emblem. The exterior of the fruit represents the body already showing symptoms of decay, but we know that out of sight lies the richness and the sweetness ripening to perfection, while all that meets the eye is hardening, fading, and withering. Its seed is in itself, as was ordained in the beginning. It exhibits a manifold life, unity in multiplicity, and multiplicity in unity. Every pomegranate has many seeds, each seed has its vitality, its germinating power to do its part towards renewing the face of the earth when the winter is past.

The ancient Greeks and Romans burnt their dead; the custom of burying was brought from the East, by the Jews, who had inherited it from their forefathers, as the Old Testament Scriptures abundantly prove. According to Prudentius, the care bestowed on the remains of the departed arose out of a loving hope that they would rise again. "There will come an age when genial warmth shall revisit these bones, and the soul resume its former tabernacle," said the ancient people.

In later ages, both burning and burying were customary with the Romans, according to circumstances and convenience; the latter was the less expensive.

We have seen that both Jews and Christians were involved together in most of the persecutions. They both made hiding-places for the living, and graves for the dead, under the surface of the earth, using or extending the catacombs when persecution rendered it necessary for both Jews and Christians to worship secretly. In the rude underground synagogue and church, each assembly of the faithful met to perform their religious services, as nearly in accordance with their ritual as straitened circumstances would permit. The catacombs being perfectly dark, artificial light was always required; terra-cotta lamps were used, and have been found in abundance, of various shape and size; thousands have been discovered. Some persons have endeavoured to trace to these services in the catacombs the custom of worshipping by lamp or candle light, but history contradicts that construction of the original motive of "candle religion," and refers it undeniably to a different source. The employment of artificial light for the mere purposes of rendering objects visible is quite distinct from the ceremonial use of it. This, against which an ancient homily on the *"peril of idolatry"* energetically declaims, appears to have been generally connected with idolatry, excepting in the case of the Jewish ritual, and was unknown to Christians until after the time of Constantine. The use of lights, being an element of pagan worship, was universally reprobated by the Church during the first three centuries. Tertullian instances the lighting of mid-day candles as a ceremony from which all wise men are exempt. He ridicules those who lavish vain lights upon the noonday. And Lactantius, who died A.D. 325, says of the pagans, "They slay rich and fat victims to God, as if He were hungry; pour libations to Him, as if He were thirsty; and burn lights, as to one living in darkness."*

In the catacombs, lamps were necessary, and many persons who there acquired the habit of worshipping by such dim, fitful light may, partly for association's sake,

* "The Church in the Catacombs." By Charles Maitland, M.D.

have preferred it. When the persecution had passed over, and the customs of peaceful times had been resumed, those subterranean meetings must have been very solemn recollections of a time when, as they prayed and sang, surrounded by the dead, God seemed very near to those who had drawn near to Him, in spite of difficulties and danger.

In the tranquil after-times, when the Church had rest, though the probability of renewed persecution remained, she encouraged the assembling of congregations in the catacombs on the anniversaries of martyrdom—on days called *Natalitia*, or birthdays, because the saints were then admitted into the unseen world. These lamp-light meetings beside the grave of a departed friend reanimated the faith of those who exhorted one another to follow the good example, and who partook together of the funereal meal provided on these occasions.

This custom, which made it sure that loving eyes would look, at least once a year, on every stone which hid from sight the bones of a martyr, whose name was inscribed thereon, gave a constant stimulus to fortitude and zeal. But the *Natalitia* celebrated after Constantine's conversion tended in a lamentable degree to secularise religious worship: the festival was thrown open in the hope of obtaining converts; and many of the pagan poor, having been fed at the expense of the Church, became suddenly convinced of the truth of Christianity.*

There was no catacomb used for martyrs alone; they were laid among the departed in the city of the dead; each has one of the narrow beds, raised tier above tier on both sides of the long, low, dark, winding passage, only wide enough for the living to pass on one by one

* "The Church in the Catacombs." By Charles Maitland, M.D.

till they gain a nook formerly used as a place of worship. Of this they are here and there reminded by a fresco, or the vestiges of one. The Jewish candlestick is unmistakably Hebrew; the Good Shepherd as decidedly Christian; for although the Jew knows his God as the Great Shepherd who protects, guides, and feeds him, yet he never thus represents Jehovah. Representations of God are nowhere allowed among Jews, except by verbal description of His attributes.

Bronze and terra-cotta lamps were used by both Jews and Christians: a few relics of them are left in the catacombs, and in some of the open sepulchres a few bones and a little dust may still be seen. Many of the stones that closed the graves have been removed to museums or churches. The palm branch has been looked upon as a symbol denoting martyrdom, but it is not to be depended on as a sign that cannot mislead. One of the prettiest couple of palm branches with a crown uniting them is inscribed to the memory of a little girl of three years old. It appears improbable that she suffered martyrdom at so early an age. A number of devices, now recognized as trade symbols, used to be looked upon as indicating the instruments by which the deceased suffered torture and death. The comb used by wool combers in conjunction with a pair of shears suggested horrible ideas. The knife and the mallets do not quite fix the occupation, as they are useful in many trades; women may have been employed in beating flax, as well as in combing wool. A pair of slippers marks the stone put up by a shoemaker to mark the grave of his "most worthy wife."

An enormous vessel, formerly supposed to be a furnace used in the martyrdom of *Victorina*, is now decidedly thought to be an ancient bushel measure filled with corn which denotes that *Victorina,* or her husband, or perhaps the head of her family, was a corn grower or a corn dealer. A saw, chisel, and adze tell that *Banto* was a carpenter.

In the catacomb of S. Calixtus, the fosser, or grave-digger, has a very elaborate monument. On either side of this *Diogenes* is seen a dove with an olive branch, the common emblem of peace. He is pictured as a man holding a pickaxe in one hand and a lamp in the other. In the background we see the walls of the chapel or nook pierced with graves closed by slabs, in front of which the digger stands; the cutting instruments and compasses used for marking out graves appear on the floor. His loose dress is marked with the cross, to indicate the faith in which he lived and died.

In an ignorant age, when very few of the multitude could read, it was well to make use of symbolic figures, which caught the eye easily, and were generally understood.

The purely allegorical symbols are very plain, such as the fish and the ship to represent the Church, the dove with the olive branch and the anchor to tell of faith and hope. The peacock, as regards its meaning, is not so clear, but it is said to have been used as an emblem of immortality. This idea was borrowed from the pagans, as were also those which ascribed a glorious meaning to the laurel crown and the palm branch; but they received additional significance when inspired writers made use of them to express typically the promises of Holy Scripture. They are, as we have seen, to be found in the burial grounds of the Jews, and may have been equally used by them in the catacombs.

Many of the written inscriptions plainly tell of martyrdom, and cannot be misunderstood, as this—

" Primitius in peace, after many torments, a most valiant martyr.

He lived thirty-eight years. . . . His wife raised this to her dearest husband, he well deserving."

And—

"Here lies Gordianus, deputy of Gaul, who was executed for the faith, with all his family: they rest in peace. Theophila, a handmaid, set up this."

A palm branch is traced on the tablet.

This stone puzzled the archæologians, as the inscription was in very bad Latin, cut in Greek characters. An observation in Julius Cæsar's account of the Gallic wars was recollected, and it threw light on the subject. Cæsar says that the Druids of Gaul were accustomed to use Greek letters in their secular transactions, and that they managed the education of the people. This accounts for Theophila's Greek. Afterwards, when she came to Rome in her master's family, she picked up a little Latin, but only by ear. Yet, notwithstanding her ignorance and other impediments, she contrived, by the aid of a stone-cutter almost as ignorant as herself, to put up this respectful memorial, which has lasted so long.

With most ancient nations the custom prevailed of enclosing in the tomb a small cup or vase supposed to contain the tears of the mourners. The Christians, though rejecting the name *lachrymatory*, retained the cup, probably to hold spices and myrrh, which were much used at the burial of the dead. The cups found in catacombs vary in shape from the tall thin lachrymatory of the heathen to the open saucer of painted glass of the fifth century. The cup often enclosed in the tomb is sometimes drawn on the gravestone. The idea which long prevailed, that these cups originally held the blood of the martyrs, was quite a mistake, which arose out of the fact that they, as well as the lower part of the grave, were often found tinged with a red colour; but this was produced by decomposition of either the bodies or the spices. The most ancient cups bear no inscription; after the end of the fourth century they were sometimes marked with inscriptions in honour of saints; but no such cups are found of the earlier Christian times.

Instruments of torture have been found in the catacombs, but their number has been greatly exaggerated. The whole stock discovered consists of three terrible hooks, called *ungula*, with which the sufferers were torn on the sides, and a large comb, which is supposed to be one used for tearing flesh. These instruments may have been buried with the martyrs. From Rabbinical writings, antiquaries have discovered that Jews who had been stoned or beheaded were interred with the swords or stones used in their execution. With regard to the Christians, a few instances were the exceptions, not the rule, which seems to have restrained resentful feeling, and to have placed around the dead only symbols of peace, of innocence, and charity, and inscriptions evincing trust in God, submission to His will, and affectionate esteem for the departed.

The phonetic signs used for expressing names are very curious; thus the name *Navira* is given by a ship, *Leo* by a lion. Two casks represent *Doleus* the father and son, *dolium* being the Latin for cask.

Porcella means a little pig. On a gravestone we see the pig, with this inscription beneath:—

"Porcella sleeps in peace. She lived three years, ten months, and thirteen days."

The tomb of a man named *Draconitius* exhibits a dragon, that of *Onager* an ass. We can imagine that the non-reading friends of these departed ones looked with loving eyes on any signs which recalled dear names and happy recollections connected with them.

One inscription states what had been paid for the grave, a sum equivalent to £1 2s. 7d. in English money.

Outside the ancient Porta Capena, near the beginning of the Appian Way, the Jews had a catacomb, which till lately has been supposed to be exclusively a Hebrew place of interment. In A.D. 1862, Raffaele Garrucci wrote a description of it, and positively expressed the opinion that it had been used only by the Jews, because the Romans could not lawfully sell a pagan burial place to Jews, and, on the other hand, Jews were not likely to wish to purchase one, but would have preferred burrowing in new ground. That appears a reasonable conclusion at which to arrive; but recent investigations have at least thrown doubt upon it.

A member of the Rothschild family was thinking of purchasing the catacomb, but abandoned the intention, because competent judges, after careful examination, pronounced it to be not entirely Hebrew, although the candlestick and other unmistakable symbols prove that a number of Jews were there laid to rest. We cannot decidedly account for this difference of opinion. Could it be possible that after the Romans had renounced paganism, the law which protected pagan cemeteries might have been repealed, and the ground sold to Jews? And perhaps the Hebrew propensity for driving a good bargain, or the idea that the hiding-places might be useful, should perilous times again put the lives of Jews in jeopardy, might have tempted them to buy.

Raffaele Garrucci thinks the rectangular room, in which is some well-preserved mosaic pavement, was a synagogue. Synagogues and burial places were often near together; and there was sure to be water for the supply of the synagogue; therefore the existence of a spring confirmed Garrucci in his opinion. The Hebrew catacomb, as it is called, is entered by passing through the vineyard Randanini, which is not far from the columbarium of the freedmen of Octavia. A columbarium was a tomb house containing regular tiers of niches, like pigeon holes. This one has nine tiers all round; every niche was made to hold one or two cinerary urns. Here and there a small bust stands beside an urn, and there are a few cups and lamps.

But to return to the Jews' catacomb, or rather to the pleasant vineyard commanding a grand view of the Alban hills, and an interesting and picturesque one of the city: but, alas! the catacomb cannot at this moment be entered; therefore it is impossible to make fresh observations. It was as accessible as are the other catacombs, until an abominable thief contrived to carry away some of the valuable curiosities. A lawsuit is going on, and until the affair is settled, no one is allowed to go in; we must therefore be satisfied with glancing over descriptions given by those who have seen it.

Augustus Hare says: "It is entered by a chamber open to the sky, floored with black and white mosaic. . . . . The following chamber has the remains of a well. Hence a low door forms the entrance of a gallery, out of which open six cubicula, one of them containing a fine white marble sarcophagus, and decorated with a painting of the seven-branched candlestick. A side passage leads to other cubicula, and to an open space which seems to have been an actual arenarium. A winding passage at the end of the larger gallery leads to the graves in the floor, divided into different cells for corpses, called *cocim* by Rabbinical writers. A cubiculum at the end of the catacomb has paintings of figures—Plenty with a cornucopia, Victory with a palm branch, and others. . . . The inscriptions are in great part in Greek letters expressing Latin words. They refer to officers of the synagogue, rulers, and scribes." This author expresses the opinion, which generally prevailed when he wrote, five years ago, that this cemetery was exclusively Jewish; and there is, he says, another small Jewish catacomb behind the basilica of St. Sebastian.

The catacombs were burrowed through mines of a volcanic kind of sand, a brittle crumbling substance. *Cubicula* are roomy caves, *ambulacres* are passages between the narrow shelf-like graves. A *Crypta arenaria* means a group of these caves and passages made in that peculiar volcanic sand.

In descriptions of these cemeteries we read that pagans, Jews, and Christians lie in the same catacomb, though perhaps in different parts of its extensive ramifications; this has lately been contradicted. The subjects of the frescoes are taken from both Old and New Testament. Of course, those from the Bible narratives may have been put up by either Jew or Christian; but there is one scriptural character of the Old Testament frequently represented. It must have been a favourite subject, not only with the early Christian artist, but also with the rulers of the early Christian Church.

The prophet Jonah is shown under three circumstances of his life. First, being thrown into the sea; secondly, being swallowed by a marine monster; thirdly, when he is thrown up by the monster on the shore. No doubt it was as a type of resurrection that the subject was selected. Moreover a fourth circumstance has often been traced—Jonah looking down upon the condemned city, while reposing under the shelter of his gourd; and in the writings of St. Augustine of Hippo we find a full explanation of the meaning. "In that," says St. Augustine, "we have an allegorical figure of what took place after the resurrection of Jesus Christ. Jonah is grieved at the conversion of Nineveh, of which he had prophesied the ruin; in the same way the converted Jews were grieved at the conversion of the Gentiles, from whom they had hitherto considered themselves entirely and for ever separated by the especial election of God, who had chosen them to be His own people, to the exclusion of all others. Jonah is grieved to see his miraculously formed gourd, which had protected him from the heat, withered as quickly and miraculously as it had at first arisen. He did not grieve over the loss of 120,000 innocent perishing souls; this did not appear very sad to the prophet; and thus also the christianized Jews distressed themselves over the loss of their special promises of temporal blessings, given particularly to them under the Old Testament.

"These ancient promises of good things to be received by them in this world were dear to them, and they did not trouble themselves about the innumerable multitude of nations who would have been excluded from the kingdom of heaven."

Saint Augustine's reasoning shows us that the Christian Church, gathered from out of every nation in his and preceding times, was not ready, not fit to receive her Lord and King, whom she was ardently longing to welcome. It shows us that her people needed not so much to be encouraged by the hope of earthly blessings as to have their aspirations raised to heavenly ones; their eyes needed to be attracted upwards, not rivetted on the earth, looking for those things which are to be accomplished when earth's Redeemer, David's Son, the Lord of all, returns.

Moreover, St. Augustine's notions, though we may not entirely agree with them, help us to more clearly see how full of mercy is the delay which tries the patience of the faithful : but it does not convince us that a promise, once made by Jehovah, which hitherto has been but partially fulfilled, can become like a withered thing that is never to revive. "*The grass withereth, the flower fadeth, but the word of our God shall stand for ever.*"

Truer than is the needle to the pole are those words to their eternal meaning. Outward agitation may shake the case that holds the compass, and the needle may tremble and quiver, and seem to have lost its mysterious connection with the pole; but directly rest is obtained it proves its fidelity to the ancient law of nature ordained by the Creator. Has any one passage in the Word of God less claim upon our faith than another? Every one which conveys a promise of material blessing must eventually be fulfilled, although it may be long withheld, while those persons who are to be the recipients are learning the relative value of temporal and spiritual blessings; so that, like Abraham, they may "be blessed, and be a blessing."

The Bishop of Hippo was not singular in condemning a self-deceptive kind of religion based on the feelings of the natural man, rooted in selfish ambition. Other chief pastors saw the danger, and endeavoured so to feed the sheep of the flock, as to strengthen them against it. Eusebius, Bishop of Cæsarea, in whose lifetime the last great persecution of the Church occurred, openly expressed the conviction that it was needed to chasten and subdue a spirit of unholy pride which had crept into the Church, and to restore purity and self-denial. An ancient homily with quaint simplicity strikes at the root of this evil, and the words written so long ago have not lost their force :—

"Let us then have faith, brothers and sisters. We are contending in the lists of the living God, and we are trained by the present life, that we may be crowned with the future. No righteous man hath reaped fruit quickly, but waiteth for it. For if God had paid the recompence of the righteous quickly, then straightway we should have been training ourselves in merchandize, and not in godliness; for we should seem to be righteous, though we are pursuing not that which is godly, but that which is gainful."

Such sound and sensible exhortations guarded persons who in a humble frame of mind gave them earnest attention. Nevertheless the evil grew, although its power was, we know, entirely under the control of Him through whom alone we can "overcome evil with good."

Yet two great evils were allowed to assume an attractive and a noble aspect. First, under what was called an Agapæ, or lovefeast, the most dangerous sentiments were fostered rather than discouraged; secondly, self-constituted teachers inflamed human passions to make their fellow-men neglect the duties of life, and court a martyr's death. Examples are given in Dr. Maitland's "Church in the Catacombs."

The lovefeast had been commented on by St. Paul in his First Epistle to the Corinthians.* Tertullian shows us what that feast had degenerated into—what it was more than a hundred years later than the apostolic age; he thus bitterly satirizes it: "Your love boils—in the kettle; your faith glows—in the kitchen; Your hope is—in the dish."

* 1 Cor. xi. 19—22, 29, 30, 33, 34.

The same author tells us how Christians were urged on to desire the crown of martyrdom by being led to think that all the most glorious promises of Holy Scripture belong only to those whose lives are literally sacrificed, who bear bodily torture and suffer death in testimony of their faith. The importance of Christian *life* was under-valued; it was distinctly separated, unnaturally disjoined from Christian death; whereas death is the last act of life; and that Good Shepherd, pictured on the walls of the catacombs, who leads His sheep through the green pastures, strengthens every faithful one, and comforts him in the dark valley, whether he die a natural or a violent death. Of all the victors who have conquered sin, triumphed over temptation, and trustfully given themselves up soul and body into God's safe keeping, we may say—

" They climbed the steep ascent of heaven
Through peril, toil, and pain.
O God, to us may grace be given
To follow in their train."

Among the grand and stimulating examples which history sets before us, those of the holy martyrs must always hold a foremost place, yet one cannot help wishing that their sufferings had never been painted as a panorama on the interior of that fine old circular church *S. Stefano in Rotondo*, or their lives collected in a " Book of Martyrs."

Dr. Maitland points out that Martyrology has its three characteristic styles, each of which indicates the period of time to which it belongs. First, the Primitive style; secondly, the Florid; thirdly, the Debased.

The primitive, as illustrated by the inscriptions in the catacombs, is pure, almost as simple as are the records of Scripture concerning the deaths of the martyrs; and the little that is added is full of natural pathos. The florid style is exaggerated, becomes exceedingly so, and by its redundance we know that the debased is not far off.

The field of the human mind, on the wilderness of this world, is that on which the Hebrew Church, the Christian Church, and every hierarchal body has to do its work and to exercise its influence. This unquestionable fact, from its very simplicity, is apt to slip out of thought, with its appendant consequences, but should be recalled when we consider the state of the churches at any given period of the world's history; for, to judge fairly, we must take into account the moral and intellectual condition of the multitudes through which a church has to carry its teaching and its discipline, and over whom it endeavours to obtain authority and power for good. The Church of Rome had to overawe the rude barbarians, and to labour for their conversion; and skilfully did she form her plans, achieve her spiritual conquests, and at the same time strengthen her temporal power, and extend and establish her dominant rule. Amidst the confusion which prevailed long after the break-up of the old Empire, and the forcible influx of new customs, manners, and habits of thought, she laid the foundations of civil, social, and educational organization. The fathers of the Church were but men; we perceive their shortcomings and mistakes more clearly than we can see the impediments they had to overcome or to circumvent. They seem to us to have been too ready to yield to the lingering heathen ideas and tastes of the people, and, on the other hand, too arbitrary and domineering. Certainly they countenanced, and even sanctioned, foolish and untruthful legends, and permitted heathenish customs to defile their lovefeasts. At meetings instituted in honour of the saints, things were said and done much more consistent with the pagan than with the Christian religion. We desire not to justify anything that was wrong; but when we reflect on what the chief pastors of the Church accomplished in those dark ages, we must gratefully acknowledge that it was a noble task, which could have been done only by the help of God.

The removal of the seat of imperial government from Rome to Constantinople made way for the seat of a chief ruler of the Church to be placed most advantageously in an independent and commanding position. The new throne in the city on the seven hills was an effectual sign of a new form of government. The crozier, which represented the crook or rod and staff of the chief shepherd, became an ensign of almost unbounded power, which was either well used or misused by the popes, as it had been by the kings and emperors of Rome, according to the personal character of each man thus exalted. Though not miraculously raised above human weakness and short-sightedness, such popes as Sylvester, Damasus, and Gregory the First did a vast amount of good, each in his generation.

The masterpiece of ecclesiastical policy was accomplished when Pope Leo the Third placed an imperial crown on the head of Charlemagne. The Church of Rome had conceived a bold project, had formed an alliance with the Carolingian house, and had revived in that family the Empire which had been dead for 300 years.

It seems that at this important crisis in the world's history the sons of Abraham were not so trodden under foot, nor so hampered by disabilities, as to be unable to take part in the excitements and duties of their day, nor was a superior man of Hebrew birth prevented from rising to eminence. One named Isaac was cabinet minister to Charlemagne, who sent him twice on confidential embassies to the Caliph Haroun Alraschid.

The mild aspect under which both Popery and Mahometanism arose, led the Jews to mistake their real nature; but no sooner were those revolutions completed, which established their power, than the gleam of sunshine on the Hebrew's path was overcast, and ages of misery succeeded. The ninth and two following centuries are appropriately called the dark ages; for Popery, in the fullest and worst sense of the expression, meaning an inhuman compound of ignorance and bigotry and superstition, reigned. It completely crushed the Jew, which is the more remarkable, because the principles that constituted it were the counterpart of that Rabbinism which had grown up in the Jewish Church, and which were indeed derived from it. What an awful amount of evil sprang out of that exaltation of human traditions over the simple truth as it is given us in Scripture, and out of the superstitious multiplication of ceremonies and forms of godliness, to neglect of its power, and that self-conceited fanatical bigotry which considered the expression of its hatred against those who differed from it as the most decisive evidence of piety towards God! Under this tyranny the prophecies against the ancient people were literally fulfilled, which makes it the more certain that those in their favour will be as exactly accomplished. The Jew did become "*a proverb*," "*a byword*," "*a reproach*," as had been foretold. Accordingly, we find them deprived of independence, kept back by unjust restrictions and prohibitions, and, later on, insulted, robbed, exiled, and slaughtered, both by their governors and their fellow-subjects.*

* "History of the Hebrew Nation." By the Rev. J. W. Brooks. Pages 501—504.

Popery imitated with wonderful exactness, not the originally pure, but the corrupted Hebrew Church, which had made "the word of God of none effect" by the traditions it had admitted. Under its rule, the most atrocious conduct toward the Jews was not only allowed, but encouraged. They were reduced to a state of political prostration, and undoubtedly, generally speaking, they fell into a condition of moral degradation, such as this treatment could not fail to produce. Individual exceptions do but confirm this rule. Nevertheless, one who knew it well assured us that the Jewish mind, the living Hebrew intellect, has held, and is holding and wielding, a wonderful power over the world.*

He further said: "The Semites exercise a vast influence over affairs, by their smallest, but most peculiar family, the Jews. There is no race gifted with so much tenacity, and such skill in organization. These qualities have given them an unprecedented hold over property, and illimitable credit. As you advance in life, and get experience in affairs, the Jew will cross you everywhere. They have long been stealing into our secret diplomacy, which they have almost appropriated;

* "I speak not of their laws which you still obey, or of their literature with which your minds are saturated; but of the living Hebrew intellect. You never observe a great intellectual movement in Europe in which the Jews do not greatly participate. The first Jesuits were Jews. That mysterious Russian diplomacy which alarms Western Europe is organized and carried on principally by Jews. That mighty revolution which is at this moment preparing in Germany, and which will be in fact a second and greater reformation, and of which so little is known in England, is entirely developing under the auspices of Jews, who almost monopolise the professional chairs in Germany. As to the German professors of this race, their name is legion."—*Benjamin Disraeli.* (Written in A.D. 1844.)

in another quarter of a century they will claim their share of open government."*

Can we doubt the existence of light more than we doubt that of darkness?

Should we further pursue the course of our subject, it will be ours to mark that "God divided the light from the darkness." We shall not clearly see how or when it was done. Who has ever seen the actual break of dawn, which occurs beyond the limits of our view, beyond our horizon?

> "The gazing eye no change can trace,
> But look away a little space,
> Then turn, and lo! 'tis there." *Keble.*

In that growing light we shall see good things that were round us, even when we saw them not. They are good because they were called into existence by the voice of God, the unchangeable Jehovah, with whom is no darkness at all; and hereafter light in full glory will show us beauty and variety, and order and design, all brought out of the chaos through which, "guided by the historic muse," we have groped our way

> ".... From age to age,
> Through many a waste, heart-sickening page." *Keble.*

The mythology of the middle ages, which has choked up the fountain-springs of modern history, is more simply poetical, therefore more pleasing, than is pagan mythology. All the streams of European history sprang up in the dark ages; they were earnestly sought and found, and in some measure cleared from the rank weeds in and around their channels, by those indefatigable hermits and monks, who collected chronicles and traditions, and compiled them, writing in their

* "Endymion." By Lord Beaconsfield. Chap. xx.

caves and cells: after awhile they, with exquisite care, illuminated their manuscripts. The bards added to the stock of early literature by celebrating the exploits of favourite heroes, and wandering minstrels composed and sang their songs, describing what they had heard and seen. From the "Lays of the Troubadours," which have been collected, we may gather what the crusaders and their contemporaries thought of the Jews. We have seen how they were treated by classical authors; it would be interesting to mark how they have been dealt with by modern writers. A sweep through our own literature, from Shakespeare to George Eliot, would give a fair example, although it might be well also to look into that of other European countries; but this work, if carried on, must be produced in another volume.

"*In those days the house of Judah shall walk with the house of Israel, and they shall come together out of the land of the north, to the land that I have given for an inheritance unto their fathers.*"—JEREMIAH iii. 18, and xxxi.

"*And they shall be one in mine hands.*"—EZEKIEL xxxvii. 19.

APPENDIX.

PROCOPIUS, a talented and highly educated Greek, searched into the antecedents and traditions of the nations whom he saw so strangely and quickly revolutionizing the world. Dean Abbadie studied the chronicles of that historian of the dark ages, in the light of the eighteenth century; and to him the idea suggested itself, that in that era so remarkably signalized by national eruption and distress of nations, the children of the twelve sons of Jacob met, being brought together for the purposes of Divine Providence, although the tribes were as insensible to the relationship, as were Joseph's brothers when they met him as a stranger bearing an Egyptian name. It may be that his life was a prototype of the fate of those tribes who were to be headed by the descendants of Ephraim, his younger son, elected to the chieftainship, whose name is often used in Scripture to designate all Israel.

On a passage in Procopius' "History of the Gauls, Persians, and Goths," Dean Abbadie remarks:—

"Perhaps if we were to search very closely into the subject, we should find that the people who made irruptions into the Roman Empire in the fifth century, and whom Procopius reduces to the number of ten, were, in fact, none other than the ten tribes of Israel, living thus far in a state of separation, keeping near the part of the world on which they had been exiled and dispersed, until they quitted that neighbourhood of the Black and Caspian Seas, their place of exile, because the land could no longer maintain them. Everything strengthens this conjecture. The extraordinary increase of the people, foretold so precisely by the prophets, the number of the tribes, the custom of living in tents, and other customs of these Scythians, like those of the children of Israel."*

Abbadie proceeds to show all the points of similarity which mark these Sycthians as a people to whom the prophecy in the tenth chapter of Zechariah, from the 6th verse, may possibly apply. In the days of the Hebrew prophets all those regions around the Black and Caspian Seas had been called the north country, because they lay northward of the then great empires of Babylonia and Persia, and in the days of Procopius all that part of the world was successively occupied, overrun by restless tribes living in tents, always ready to migrate, yet gaining power enough to make them formidable enemies to the divided Roman Empire. As well as the light of his times permitted, Procopius wrote the histories of several of the so-called barbarian nations, which more than a thousand years later were read by Dean Abbadie. As we read his comments, it seems that in his time it was not as decidedly ascertained as it now is, that Scythian was not the name of any particular race, but was originally a word applicable to all nomadic people wandering on for pasturage. Abbadie was a man of deep learning, and the peculiar circumstances of his life had made him widely acquainted with the European world. He came to England with King William the Third, who made him Dean of Killaloe in Ireland, and Minister of the Savoy in London.

* "Le Triomphe de la Providence," tome ii. 177. Par le Dr. Abbadie. Amsterdam, 1723.

Abbadie did not trace the tribes beyond the age of Constantine, not further than the period which, though extending beyond his time, may well bear the name of the Emperor who inaugurated it; and which was indeed a blessed time of rest to the Christians after the persecutions through which the Church had passed under the pagan emperors. But we cannot think with Abbadie that all Isaiah's grand predictions, and Jer. xxxi., and the Book of Micah received complete ultimate fulfilment in the age of Constantine; and likewise several passages in the Book of Hosea, metaphorical prophecy which Abbadie decidedly applies to the Israelites, but thinks that admission into the Christian Church, in a figurative sense, entirely fulfilled them. He was so perfectly satisfied with the glorious view of all those barbarous nations brought together by God's guiding providence, in order that they might be within hearing of the gospel; he rejoiced so contentedly in the knowledge that, one after another, they became converted, either before or soon after they had settled themselves, and thus formed Christian kingdoms, all comprehended in the one fold of the Church, that he cared to go no further. Evidently his mind was completely filled with the idea that the blessed privilege of being a member of Christ's Church so far surpasses that of being a son of Abraham, that the latter distinction is quite merged in the former. Very literally did he understand the third chapter of St. Paul's Epistle to the Colossians. He looked upon the inheritance referred to in verse 24 as a spiritual birthright, as far superior to any earthly heritage, even to all that is earthly in that of the sons of Abraham and the royal line of David, as is the immortal spirit in man superior to his earthly tenement. From the depths of his heart, Abbadie repeated the words of the Apostle to the Gentiles: "The new man is renewed in knowledge, after the image of Him that created him, where there is neither Greek nor Jew, circumcision nor uncircumcision, barbarian, Sycthian, bond nor free: but Christ is all, and in all."

Abbadie had translated the liturgy and psalmodies of the Church into different languages, and he felt perfectly happy in the thought that in the Christian Church all the descendants of Abraham, and all the families of the earth are united as the members of one family, enjoying the richest and best heritage, and that they all sing together the songs of Zion, calling the God of Israel their God, and Abraham their forefather. This view filled Abbadie's heart with fervent gratitude; and believing, as he did, that Israelites were comprehended in the enormous masses of invaders that fell upon Rome, seeming to destroy civilization, and threatening to bring back chaos, but which were ere long reduced to order under settled governments, Abbadie felt that they and their children had every right to sing with one accord, "Blessed be the Lord God of Israel, for He hath visited and redeemed His people," and to repeat all passages from both the Old and New Testament which are incorporated into the liturgies of the Universal Church of Christ. This new embodiment of holy words did not disprove the higher antiquity of their origin, did not alter their signification, nor weaken their claims, as portions of the Word of God, on man's trustful faith.

Abbadie's ideas are tinged with Calvinism; when studying his life, one sees it could hardly be otherwise. He was born of Huguenot parents in the south of France, and educated in his boyhood by the celebrated La Placette, before the revocation of the Edict of Nantes, which blighted the hopes and prospects of his early manhood. His life work was done in Paris, in Brandenburg, then just developing into the kingdom of Prussia, in Holland, in Ireland and England. In the Reformation, a work of centuries, Abbadie did his part carefully as a theological writer. He arrived in England just at that crisis of our history which we call the Revolution. As to his opinions with regard to the ten tribes, he held them in an enquiring rather than in a dogmatical spirit. The subject was one of the popular topics of his day, and nothing that was written upon it by those who thought they had found all the lost tribes, or who expected to find them all hidden in narrow secluded localities, or perhaps at the North Pole, satisfied him. How could a race which, according to the word of God, was to increase rapidly, and some of its nations were to spread very vigorously and widely, and every one was to have some kind of power, continue, through rolling ages, to be concealed in the secret places of the earth?

It is an open question: we did not open it, and perhaps we cannot close it. Dean Abbadie opened it two hundred years ago, but not at all widely. His ideas, though not on the whole coinciding with those of the Jews on the subject of the dispersion of the ten tribes, yet agree with them in one respect. He continually remembered, and used in argument, the Scriptural simile of seed dispersed over fields by a husbandman, not sown by the winds. Seed does not lose its identity by being sown; it is still wheat or barley or flax: by it we identify the field as one of wheat or barley or flax; the ground is marked by what it has reproduced.

If Abbadie had thought about the kingdoms which arose out of the division of the Roman Empire, no one could have been more capable of doing so dispassionately, unbiassed by natural prejudices. By birth he was a

Frenchman. He loved, no doubt, his childhood's home and the kind pastor to whom he owed so much, but he had little reason to love a kingdom which in that day was not worthy of its noblest subjects. Neither a Prussian, a Dutchman, an Irishman, nor an Englishman, he dwelt with each of these people, was a leading man among them—was one with them in days of excitement and trouble, when sympathy is awakened which does not pass away as though it had not been. And he had known their great men, had stood before their kings, had gained the confidence of princes and sovereigns, and had used his influence on behalf of persons and classes of persons who needed consideration in hard times; but, wide as was the scope taken by his intelligence, yet he did not at all go into the origin of modern kingdoms and states in the dark ages. This has been done by trustworthy historians of all the leading nations, among whom our own Sharon Turner maintains a good reputation.* Many persons who now look into the question opened by Dean Abbadie, believe that they see much more than he did. That is very likely; knowledge is a growing light, increased by the rapidity of locomotion, and enterprising explorers have traversed and examined vast tracts of the world, which two centuries ago was all unknown land.†

* "The Saxon was one of the Gothic States, and it was as far west as the Elbe in the days of Ptolemy. The Saxons were therefore in all likelihood as ancient visitors of Europe as the Belgæ, the Germans, or any other Gothic tribe. Their situation seems to indicate that they moved among the foremost columns of the vast Gothic emigration; but the particular date of their arrival on the Elbe, or their particular derivation, it is impossible to prove, and therefore unprofitable to discuss."—*From "History of the Anglo-Saxons,"* vol. i., page 22.

† Daniel xii. 4.

Since Abbadie's time several travellers have felt convinced that they have discovered some tribe, or portion of a tribe of Israelites. Most interesting is Dr. Wolff's account of those he found in Afghanistan.

The Rev. Jacob Samuel, of Bombay, a converted Jew, describes what he believes to be a remnant of Israel, dwelling in Dagistan, on the ridge of the Caucasus, which divides Georgia from the Caspian Sea. These people have many customs which led this Hebrew traveller who found them to believe in their Israelitish origin. Dr. Samuel particularly remarks on their way of fighting their neighbour, the mounted Cossack. They strike at the heels of his horse, which reminded him of the Patriarch Jacob's prophetic blessing: "Dan shall be a serpent by the way, an adder in the path, that biteth the horse-heels, so that his rider shall fall backwards."[*]

Their cunning dexterity in war is proverbial. They had never seen a printed book until the Russians conquered Georgia, but they possess the Pentateuch written in the ancient Hebrew character, not the Chaldaic, as are the copies preserved by the Jews; and they have none of the portions supposed to have been written by Ezra.[†]

The destiny of each son of Jacob is distinctly given in the eloquent language of inspired prophecy, as expressed by the dying father when he blessed his sons, and by Moses before he went up to the top of Pisgah, to see the land which the Israelites were about to enter, though he was not to lead them over the river. The future of Joseph and his sons is particularly described in magnificent allegorical language.[‡]

---

[*] Genesis xlix. 17.
[†] "The Remnant Found." By the Rev. J. Samuel. Hatchards. 1841.
[‡] The blessing of Joseph, Gen. xlix. 22—27; Deut. xxxiii. 13—18.

The blessing pronounced upon Asher is remarkable.* As well might we try to count the stars of heaven and the sand of the seashore, as to reckon the multitude of persons, gathered from every generation, from under every kind of trouble and anxiety, from soldiers on the battle-field, and sufferers on the bed of death, who have been helped and comforted by those few words, "As thy days, so shall thy strength be." Though we cannot count them, it does us good to look up to heaven and down upon the earth.†

That overflow of blessing poured into Asher's cup, of which, in the fullest, clearest, most literal sense, all the families of the earth have partaken, cannot have left the cup dry. It is the most precious heritage of those children included in Asher's portion of good things, and they are holding it wherever they may be. Surely not an iota of a promise made by God through His inspired prophets can any one of those tribes have lost!

Asher did not in ancient times gain worldly renown—the tribe did not produce a judge or a hero. One name alone shines out of the general obscurity—the aged widow Anna, who saw the infant Saviour in the Temple, " and gave thanks unto the Lord, and spoke of Him to all them that looked for redemption in Jerusalem."

When all the tribes were living in the Holy Land, the ten which formed the kingdom of Israel were often called Ephraim, just as the name Judah included Judah and Benjamin. Ephraim was a very numerous tribe, and was allowed to exercise some control over the others. This fact, and also that to it belonged the ancient town of Shiloh, where Joshua set up the tabernacle and divided the land, should be borne in mind

---

* The blessing of Asher, Deut. xxxiii. 24, 25.
† Genesis xv. 5, xxii. 17.

when we read the prophetical books. Zechariah, who distinctly predicts the restoration of the ten tribes, by the names of Joseph and Ephraim, cannot refer to the return of such of their people as came back with their brethren of Judah. He wrote after the Jews had returned from Babylon; his prophecies concerning the still scattered tribes must therefore relate to an event which has not yet come to pass.

Dr. Latham states with regard to the Hebrew race, that the ten tribes have either become extinct or incorporated, that the Jews are not incorporated, but dispersed, and have lost national existence.* The continuance of Jewish nationality in spite of dispersion is seen more clearly by an historian than by an ethnologist.

Dr. Latham's statement (see foot-note) fits in remarkably with Dean Abbadie's idea that the ten tribes were mixed with only their own old home neighbours and the Samaritans who had occupied their vacated land, employing and dwelling with the poorest Israelites who had been left behind; that these people, all monotheists, were held in a state of separation from the heathen until after the Gospel had been proclaimed to them, and they had had the opportunity of receiving or

---

* Beni Israel Hebrews—The twelve tribes. Area, Palestine.
Divisions.—Samaritans and ten tribes.
Jews, tribes of Judah and Benjamin.

"Division 1.—Samaritans ten tribes, and Galileans. Canonical books. The Pentateuch.

"Alphabet—A nearer approach to the Phœnician than the Jewish, probably an older form.

"National existence terminated A.D. 721, since then either extinct or incorporated.

"Division 2.—The Jews' national existence terminated A.D. 89. Since then dispersed, but not incorporated.

"The Jews are still often considered a nation by reason of their maintaining a national religion and national customs."

rejecting it; that multitudes of Israelites were admitted into the Christian Church, before, as a nation, they were spread and lost sight of, ere many centuries had passed away.

Ethnologists use the terms *incorporation, fusion,* or *infusion, absorption,* and others.* The distinctive meaning of each of such words should be firmly grasped, while at the same time we bear in mind the fundamental truth, that words are signs of ideas.

The more closely we reflect on *incorporation,* the more are we convinced of the fulness of its meaning. Our food is incorporated in our bodies; every sort does its own duty, gives one kind of required strength. Within the bosom of our mother earth are formed rocks, metals, and jewels; all are incorporated in the terrestrial globe. In due time each substance becomes distinguishable by man, and is discovered. Can we not conceive it possible that under the direction of a special providence the ten tribes may have been so incorporated in other nations that they may hereafter be distinguished?

Particular tribes may have been incorporated into certain races or families of the earth, which, blessed by the infusion of the Abrahamic element, may have received distinctive recognizable qualities developing in course of time. Whether all the complete tribes, or severed portions of them, are being dealt with alike, or are being

---

* "A superior race cannot be absorbed in an inferior.—The fact is, you cannot destroy a fact, a simple law of nature, which has baffled Egyptian and Assyrian kings, Roman emperors, and Christian inquisitors. No penal laws, no physical tortures can effect that a superior race should be absorbed in an inferior, or be destroyed by it. The mixed persecuting races disappear, the pure persecuted race remains."—*Coningsby.* By Benjamin Disraeli.

ruled variously by a manifold exertion of Divine mercy, we know not. But whether unitedly or separately they have been incorporated, or whether as pure Israelites they are existing on the surface of the earth, as flowers and fruits of Palestine are found, called by new or altered names in different languages, flourishing in distant lands to which they have been transplanted, or in which they have been sown: however that may be, surely they will be discovered, known by their characteristics and also by the condition in which they will be found. We know that in the latter days they will be giving glory to God by bearing witness to the unfailing truth of Scriptural prophecy, from the Book of Genesis to that of the Revelation of St. John.*

Abraham, when called and blessed by the Lord, that he might be a blessing, must have thought on God's previous goodness towards him; and when blessed again, after he had separated himself from the wickedness of Sodom, and again after the great trial of his faith, he must have remembered how he had been hitherto blessed —how he had been called and led from his father's house. Every noteworthy scene and adventure he and those who accompanied him had met with on the journey must have been fresh in his recollection. Memories of the past invigorated his faith; but, as regards the future, he can have formed but vague ideas as to how and when God's promises would be fulfilled, although he firmly believed in them. And thus was it also with St. John. Most likely he understood those portions of the revelation he was inspired to write, which related to the past— to the five fallen forms of Roman government. The form existing in his day was the imperial government. Beyond this St. John in the power of the Spirit could

* Genesis xii. 3, xiii. 14, xxii. 17; Rev. vii. 3—9, xxi. 12.

prophesy.* He painted in vivid words a series of terrible or glorious allegorical pictures, which he may not himself have understood. That in Rev. xvii. 12 represents ten European kingdoms which arose from the upheaving and breaking of the Roman power. Mighty, cruel, and world-wide was it in St. John's day, yet it was doomed to pass away from the west and from the east; but when its sun had quite gone down, an after-glow revived, and spread and faded. During the course of many generations imperialism existed in the person of the Emperor of Germany, who was styled Emperor of the Holy Roman Empire until A.D. 1806, when Napoleon compelled Francis the Second to renounce the throne and relinquish the title.†

* Rev. i. 10.

† "From the explanation given in Rev. xvii. 10, 11, we learn that the seven heads represent seven kings or forms of the supreme government, of which five were fallen or past in St. John's days. One then existed, and another was to come and to continue a short space. It is added that this seventh form of kingship, or government, would be so modified as to form an eighth. The five fallen forms of Roman government, we gather from Tacitus, were the—(1) Kingly, (2) the Consulate, (3) the Decemvirate, (4) the Military Tribuneship, (5) the Triumvirate. Tacitus gives six, but especially says of the Dictatorship, that it was only taken as a temporary office. . . . In Rev. xvii. 12, the ten horns are said to represent ten kings or kingdoms, which are to arise out of the Roman power, weaker in their nature than the empire out of which they spring, as we learn from the clay being mixed with iron in the toes of Nebuchadnezzar's image. These are plainly commonwealths of Europe which rose on the overthrow of Rome in the fourth and fifth centuries, by the Gothic nations. Even Machiavel makes these out to be just ten, and Schlegel, in his "Philosophy of History," says they have always on an average been ten." (Abridged from "Palestine Repeopled," by Rev. James Neil, B.A., formerly Incumbent of Christ Church, Jerusalem. Published by Nisbet, Berners Street.)

v

www.ingramcontent.com/pod-product-compliance
Lightning Source LLC
Chambersburg PA
CBHW051248300426
44114CB00011B/934